(Cap) CAPIT[ALIZATION]

Y0-BWF-084

1 Sentence	[...] mes
2 Direct Quotation	10 Father, Mother, etc.
3 Poetry	11 I
4 Outline	12 Initials
5 Resolution	13 Proper adjectives
6 After interjection	14 Noun followed by numeral
7 Title	15 Salutation, closing
8 Proper nouns	16 Certain abbreviations

(Punc) PUNCTUATION *Pages 107–136*

1 Period	8 Apostrophe
2 Question Mark	9 Hyphen
3 Exclamation Point	10 Dash
4 Comma	11 Parentheses
5 Semicolon	12 Brackets
6 Colon	13 Dots
7 Quotation Marks	14 Underlining

(Dic) DICTION *Pages 137–188*

Enunciation	Vocabulary Enrichment	Figures of Speech	Idioms, Colloquialisms	Slang
Dic 1	Dic 2	Dic 3	Dic 4	Dic 5
	Triteness	Wordiness	Euphony	Faulty Diction
	Dic 6	Dic 7	Dic 8	Dic 9

(Sp) SPELLING *Pages 189–212*

Pronunciation	Meaning	Rules	Plurals	Possessives
Sp 1	Sp 2	Sp 3	Sp 4	Sp 5
	Contractions	Hyphenated Words		
	Sp 6	Sp 7		

(EF S) EFFECTIVE SENTENCES *Pages 213–270*

Fragments	Unity	Coherence	Clarity	Subordination
EF S 1	EF S 2	EF S 3	EF S 4	EF S 5
	Emphasis	Variety		
	EF S 6	EF S 7		

ENGLISH HANDBOOK

Matilda BAILEY

Gunnar HORN

AMERICAN BOOK COMPANY

New York   Cincinnati   Chicago

Boston   Atlanta   Dallas   San Francisco

Copyright, 1954, by

AMERICAN BOOK COMPANY

Copyright, 1949, by American Book Company

All rights reserved.
No part of this book protected by the above copyright
may be reproduced in any form
without written permission of the publisher.

Manufactured in the United States of America

E.P. 3

Acknowledgments

For the use of copyrighted material the authors wish to thank the following:

American Book Company: For the material from *A History of American Letters* by Walter Fuller Taylor, on which many of the exercises in chapters 3, 4, and 5 are based.

Bostick & Thornley, Inc.: For the excerpt from *Mellowed by Time* by Elizabeth O'Neill Verner. Used by permission of the publishers.

Thomas Y. Crowell Company: For the selection from *How to Read Better and Faster* by Norman Lewis.

Crown Publishers: For the selection from *A Treasury of American Folklore*, copyright 1944 by B. A. Botkin. Reprinted by permission of Crown Publishers.

Dodd, Mead & Company: For the excerpts reprinted by permission of Dodd, Mead & Company, Inc. from *Excuse It, Please!* by Cornelia Otis Skinner. Copyright, 1936, by Cornelia Otis Skinner; and the excerpt reprinted from *Dere Mable* by Edward Streeter. By permission of Dodd, Mead & Company, Inc. Copyright, 1918, 1945, by Edward Streeter.

Encyclopædia Britannica: For the quotations used by permission.

Harper & Brothers: For the excerpts from *My Life and Hard Times* by James Thurber; *One Man's Meat* by E. B. White; *Inside U. S. A.* by John Gunther; and *Life on the Mississippi* by Mark Twain.

Harcourt, Brace and Company, Inc.: For the quotations from *An Introduction to the Study of Literature* by R. P. Boas and E. E. Smith; and the excerpt from *Better Writing* by Henry Seidel Canby.

Mrs. Elmer Hiers: For the selection which originally appeared in *Coronet*, May, 1948.

Houghton Mifflin Company: For the excerpts from *Riverby* by John Burroughs; and the excerpt from *Ponkapog Papers* by Thomas Bailey Aldrich.

J. B. Lippincott Company: For the excerpt from *What Is Music?* by John Erskine.

McClelland and Stewart, Limited, Toronto: For the selection from *The Book of Ultima Thule* by Archibald MacMechan.

A. P. Watt & Son and the Owners of the Copyright: For the extract from "The Fact," an essay which appears in *Friendship and Happiness* by Arnold Bennett.

Yale University Press: For the quotation from *Chimney-Pot Papers* by Charles S. Brooks.

PREFACE

Once a man bought an expensive set of encyclopedias and then set himself the arduous and foolish task of reading them straight through. Fortunately there are few persons who misuse a reference book in such a way. Encyclopedias, dictionaries, and handbooks—even this *English Handbook*—offer various kinds of specific information. Francis Bacon once said, "Some books are to be tasted, others to be swallowed." Surely handbooks belong to the first classification. *English Handbook* deals with those topics in English which most persons are constantly finding essential. The topics can be easily referred to for concentrated study.

In using *English Handbook*, you will be aware of certain points basic to its plan of development.

PLACEMENT. *English Handbook* has been built with such an over-all conception of needs in the field of English as to permit its use at various levels. Because of its ample development of language concepts, it can be used in any of the high-school grades as well as in college classes. It can be used by students or by "the man in the street"; it can be used by academic or by vocational groups; it can be used to supplement a textbook or as a textbook itself. Because of the manner in which the material has been organized and presented, the instructor may use *English Handbook* wherever and however he wishes.

COVERAGE. The Contents will indicate the scope of material covered in this book. The first two chapters deal with grammar and usage; and, as will be seen, they fully cover these two related subjects. The grammar chapter gives a *complete* coverage of the principal concepts of grammar. This plan is in contrast to that of concentrating on only two or three concepts, presumably those of importance, as followed by some handbooks. Since no two classes and no two individuals suffer from exactly the same ills, the complete coverage gives each instructor an opportunity to choose wisely in terms of actual needs. The diagrams will serve as a visual aid. The usage items treated in Chapter 2 are closely related to the concepts developed in Chapter 1. They are, moreover, those which the best research shows are the most important and appear most frequently.

In addition to the full development given such matters as capitalization, punctuation, diction, and spelling, considerable emphasis has been placed upon the *application* of skills. Chapter 7 shows specifically various ways by which the student can improve his own sentences. Chapter 8 continues this emphasis by showing how sentences can be effectively woven into good paragraphs. Chapters 10 and 11 are provided because teachers everywhere agree that the research paper, also known as the term paper and the term report, leads students to skillful employment of library techniques, to effective organization of ideas, and to logical presentation of material. To facilitate proofreading and revision, the last chapter in the book outlines the important mechanical elements necessary in making corrections.

Since Chapter 9 — letter writing — illustrates one aspect of the philosophy of this handbook, it deserves special consideration. This chapter has been included in the hope that it will give practical help to vocational and commercial groups as well as to the so-called academic classes. Throughout the handbook, an attempt has been made to meet the needs of *all* groups. Academic, commercial, and vocational students will all find help.

FLEXIBILITY OF USE. A handbook, according to the general conception, is a book into which one dips whenever the need arises. This method of use indicates, therefore, that the chapters are not necessarily arranged in a logical or sequential pattern. Certainly the chapters in *English Handbook* may be used in any order that the instructor or the student wishes.

USE OF SYMBOLS. The end sheets of this book show fully a system of symbols which an instructor may use in the correction of papers. Many will disregard them entirely, preferring to use the general *Sp*, *S*, *Par* (or ¶), and so on. Others will wish to be more specific and will use the general symbol plus the number which tells the student exactly wherein his error lies.

An effort has been made to keep the system of symbols in this handbook just as simple as possible. Each new concept begins with the number 1, and in this way the numbers are kept low. Moreover, as you will see, never at any time does the numbering involve the confusing use of the decimal point. If instructors use the symbols suggested, students can readily refer to the end sheets, determine their errors, do the necessary remedial work, and make the corrections on their papers. Familiarity with the system of symbols will enable a student to make his corrections quickly and exactly.

DRILL MATERIAL. The wealth of exercise material given in *English Handbook* is obvious at a cursory glance. As each language principle is presented, illustrations are provided to show its application. Exercise material is then given to clinch the concept. Moreover, at various appropriate points, review exercises are provided; these exercises concentrate on a number of concepts taught in the chapter.

As important as drill is in the establishment of ideas, it can be deadly unless some effort is made to give it vitality and reality. In *English Handbook*, students are encouraged to apply to their own particular problems the information which they have gained. Moreover, as you will see, the exercise material throughout the book is woven around interesting subject matter. Consequently, while a student is working an exercise, he is at the same time reading interesting and worth-while subject matter. Sometimes the by-products of learning can have the same valuable results as had the famous arrow that was shot into the air.

There are many other things which might be said about the use of *English Handbook*. Probably the most important lies beyond the realm of the book itself. It is possible for a letter to be mechanically correct and still be duller than last year's gossip. A person's speech may exemplify correct enunciation and pronunciation and all the precise laws of grammar and yet plunge listeners into a mental coma. The point is obvious: of first importance always is the idea. Nourishment of the mind and heart is as essential as is that of the body. A handbook, then — this handbook, for example — when used wisely, becomes not the end but the means to the end; namely, the improvement of speaking and writing.

The authors take this opportunity to thank the following persons for their assistance with this book: Miss Janet H. Nixon, librarian of the Clairton High School, Clairton, Pennsylvania; Miss Alice Horsfall, librarian, Miss Esther Weitkamp, head of the Commercial Department, and the members of the English staff of the Benson High School, Omaha, Nebraska.

CONTENTS

(The topics marked with an asterisk include exercise material.)

vii

Contents

Contents

Contents

GRAMMAR

SENTENCE STRUCTURE

The word *sentence* may mean different things to different persons. It may mean an opinion given after deliberation. To a criminal, it may mean ten years in jail. To most persons, however, it means a unit of thought. But still the variation continues. For all of us, the following conversation contains understandable units of thought:

> "Howdy! Long time no see."
> "Been away."
> "Where?"
> "Fishing in Canada."
> "Catch anything?"
> "Not to speak of. A few suckers."
> "Tough luck. Well, so long."

A little girl once said of a sentence fragment that she was examining, "If it's not a sentence, it's sure enough hinting at it." The groups of words in the conversation above are "hinting" at sentences, but they are *not* actually complete sentences.

S   Definition of Sentence

A <u>sentence</u> is a group of words that expresses a complete thought. It contains a subject and a predicate.

The <u>subject</u> of a sentence tells whom or what the sentence is talking about, and the <u>predicate</u> tells something about the subject.

When you are doubtful about whether a group of words is a sentence or merely a fragment, apply the subject-predicate test. This can be done with all kinds of sentences — simple, compound, complex, and compound-complex.

S 1   Simple Sentences

A <u>simple sentence</u> has one subject and one predicate, either or both of which may be compound.

If a simple sentence has only one subject and one predicate, it is said to have a *simple subject* and a *simple predicate*. The simple subject is the most important word in the complete subject, and the simple predicate is always a verb or a verb phrase.

  S. S. S. P.
Times change.

Times	change

If a simple sentence has two or more simple subjects, it is said to have a *compound subject*.

  C. S.   C. S. S. P.
Customs and *manners vary.*

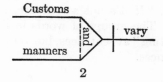

If a simple sentence has two or more simple predicates, it is said to have a *compound predicate.*

S. S.   C. P.   C. P.
Yesterday ends and *is forgotten.*

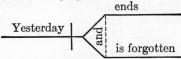

Moreover, both parts may be compound.

C. S.   C. S.   C. P.   C. P.
You and *I may remember* and *smile.*

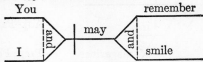

EXERCISE. Point out the simple and compound subjects and predicates in the following. Two groups of words may trick you; they do not meet the subject-predicate test.

1. Magazines and newspapers record.   2. History is caught.
3. Events and people and styles.   4. Posterity may be amused.
5. Changes and modifies.   6. Architecture and furniture alter.
7. Transportation and communication grow and expand.
8. Amusements vary.   9. You and I are interested.   10. We read and laugh.

Enlarging the Simple Sentence

The addition of modifying words and phrases does not change the structure of the simple sentence.

Adjectives and adverbs may be added.

S. S.   S. P.
Women's styles change *greatly.*

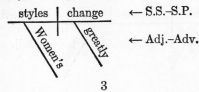

← S.S.–S.P.

← Adj.–Adv.

Prepositional phrases may be added.

S. S.   S. P.
Styles *of dresses* go *in cycles*.

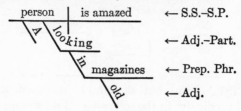

Participial phrases may be added.

S. S.   S. P.
A person *looking in old magazines* is amazed.

| person | is amazed | ← S.S.–S.P. |

← Adj.–Part.

← Prep. Phr.

← Adj.

Infinitive phrases may be added.

S. S.   S. P.
An inclination *to laugh* comes naturally.

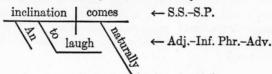

The addition of words to complete the meaning of the verb does not change the structure of the simple sentence.

A *direct object* may complete the meaning of the verb.

S. S.   S. P.
A 1929 fashion magazine pictures amazing *styles*.

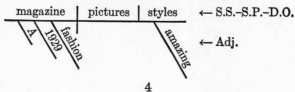

An *indirect object* may complete the meaning of the verb.

      s. s. s. p.
The ungainly lines give *us* a shock.

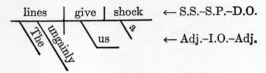

    ←S.S.–S.P.–D.O.

    ←Adj.–I.O.–Adj.

An *objective complement* may help to complete the meaning of the verb.

s. s.   s. p.
We certainly consider them poor *taste*.

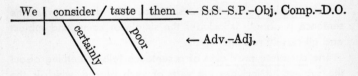

← S.S.–S.P.–Obj. Comp.–D.O.

← Adv.–Adj,

A *predicate noun* may complete the meaning.

    s. s. s. p.
Men's styles were also amazing *creations*.

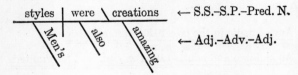

    ←S.S.–S.P.–Pred. N.

    ←Adj.–Adv.–Adj.

A *predicate adjective* may complete the meaning.

    s. s. s. p.
The pictures seem *ridiculous*.

| pictures | seem \ ridiculous |

←S.S.–S.P.–Pred. Adj.

← Adj.

5

A *predicate pronoun* may complete the meaning.

s s.   s. P.

The victims fortunately were not *you* and *I*.

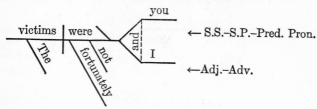

Despite all these additions, the basic structure of the simple sentence remains the same: it has a subject and a predicate, either or both of which may be compound.

The <u>complete subject</u> of a sentence tells whom or what the sentence is about. It includes the simple or compound subject and all closely related words.

The <u>complete predicate</u> of a sentence tells something about the subject. It includes the verb or verb phrase, which is the simple predicate, and all closely related words.

In the following examples, the complete subjects have been underlined once; and the complete predicates have been underlined twice.

s. s.   s. P.
<u>Amusements in the late 1920's</u> <u><u>differed also.</u></u>

c. s.   c. s.   s. P.
<u>All children and adults</u> <u><u>take the "talkies" for granted.</u></u>

EXERCISE. Apply the subject-predicate test to each of the following. Find the complete subject and the complete predicate, and then point out the simple or compound subject and the simple or compound predicate. You will find that two of the sentences do not pass the test.

1. The first important movie was produced in 1914. 2. It was *The Birth of a Nation*. 3. The year 1927 marks the first

popular talking movie. 4. It was called *The Jazz Singer*. 5. Al
Jolson sang and acted in that picture. 6. Movie history in
that tear-jerker. 7. Many actors and actresses of the silent
screen failed in the "talkies." 8. Sound helped in the development of the animated cartoon. 9. Mickey Mouse and Minnie
Mouse rose very quickly to fame. 10. The first color films
in the 1930's. 11. *Toll of the Sea* and *Becky Sharp* astounded
movie-goers during that period. 12. The three-dimensional
film was still in the future.

Kinds of Sentences

Sometimes in applying the subject-predicate test to sentences, one must play the role of detective. The subject of
a sentence does not always stand first; and, for this reason,
one needs to be wary. Let's consider the varying placement of subjects and predicates in the four kinds of sentences as they are regarded according to meaning —
declarative, interrogative, exclamatory, and imperative.
The examples below illustrate these kinds of sentences in
simple structure only. Compound, complex, and compound-complex sentences may also be written as declarative, interrogative, exclamatory, and imperative sentences.

A <u>declarative sentence</u> makes a statement. It ends with a
period.

Notice the placement of the subjects and the predicates
in the following sentences:

REGULAR ORDER: Miniature *golf boomed* in the late 1920's.

INVERTED ORDER: To a man from Tennessee *goes* the *credit*
for starting that sport.

INVERTED ORDER THROUGH THE USE OF AN EXPLETIVE: There
were thousands of these courses in America.

INTRODUCTORY PHRASE: In their mad pursuit of pleasure,
Americans were willing to try anything.

7

An <u>interrogative sentence</u> asks a question. It ends with a question mark.

> S.S. S.P.
> What *figures were* popular in radio?
> S.P. S.S. S.P.
> *Can you identify* the names Gosden and Correll?

An <u>exclamatory sentence</u> expresses strong or sudden feeling. It ends with an exclamation point.

> S.S. S.P.
> What an easy question *you have asked!*
> C.S. C.S. S.P.
> How popular *Amos 'n' Andy have been!*

An <u>imperative sentence</u> gives a command. It ends with a period or an exclamation point. The subject of an imperative sentence is always *you*, understood.

> S.S. S.P.
> (You) *Name* some of their amusing expressions.
> S.S. S.P.
> (You) *Help* me quickly!

EXERCISE 1. What kind of sentence is each of the following, and what punctuation mark should each have?

1. There were big names in the headlines twenty years ago
2. Make a list of them   3. Among the names will be those of Herbert Hoover, Calvin Coolidge, and Thomas A. Edison
4. Samuel Insull was then at the peak of his career   5. Have you heard of Bobby Jones, the champion golfer   6. How avidly American businessmen, dressed in their plus fours and checked sweaters and caps, were turning to golf   7. Al Smith of the "sidewalks of New York," having lost to Hoover in 1928, was building a new career   8. To him went the presidency of the great Empire State, Inc   9. What exciting days those must have been   10. Do you think our days are any less exciting

EXERCISE 2. In the sentences in EXERCISE 1, point out the simple subjects and predicates. Then point out the complete subjects and predicates.

8

S 2   Compound Sentences

The simple sentence — whether it is declarative, interrogative, exclamatory, or imperative — is basic to all sentence structure. From it are built compound, complex, and compound-complex sentences.

A compound sentence, as its name indicates, is made up of two or more independent parts of equal value.

A <u>clause</u> is a part of a sentence that has a subject and a predicate.

An <u>independent,</u> or principal, <u>clause</u> is one that makes sense standing alone.

When two or more independent clauses are properly joined to make one sentence, they form a <u>compound sentence.</u>

SIMPLE SENTENCES: Babe Ruth was the big name in baseball. Bobby Jones was capturing the honors in golf.

COMPOUND SENTENCE: Babe Ruth was the big name in baseball, and Bobby Jones was capturing the honors in golf.

With compound sentences, the subject-predicate test is just as easy to make as with simple sentences. Each independent clause must contain a subject and a predicate.

<small>S. S.</small>   <small>S. P.</small>   <small>S. S.</small>

<u>Lou Gehrig</u> <u>was another idol of baseball</u>, and <u>Helen Wills</u>

<small>S. P.</small>

<u>was a popular tennis star</u>.

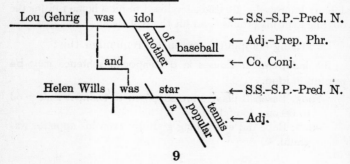

Do not confuse compound sentences with simple sentences which contain compound parts.

COMPOUND SENTENCE: The <u>1920's</u> <u>were happy-go-lucky</u> <u>times</u>; and, consequently, <u>amusements</u> <u>flourished</u>.

SIMPLE SENTENCE WITH COMPOUND SUBJECT: <u>Babe Ruth</u> and <u>Lou Gehrig</u> <u>were national heroes</u>.

EXERCISE 1. Determine whether each of the following is a simple or a compound sentence. Then point out the simple and compound subjects of the independent clauses. One group of words will not pass the subject-predicate test.

1. Babe Ruth died in 1948, and with his death America lost its most colorful figure of baseball. 2. In 1927, Babe Ruth hit sixty home runs and thus set a record. 3. At the start of his career, he was a pitcher; but at the end, he was a batter. 4. In addition to his remarkable skill, Babe Ruth was a colorful figure on the diamond and won the hearts of the fans. 5. Magnificent in victory, and equally magnificent in defeat. 6. During the World Series of 1926, the Babe received a letter from the father of a boy in New Jersey. 7. The boy was very ill, and the doctors did not expect him to recover. 8. The father asked Babe for an autographed ball for his son Johnny. 9. The next day Johnny received two autographed balls; and with this new interest in life, Johnny improved. 10. Babe promised to hit a home run for the boy; he kept his promise and hit three of them.

In writing compound sentences, remember this:

The independent clauses in a compound sentence must be related in idea.

> POOR: Baseball players are supposed to train; it isn't good to become too fat.
> GOOD: Babe did everything grandly; even his appetite was grand.

10

In writing compound sentences, one must remember also certain rules of punctuation.

1. When independent clauses are combined by the co-ordinate conjunctions *and*, *but*, or *or*, a comma is used before the conjunction.

> Babe ate hot dogs by the pound, and he drank soda pop by the case.

2. When independent clauses are combined without a co-ordinate conjunction, a semicolon is used between them.

> Babe ate hot dogs by the pound; he drank soda pop by the case.

3. When one or more independent clauses contain a comma, a semicolon is used before the conjunction.

> Babe, the greatest champion of them all, ate hot dogs by the pound; and he drank soda pop by the case.

EXERCISE 2. Find among the following pairs of sentences those which are related closely enough in idea to be combined into compound sentences. Write them correctly as compound sentences.

1. Babe Ruth received tremendous salaries. He also spent freely.
2. From 1927 to 1929, he received $70,000 a year. For the next two years, he received $80,000 a year.
3. Those were huge salaries. That of the President of the United States was only $75,000 a year.
4. The Babe ran up many records. He competed in ten World Series.
5. He always attracted the crowds. This ability caused the Yankee Stadium to be known as his contribution to baseball.
6. In 1936 he was elected to baseball's hall of fame at Cooperstown, New York. In the balloting, he ran second only to Ty Cobb.
7. Sultan of Swat was one name for him. Bambino was another.

S 3 Complex Sentences

As you have seen, a compound sentence is valuable in relating ideas of equal importance. But sometimes ideas may be combined which are *not* of equal value; one idea may be more important than the other. In such situations, the complex sentence is the kind to use.

A dependent, or subordinate, clause is one that does not express a complete thought but depends on an independent, or principal, clause to give it meaning.

A sentence that has one independent clause and one or more dependent clauses is called a complex sentence.

In the following examples, the independent clauses have been underlined once; and the dependent clauses, twice.

Ind. Cl.   Dep. Cl.
Another name which was in the headlines was that of
Ind. Cl
Richard E. Byrd.

Ind. Cl.   Dep. Cl.
You know that he flew over the South Pole.

Dep. Cl.   Ind. Cl.
As you can see, this was an age of adventure.

Some persons make the mistake of using dependent clauses as though they were sentences. Certainly it doesn't make sense to say simply *which was in the headlines* or *that he flew over the South Pole* or *As you can see* without enlarging upon these words. Each of those groups of words depends upon something else to give it meaning.

Dependent clauses, like independent clauses, have subjects and predicates.

S. S.   S. S. S. P.   S. P.
Many who had spare money speculated in stocks.

S. S.   S. P   S. S.   S. P.
When the market broke, thousands were ruined.

In the two examples, *who had spare money* and *When the market broke* are the dependent clauses. In the first, *who* is the simple subject and *had* is the simple predicate. In the second, *market* is the simple subject and *broke* is the simple predicate. Notice in the two examples the simple subjects and simple predicates of the independent clauses.

EXERCISE 1. Apply the subject-predicate test to each of the following. As you copy the sentences, make whatever corrections are necessary to complete them.

1. When Calvin Coolidge was President, years of prosperity. 2. His administration, which extended from 1923 to 1929. 3. As the stock market seemed an easy way to make money. 4. A share of stock which on one day might be worth a hundred dollars. 5. When the stock market crashed on October 29, 1929. 6. Hard to believe that years of bad times were ahead. 7. When factories closed down. 8. Those who had been rich. 9. The poor who had no jobs or money. 10. Because there was a world-wide depression. 11. That "prosperity was just around the corner" a kind of whistling in the dark. 12. A program which gave assistance to banks and industries. 13. Gradually as the years passed. 14. Prosperity which was long awaited.

Dependent clauses may be used (1) as adjectives, (2) as adverbs, and (3) as nouns.

An underline{adjective clause} is a dependent clause that modifies a noun or a pronoun. The relative pronouns *who*, *whom*, *whose*, *which*, and *that* are commonly used to introduce adjective clauses.

Ind. Cl.   Adj. Cl.   Ind. Cl.
The fear *that people felt* was contagious.

fear | was \ contagious   ← Ind. Cl.: S.S.–S.P.–Pred. Adj.

← Adj.

people | felt | that   ← Adj. Cl.: S.S.–S.P.–D.O.

Occasionally the relative pronoun is omitted.

There had been other depressions (*that*) America had known.

Occasionally the words *when* and *where* introduce adjective clauses.

The years 1857, 1875, and 1893 were times *when* this country suffered.

EXERCISE 2. Point out the adjective clauses in these sentences:

1. Surely there had been other depressions which this country struggled through.   2. The depression that struck in the 1930's, however, was one which was a part of a very complex situation.   3. Great masses of the people were drawn from the farms, where they were independent agents, to factory jobs, where they were dependent upon those who owned the factory.   4. The increase in population, which showed a sharp rise, placed a strain on employment.   5. The age of pioneering, which meant opportunity for everyone, was practically at an end.

EXERCISE 3. How can the following pairs of choppy sentences be joined through the use of adjective clauses?

1. The early 1930's were strange times.   They were marked with anguish and uncertainty.
2. Gangsters and racketeers became headline news.   One read about them constantly.
3. Legs Diamond, Dutch Schultz, and Al Capone were headlined. All Americans knew about them.
4. The crime wave was something.   It could not be ignored. For a time it could not be controlled.
5. A stock-market crash, a depression, and a crime wave spread gloom over the country.   It could be cut with a knife.

An <u>adverbial clause</u> is a dependent clause that modifies a verb, an adjective, or an adverb.

A <u>subordinate conjunction</u> joins a dependent clause to an independent clause.

Some subordinate conjunctions are:

after	for	so that	until
although	if	than	when
as	in order that	that	where
as if	lest	though	whereas
because	provided	till	whether
before	since	unless	while

Adv. Cl.   Ind. Cl.

<u>If you study the record,</u> you will find ridiculous things, too.

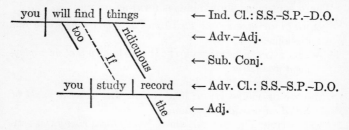

← Ind. Cl.: S.S.–S.P.–D.O.

← Adv.–Adj.

← Sub. Conj.

← Adv. Cl.: S.S.–S.P.–D.O.

← Adj.

EXERCISE 4. Find the adverbial clause in each of these sentences, and indicate the word that it modifies:

1. When miniature golf was born, a new craze began. 2. It became popular because it absorbed people's minds. 3. Before the craze had ended, the boom had netted $125,000,000. 4. Wherever you looked, you would see people knocking golf balls around miniature golf courses. 5. When Garnet Carter established this pastime in Florida in the winter of 1929–1930, he probably did not foresee its tremendous popularity.

EXERCISE 5. The choppy sentences in each of the following groups can be joined through the use of at least one adverbial clause. In making the necessary combinations, remember that an introductory adverbial clause is set off by a comma.

1. You are looking for other strange signs of those times. You will notice the craze for flag-pole sitting.

2. Someone craved publicity. He roosted on a pole or in a tree. He set a record.

3. For publicity some people sat on poles. Others sought it in marathon-dancing contests.

4. They would go through all kinds of physical tortures. They wished to set new records.

5. People worry. They want a means to forget. They frequently turn to strange pastimes.

A noun clause is a dependent clause that is used as a noun.

These sentences show clauses used as nouns:

> SUBJECT OF SENTENCE: *That times were becoming worse* was obvious.
>
> SUBJECT AFTER EXPLETIVE *IT*: It was known *that unemployment was rising.*
>
> DIRECT OBJECT: People knew *that life was not easy.*
>
> OBJECT OF PREPOSITION: The nation was in *what might be called an unsound condition.*
>
> APPOSITIVE: The fact *that unemployment was rising* was serious.
>
> PREDICATE NOUN: This rising tide was *what frightened the nation.*

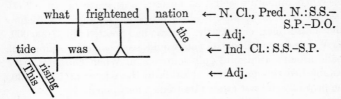

EXERCISE 6. Point out the noun clauses in these sentences, and tell how each is used:

1. Everyone knows that the early 1930's were black years.
2. The fact that bread lines increased was one evidence.   3. That thousands were evicted from their homes was another evidence.
4. It was known that several hundred thousand persons were homeless.   5. Help was what they needed desperately.

S 4   Compound-Complex Sentences

As the name indicates, the compound-complex sentence combines the qualities of the compound and the complex sentences.

A <u>compound-complex</u> sentence is made up of two or more independent clauses and one or more dependent clauses.

    Ind. Cl.   Dep. Cl.   Ind. Cl.

<u>We know</u> <u>how poverty oppresses</u>, and <u>poverty brings des-peration.</u>

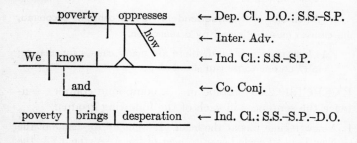

← Dep. Cl., D.O.: S.S.–S.P.

← Inter. Adv.

← Ind. Cl.: S.S.–S.P.

← Co. Conj.

← Ind. Cl.: S.S.–S.P.–D.O.

EXERCISE 1. Point out the independent and dependent clauses in the following compound-complex sentences. Then apply to them the subject-predicate test. Diagram the sentences if you wish.

1. When people are desperate, crime rises; and the situation grows worse. 2. The story of Jean Valjean in *Les Misérables* is an example of what can happen, and that story can be duplicated many times. 3. Thievery rose; and then because the profits were higher, another crime came into prominence. 4. Papers described a wave of kidnaping; and when the American public read of it, they were stunned. 5. The era, which had been black enough, had reached the bottom; it couldn't possibly go any lower.

In writing compound-complex sentences, there are three rules of punctuation to remember.

1. Independent clauses may be joined by *a conjunction and a comma*.

> Conditions were bound to improve, and they did as time went on.

2. Independent clauses may be joined by *a semicolon without a conjunction*.

> There is a pendulum that swings both ways; good times follow bad times.

3. When one of the independent clauses contains a comma, the clauses must be joined by *a semicolon*.

> As historians point out, there are many causes for change; and no one cause can stand alone.

EXERCISE 2. Combine into a compound-complex sentence the sentences in each of the following groups:

1. A new regime was at the helm. It went by the name of the New Deal. People began to hear of the AAA, the TVA, the CCC, and the NRA.
2. The alphabetical combinations may have bothered some. Most Americans hoped one thing. Would these organizations bring relief?
3. The CCC concentrated on conservation work. It was badly needed. The AAA took over the administration of crop control to aid the farmers.
4. The Tennessee Valley Authority built Federal dams. They helped to conserve the land in the Tennessee Valley. They provided for cheap electric power. Everyone knows this. This experiment was one of the most ambitious of the New Deal projects.
5. There was a trend toward shorter working hours. Statisticians will point this out. There was also a trend toward longer play hours.

Review Exercises

EXERCISE 1, KINDS OF SENTENCES. Identify each of the following sentences as to kind — simple, compound, complex, or compound-complex:

1. Places of amusement increased in tremendous numbers.
2. According to one authority, the number doubled in ten years.
3. Small communities installed swimming pools, and big cities built huge bathing beaches. 4. When you visit New York, you should go to Jones Beach, where thousands of people enjoy themselves. 5. Persons who could afford it took up skiing, and those who could not afford it enjoyed newsreels of the sport. 6. Everyone who could was becoming a devotee of sports. 7. Some took up bicycling; others tried softball. 8. Sports clothes were definitely the rage. 9. Women wore overalls and play suits, and men daringly appeared in bright-colored outfits. 10. The world seemed gay again.

EXERCISE 2, DIAGRAMING. Diagram the ten sentences given in the exercise above.

EXERCISE 3, APPLICATION OF PRINCIPLES. Write sentences of your own which illustrate the following kinds:

1. Simple sentence with simple subject and predicate
2. Simple sentence with compound subject
3. Simple sentence with compound predicate
4. Simple sentence with compound subject and predicate
5. Simple sentence in inverted order
6. Compound sentence
7. Complex sentence with adjective clause
8. Complex sentence with adverbial clause
9. Complex sentence with noun clause
10. Compound-complex sentence

19

VERBS

V Definitions

A <u>verb</u> either expresses action or shows a state of being.
A verb that is made up of two or more words is called a
<u>verb phrase.</u>

V 1 Kinds of Verbs

Since verbs perform differently, we classify them as to
kinds. The two kinds are *transitive* and *intransitive*.

A <u>transitive verb</u> is one that passes its action over to a receiver.

The receiver of the action may be a *direct object*.

The last decade *fostered* colorful figures.

The receiver of the action may be the *subject*.

Colorful figures *were fostered* by the last decade.

An <u>intransitive verb</u> is one that does not pass its action over
to a receiver.

Sometimes an intransitive verb is complete in itself.

Franklin D. Roosevelt certainly *ranks* high.

Sometimes an intransitive verb is a linking verb, connecting a word in the predicate with the subject.

His personality *was* dynamic.

All forms of the verb *to be* are linking verbs; and, in
some constructions, the verbs *seem, become, look, feel, taste,
sound,* and *grow* are also linking verbs.

EXERCISE. Identify the verbs in the following sentences, and tell what kind each is — transitive or intran-

sitive. Tell whether each intransitive verb is complete or linking.

1. F. D. R. became the personification of the New Deal. 2. Frequently he spoke to the American people over the radio and explained the issues of the day. 3. His "Fireside Chats" were heard by millions. 4. Thus, through the medium of the radio, the American people heard the President of the United States; and, as a consequence, they felt close to the operation of the government. 5. Roosevelt was undoubtedly one of the most colorful figures in the 1930's; but there were others, too.

V 2   Verbals

Some persons confuse verbals and verbs. A verbal has some of the qualities of a verb, but it does the work of a noun, an adjective, or an adverb. Notice the verbs and verbals in these sentences:

             Verbal   Verb
J. Edgar Hoover, *known* to many, *rose* to fame.
 Verb   Verbal
It *is* easy *to quote* his accomplishments.
Verbal   Verb Verbal
Tracking criminals *seems to be* his hobby.

The three kinds of verbals are (1) participle, (2) infinitive, and (3) gerund.

A participle is a verbal used as an adjective.

PRESENT PARTICIPLE: Hoover, *directing* the F.B.I., got results.

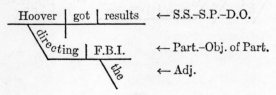

Hoover | got | results   ← S.S.–S.P.–D.O.

directing | F.B.I.   ← Part.–Obj. of Part.

the   ← Adj.

PAST PARTICIPLE: Laws, *passed* by Congress, gave the F.B.I. power.

PERFECT PARTICIPLE: Hoover, *having gained* this power, set to work.

An infinitive is a verbal that is usually introduced by the word *to*. It may be used as a noun, an adjective, or an adverb.

USED AS NOUN: *To catch* John Dillinger was a goal.

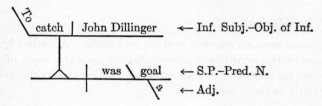

USED AS ADJECTIVE: Dillinger had the ability *to disguise* himself.

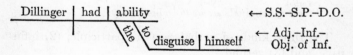

USED AS ADVERB: The F.B.I. worked hard *to trap* Dillinger.

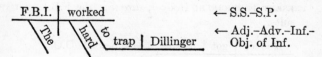

22

A **gerund** is a verbal, ending in *ing,* that is used as a noun.

GERUND SUBJECT: *Tracking* Dillinger was not easy.

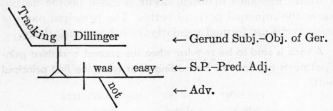

← Gerund Subj.–Obj. of Ger.

← S.P.–Pred. Adj.

← Adv.

GERUND PREDICATE NOUN: The first job was *finding* him.

GERUND DIRECT OBJECT: Dillinger apparently enjoyed *fighting.*

GERUND OBJECT OF PREPOSITION: He had ways of *eluding* the police.

GERUND APPOSITIVE: His method, *shooting* and *killing,* eventually came to an end.

EXERCISE. In the following sentences, point out each verb and each verbal. Indicate what kind each verbal is and how it is used in the sentence.

1. The American public, aroused by the horror of the crime wave, followed the man hunt with interest. 2. One of the greatest of crimes, occurring in the early 1930's, had awakened public interest to the necessity for suppressing crime. 3. Melvin Purvis, chosen by Hoover to lead the man hunt, followed Dillinger to Chicago. 4. Having received information concerning Dillinger's plan to go to a movie, Purvis parked his car in front of the theater and waited. 5. Scanning each face was his next job. 6. By dyeing his hair and disguising himself by means of plastic surgery, Dillinger hoped to avoid detection; but Purvis recognized him. 7. Purvis and the other F.B.I. men waited until Dillinger had seen the movie and was ready to leave the theater. 8. At a prearranged signal from Purvis, the F.B.I. men closed in. 9. Capturing Dillinger was the start of a campaign to rid this country of undesirables. 10. Very soon children could be seen playing G-men.

V 3   Regular and Irregular Verbs

Many mistakes in usage occur because people do not know the principal parts of verbs. The principal parts of some verbs are formed regularly; of others, irregularly.

A verb is said to be **regular** when the second and third principal parts are formed by adding *d* or *ed* to the first principal part.

PRESENT	PAST	PAST PARTICIPLE
dive	dived	dived
walk	walked	walked

A verb is said to be **irregular** when the principal parts are formed in a variety of ways.

PRESENT	PAST	PAST PARTICIPLE
swim	swam	swum
do	did	done
lie	lay	lain
take	took	taken

EXERCISE. Give the principal parts of each of the following. Consult your dictionary whenever you are in doubt.

am (be)	begin	burst	drink
freeze	lend	shine	shrink
spring	swing	wear	think
wring	forsake	catch	kneel
strive	slink	creep	sting
bite	dig	slay	tread
weave	dwell	teach	see
steal	set	omit	ring
lay	rise	get	forget
fling	eat	go	dream
attack	blow	lead	mean
bid	cling	rid	prove
broadcast	drown	show	wake

V 4 Tense

On the three principal parts are built the six tenses.

PRINCIPAL PARTS	TENSES
Present:	Present and Future
Past:	Past
Past Participle:	Present Perfect, Past Perfect, Future Perfect

The following shows the conjugation of the six tenses:

PRESENT TENSE

Singular	Plural
I catch	we catch
you catch	you catch
he, she, it catches	they catch

PAST TENSE

I caught	we caught
you caught	you caught
he, she, it caught	they caught

FUTURE TENSE

I shall catch	we shall catch
you will catch	you will catch
he will catch	they will catch

PRESENT PERFECT TENSE

I have caught	we have caught
you have caught	you have caught
he has caught	they have caught

PAST PERFECT TENSE

I had caught	we had caught
you had caught	you had caught
he had caught	they had caught

FUTURE PERFECT TENSE

I shall have caught	we shall have caught
you will have caught	you will have caught
he will have caught	they will have caught

The auxiliary verbs *do, does, am, is,* and *are* are also sometimes used to indicate present tense or action in progress; and *did, was,* and *were,* to indicate past tense.

EXERCISE. What is the tense of each of the following?

1. he rode
2. he has written
3. I am throwing
4. they will have sung
5. it will sink
6. he has heard
7. we did beat
8. we are falling
9. it breaks
10. they have been
11. it will wear
12. we had shaken
13. they took
14. it had shrunk
15. he drew
16. they had lent
17. I shall burst
18. they have grown
19. they ate
20. you had fought
21. I teach
22. he will have run
23. they will dig
24. it has paid
25. we do give
26. I shall have done

Sequence of Tenses

Make the verbs of the subordinate and principal clauses agree logically.

WRONG: The people see that another young man was making the headlines.

RIGHT: The people *saw* that another young man *was making* the headlines.

WRONG: They saw that he has begun a fight against crime.

RIGHT: They *saw* that he *had begun* a fight against crime.

WRONG: He was in office only a short time when his efforts began to show results.

RIGHT: He *had been* in office only a short time when his efforts *began* to show results.

WRONG: He says he would eliminate racketeering.

RIGHT: He *says* he *will eliminate* racketeering.

RIGHT: He *said* he *would eliminate* racketeering.

Use the present tense when referring to something that is permanently true.

WRONG: We recognize that the man's name was Dewey.
RIGHT: We recognize that the man's name *is* Dewey.

EXERCISE. Nine of the following sentences contain errors in verb sequence. How can they be corrected?

1. We know this happens in 1935. 2. History said that racketeering has become big business in those days. 3. Dewey promised he will clean up the rackets in New York. 4. The people know he would keep his word. 5. Over two hundred restaurants pay for the "protection" that the racketeers gave them. 6. Men in the poultry business feared Toots Herbert until Dewey puts him in prison. 7. Dewey got convictions despite the fact that witnesses were afraid to talk. 8. When Dewey was elected district attorney, he only started on his drive. 9. Everyone knows that crime could be controlled when a concerted drive against it was made. 10. The G-men and Dewey showed the world that crime didn't pay.

V 5   Voice

The <u>active voice</u> shows the subject as the actor.

The <u>passive voice</u> shows the subject as the receiver of the action.

Only transitive verbs have voice.

ACTIVE VOICE: The Federal authorities finally *controlled* crime.
PASSIVE VOICE: Crime *was* finally *controlled* by the Federal authorities.

EXERCISE. List the verbs in these sentences, and give the voice of each:

1. In 1933 a new calamity struck a large part of the United States. 2. On November 11, 1933, South Dakota was overwhelmed by the first of the great dust storms that it suffered. 3. The people were enveloped by a great storm of black dust.

4. It was rich topsoil that was being blown by the great gusts of wind. 5. Here, indeed, was a horror that could not be controlled.

V 6   Mood

The **mood** of a verb shows how its action or state is thought of. The three moods are (1) *indicative,* (2) *imperative,* (3) *subjunctive.*

A verb in the **indicative mood** indicates a fact.

The dust storms *brought* suffering and destruction.

A verb in the **imperative mood** indicates a command.

Describe the appearance of a dust storm.

A verb in the **subjunctive mood** indicates a condition contrary to fact, a doubt, or a wish.

If I *were* in your class, I would show you some pictures.
I wish soil conservation *were* rigidly enforced.
It looks as if it *were* a national necessity.

The indicative and imperative moods are used most frequently. The subjunctive mood is being used less and less; the verb *to be* is the last one in which there are many changes in form. The present and past tenses in the subjunctive mood of *to be* are as follows:

PRESENT		PAST	
Singular	Plural	Singular	Plural
if I be	if we be	if I were	if we were
if you be	if you be	if you were	if you were
if he, she, it be	if they be	if he, she, it were	if they were

In most other verbs, the *s* (or *es*) at the end of the third person singular in the present tense of the indicative mood is dropped to form the subjunctive mood (*if he go, if he see*). The following shows the complete conjugation of the verb *to drive* in all three moods:

Indicative Mood

PRESENT TENSE

Active Voice

Singular	Plural
I drive	we drive
you drive	you drive
he drives	they drive

Passive Voice

Singular	Plural
I am driven	we are driven
you are driven	you are driven
he is driven	they are driven

PAST TENSE

I drove	we drove
you drove	you drove
he drove	they drove

I was driven	we were driven
you were driven	you were driven
he was driven	they were driven

FUTURE TENSE

Active Voice

Singular	Plural
I shall drive	we shall drive
you will drive	you will drive
he will drive	they will drive

Passive Voice

I shall be driven	we shall be driven
you will be driven	you will be driven
he will be driven	they will be driven

PRESENT PERFECT TENSE

Active Voice

Singular	Plural
I have driven	we have driven
you have driven	you have driven
he has driven	they have driven

Passive Voice

I have been driven	we have been driven
you have been driven	you have been driven
he has been driven	they have been driven

PAST PERFECT TENSE

Active Voice

I had driven   we had driven
you had driven   you had driven
he had driven   they had driven

Passive Voice

I had been driven   we had been driven
you had been driven   you had been driven
he had been driven   they had been driven

FUTURE PERFECT TENSE

Active Voice

Singular   Plural

I shall have driven   we shall have driven
you will have driven   you will have driven
he will have driven   they will have driven

Passive Voice

I shall have been driven   we shall have been driven
you will have been driven   you will have been driven
he will have been driven   they will have been driven

Subjunctive Mood

PRESENT TENSE

Active Voice

if I drive   if we drive
if you drive   if you drive
if he drive   if they drive

Passive Voice

if I be driven   if we be driven
if you be driven   if you be driven
if he be driven   if they be driven

30

PAST TENSE
Active Voice

if I drove   if we drove
if you drove   if you drove
if he drove   if they drove

Passive Voice

if I were driven   if we were driven
if you were driven   if you were driven
if he were driven   if they were driven

PRESENT PERFECT TENSE
Active Voice

if I have driven   if we have driven
if you have driven   if you have driven
if he have driven   if they have driven

Passive Voice

if I have been driven   if we have been driven
if you have been driven   if you have been driven
if he have been driven   if they have been driven

Imperative Mood

PRESENT TENSE
(You) Drive!

EXERCISE. Choose the correct verb forms for the following sentences:

A dust storm made it seem as if it (1. was, were) night. (2. Pretend, Pretends) that we (3. are, were) in the midst of one now. The black dirt (4. rush, rushes) through the air. If I (5. was, were) good at description, I would make you realize how the dirt (6. tastes, taste). I do wish I (7. was, were). (8. Put, Puts) a handkerchief over your nose and mouth because the dust (9. penetrates, penetrate) to your lungs. Your eyes smart as if the dust (10. was, were) fire.

31

NOUNS

N   Definition

A <u>noun</u> is the name of a person, place, or thing.

N 1   Kinds of Nouns

As you have seen, some nouns, or name words, begin with capital letters; others do not. Because of this fact, nouns are classified according to two kinds — *common nouns* and *proper nouns.*

A <u>common noun</u> is the name of any one of a class of persons, places, or things; it does not begin with a capital letter.

   inventor   continent   river   street

A <u>proper noun</u> is the name of a particular person, place, or thing; it always begins with a capital letter.

   Edison   Asia   Ohio River   Main Street

EXERCISE 1. Find the proper nouns among the following, and write them correctly:

1. modern poetry
2. argentina
3. boston red sox
4. empire
5. independence day
6. south dakota
7. harry jones
8. football
9. adirondacks
10. freedom
11. walt disney
12. congress
13. high school
14. hotel
15. peter rabbit

Another kind of noun is the *collective noun;* it may be either common or proper.

A <u>collective noun</u> refers to a group. When it refers to a group as a whole, it takes a singular verb. When the individual members of the group are considered, it takes a plural verb.

   herd   team   jury   Senate

   SINGULAR: The farmer's *herd was* killed by the dust.
   PLURAL: The *herd were found* in scattered parts of the field.

EXERCISE 2. Choose the correct verbs for these sentences:

1. The entire class (was, were) on time.   2. The group (is, are) interested in the project.   3. The jury (was, were) disagreeing among themselves.   4. The squad (is, are) going to the lockers. 5. The choir (has, have) finished the morning anthem.

N 2   Gender

Nouns and pronouns have three <u>genders:</u> <u>masculine</u> (*man, he*), <u>feminine</u> (*woman, she*), and <u>neuter</u> (*school, it*). Nouns have a fourth gender called <u>common gender,</u> which refers to words that may be either masculine or feminine (*teacher, person*).

Knowledge of gender of pronouns is important because of possible usage errors; knowledge of gender of nouns is important chiefly from the point of view of vocabulary.

The distinction between masculine and feminine gender of nouns is made in the following ways:

1. By compounding elements:

MASCULINE	FEMININE
man	woman
merman	mermaid
manservant	maidservant

2. By adding to or changing an ending:

giant	giantess
adventurer	adventuress
executor	executrix

3. By using different words:

rooster	hen
husband	wife
king	queen

EXERCISE. Write the opposite of each of these:

1. goose	6. mare	11. landlady	16. tiger
2. gentleman	7. aviator	12. nun	17. sir
3. doe	8. emperor	13. patron	18. peacock
4. actor	9. heifer	14. bachelor	19. host
5. marchioness	10. duke	15. female	20. ewe

N 3   Number

The term <u>number</u> is used to distinguish between one and more than one. A noun or a pronoun that indicates one in number is <u>singular</u>; a noun or a pronoun that indicates more than one is <u>plural</u>. Thus, *house* and *it* are singular; *houses* and *we* are plural.

On pages 201 to 203 are listed the principal rules for making nouns plural. Study those rules; then do the exercise.

EXERCISE. Write the plural of each of these nouns:

1. beef	10. basis	19. A	28. cupful
2. army	11. hoof	20. crocus	29. 10
3. antenna	12. buffalo	21. oath	30. tooth
4. beau	13. alumnus	22. piano	31. latch
5. handful	14. grouse	23. datum	32. potato
6. handkerchief	15. hoe	24. attorney	33. crisis
7. volcano	16. lily	25. valise	34. trade-union
8. index	17. mouse	26. money	35. tax
9. son-in-law	18. swine	27. cactus	36. embargo

N 4   Case

<u>Case</u> is important in that it shows the relationship of a noun (or a pronoun) to other words in a sentence. The three cases in the English language are <u>nominative</u>, <u>possessive</u>, and <u>objective</u>.

NOMINATIVE CASE

In the nominative case, the following are the most important uses of nouns:

1. SUBJECT OF A SENTENCE AND OF A DEPENDENT CLAUSE

When the dust *storms* ended, the *fields* were gone.

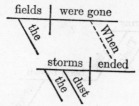

2. PREDICATE NOUN

The fields were *deserts* of sand.

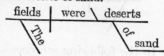

3. NOUN OF DIRECT ADDRESS

Students, the devastation was horrible.

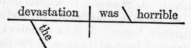

4. APPOSITIVE, WITH THE NOUN IN THE NOMINATIVE CASE

The farms, barren *wastes,* were worthless.

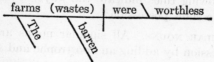

5. EXCLAMATION

Oh, the *misery* of it!

6. NOUN IN ABSOLUTE PHRASE

Their *farms* having been blown away, the people had nothing.

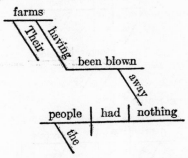

EXERCISE 1. In the following sentences, list the nouns that are in the nominative case. Tell how each is used.

1. During 1934 and 1935, thousands of square miles were destroyed by dust storms. 2. The families whom these farms supported were ruined. 3. Students, thousands of them suddenly were paupers. 4. These persons finding themselves homeless, a tremendous migration began. 5. John Steinbeck, a contemporary American novelist, has told the story in *The Grapes of Wrath*.

POSSESSIVE CASE

The following rules indicate the ways by which nouns are made to show possession:

1. SINGULAR NOUNS. All singular nouns are made to show possession by adding an apostrophe and *s*.

    boy — boy's   James — James's

The only exception to this rule occurs when there are too many *s's* or *s* sounds close together (*princess' slipper*). Possession may then be shown by adding merely the apostrophe.

36

2. PLURAL NOUNS. (a) Plural nouns that end in *s* are made to show possession by adding an apostrophe.

boys — boys'   Smiths — Smiths'

(b) Plural nouns that do not end in *s* are made to show possession by adding an apostrophe and *s*.

children — children's   sheep — sheep's

3. COMPOUND WORDS. Hyphenated compound words, both singular and plural, are made to show possession by adding an apostrophe and *s* to the last word.

father-in-law — father-in-law's
fathers-in-law — fathers-in-law's

4. JOINT OR SEPARATE OWNERSHIP. (a) When two or more persons own something jointly, possession is shown by adding the sign of possession to the last word.

Jack and Jill's pail   boys and girls' attitude

(b) When two or more persons own something separately, possession is shown by adding the sign of possession to each name.

Jack's and Jill's clothes   boys' and girls' gym classes

Since possessive nouns are used as adjectives, they are diagramed as adjectives.

EXERCISE 2. Make a chart showing the singular, singular possessive, plural, and plural possessive of each:

1. mother-in-law	9. corpse	17. beau
2. alto	10. ox	18. nurse
3. calf	11. hanger-on	19. wife
4. witch	12. baby	20. turkey
5. Chinese	13. man and woman	21. dwarf
6. sheep	14. alumnus	22. deer
7. Jones	15. maid of honor	23. parent
8. monkey	16. goose	24. passer-by

OBJECTIVE CASE

In the objective case, the following are the most important uses of nouns:

1. DIRECT OBJECT

   The great dust storms had their *causes*.

   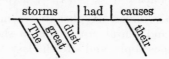

2. INDIRECT OBJECT

   The experience taught *America* a costly lesson.

   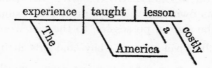

3. OBJECT OF A PREPOSITION

   In the last *century*, herds grazed on **the** *plains*.

   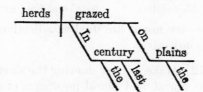

4. OBJECTIVE COMPLEMENT

   The light rainfall made agriculture a difficult *matter*.

   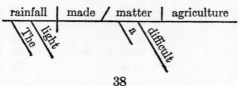

5. ADVERBIAL OBJECTIVE

The unbroken plains stretched *hundreds* of miles.

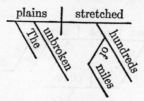

6. APPOSITIVE, WITH THE NOUN IN THE OBJECTIVE CASE

World War I drove the farmers, poor *homesteaders*, into the production of wheat.

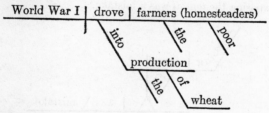

7. SUBJECT OF AN INFINITIVE

The government urged the *people* to plow.

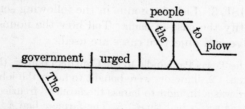

8. OBJECT OF AN INFINITIVE

The plains were broken to raise *food*.

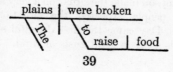

9. OBJECT OF A PARTICIPLE

The farmers, breaking the *plains*, took the first step to disaster.

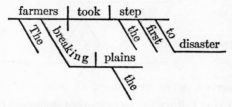

10. OBJECT OF A GERUND

Exposing the *topsoil* was a mistake.

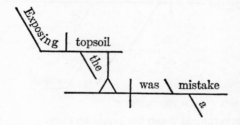

EXERCISE 3. List the nouns in the following sentences, and identify the case of each. Tell how the nouns in the nominative and objective cases are used.

1. From the Texas Panhandle to the Canadian border, the plains were broken. 2. Tractors were bought to hurry the job. 3. In 1930, there was a drought to harass the farmers' frenzied efforts. 4. That year was a bad time. 5. The farmers had a bad time the next year, too. 6. The year 1933, a fateful one, was the climax to their troubles. 7. The sun gave the people no relief. 8. The blowing topsoil made the situation a very serious problem. 9. Perhaps the people expected the situation to improve. 10. On Armistice Day came the first dreadful storm, sweeping the people's lands away in great gusts of wind.

PRONOUNS

P   Definition

A <u>pronoun</u> is a word used in place of a noun to refer to it or to point it out.

P 1   Kinds of Pronouns

There are several kinds of pronouns — *personal, relative, interrogative, indefinite, demonstrative, intensive,* and *reflexive.*

The <u>personal pronoun</u> is one that distinguishes the speaker, the person spoken to, or the person, place, or thing spoken of. With the exception of the word *it,* personal pronouns refer only to persons.

	NOMINATIVE CASE	POSSESSIVE CASE	OBJECTIVE CASE
Singular			
First Person	I	my, mine	me
Second Person	you	your, yours	you
Third Person	he, she, it	his, her, hers, its	him, her, it
Plural			
First Person	we	our, ours	us
Second Person	you	your, yours	you
Third Person	they	their, theirs	them

A pronoun that relates, or refers, to a preceding word and at the same time connects two clauses of a sentence is called a <u>relative pronoun.</u> The relative pronouns are *who, whose, whom, that,* and *which.*

> Housewives *who* suffered through the dust storms have stories to tell.
> Those *whose* endurance was great managed to survive.
> They were the ones *whom* necessity drove to strange actions.

41

Interrogative pronouns are those used in asking questions — *who, whose, whom, which,* and *what.*

> *Who* knows one device used by the housewives?
> *Whom* did you ask?

A pronoun that does not refer to a definite antecedent is called an indefinite pronoun.

It is necessary to know whether an indefinite pronoun is singular or plural. If it is the subject of the sentence, the predicate must agree with it in number; and personal pronouns referring to it must agree in number also.

These indefinite pronouns are singular:

another	each	neither	nothing
anybody	either	nobody	one
anyone	everybody	no one	someone

These indefinite pronouns are plural:

many	both	few	several

The indefinite pronouns *some, all,* and *none* may be either singular or plural, according to their use.

> *Everyone does his* best.
> *Many were* soon to lose *their* farms.
> *None* of the persons *was* successful. (meaning *not one*)
> *None* of the devices against the dust *were* sufficient. (meaning *not any*)

Pronouns used to point out are called demonstrative pronouns. *This* and *these* refer to things near by; *that* and *those* refer to things farther away.

> *This* is a true story.
> *Those* which you told me last week were tall tales.

Intensive and reflexive pronouns are compound forms of personal pronouns plus the word *self* or *selves.*

The intensive pronoun is used for emphasis.

The goddess Patience *herself* could not succeed.

The reflexive pronoun refers the action of the verb back to the subject.

Some housewives bought *themselves* gummed sealing tape to seal the windows.

EXERCISE. List the pronouns found in these sentences, and identify each as to kind:

1. The women found their efforts futile in their fight against the great dust storms. 2. The men themselves were powerless in their struggles. 3. The roads which they had built were gone. 4. The fields that they had cultivated were covered with sand. 5. No one saw any hope for himself and his family. 6. Who could possibly save any of them in this extremity? 7. That was a question which nobody could answer. 8. The farmers themselves, who had broken the plains, had brought this about. 9. Now they were the ones who suffered. 10. This is the way of life as everyone knows it to be.

P 2   Gender

See page 33 for a discussion of gender.

P 3   Number

See page 34 for a discussion of number.

P 4   Case

Pronouns, like nouns, have <u>case</u>. Pronouns (and nouns) are said to be in a particular case — <u>nominative</u>, <u>possessive</u>, <u>objective</u> — because of their use in sentences.

Turn to the declension of the personal pronouns on page 41.

Pronouns have the following uses in sentences. See the discussion of the uses of nouns, pages 34 to 40, for an amplification of this work.

NOMINATIVE CASE

1. SUBJECT OF A SENTENCE OR OF A DEPENDENT CLAUSE
2. PREDICATE PRONOUN
3. APPOSITIVE, WITH THE NOUN IN THE NOMINATIVE CASE
4. PRONOUN IN ABSOLUTE PHRASE

POSSESSIVE CASE

The possessive forms of pronouns are used as adjectives even though they are pronouns.

Their one *hope* was migration. (*Their* modifies *hope.*)

Desperation was *theirs*. (*Theirs* is a predicate adjective.)

OBJECTIVE CASE

1. DIRECT OBJECT
2. INDIRECT OBJECT
3. OBJECT OF A PREPOSITION
4. APPOSITIVE, WITH THE NOUN IN THE OBJECTIVE CASE
5. SUBJECT OF AN INFINITIVE
6. OBJECT OF AN INFINITIVE
7. OBJECT OF A PARTICIPLE
8. OBJECT OF A GERUND

EXERCISE 1. Point out the pronouns in these sentences. Give the case of each, and tell how it is used.

1. In 1934 and 1935, the migration, which lasted for years, began.
2. According to records which we have, 200,000 persons had migrated from their homes by 1939. 3. They moved in old automobiles and trucks, taking with them their few possessions.

4. These were the ones whom nature had ruined, and with them were others whom the mechanization of farming had made jobless. 5. To give them help was the responsibility of everyone, but the situation was so enormous that no one could cope with it.

EXERCISE 2. Choose the correct pronoun forms from the parentheses:

You and (1. I, me) should look at the records. Between you and (2. I, me), they are startling. Authorities (3. who, whom) have studied the problem say that the migration left a depopulated section of the country. (4. Who, Whom) could make a living on a farm of sand? Anyone (5. who, whom) circumstance has ever forced to try it knows from (6. his, their) own experience the insurmountable difficulty. One authority, (7. who, whom) you all know, says that almost 3000 houses were abandoned in Colorado. It was (8. he, him) (9. who, whom) counted 1500 abandoned homesites. Certainly everyone can interpret for (10. himself, hisself) the seriousness of the situation.

EXERCISE 3. Write sentences of your own using each of the following:

he and I	Bob and me
between Mary and him	for Ellen and us
was she	John to be him
who	whom you know
whom	who spoke to me
this	those

EXERCISE 4. Write sentences using a pronoun in each of these constructions:

1. appositive in nominative case
2. object of a participle
3. subject of a dependent clause

ADJECTIVES

Adj   Definition

An <u>adjective</u> is a word that modifies a noun or a pronoun.

An adjective performs the following functions in a sentence:

1. It may describe: *bad* weather.
2. It may point out: *this* story.
3. It may give a number: *three* pigs.
4. It may be indefinite: *several* persons.
5. It may be an article: *the* result.
6. It may be derived from a proper noun: *American* people.
7. It may be a noun used as an adjective: *soil* erosion.
8. It may be a possessive noun: *Mary's* answer.
9. It may be a possessive pronoun: *her* answer.
10. It may be a compound word: *worth-while* idea.

An adjective may also be used as a predicate adjective or as an objective complement.

PREDICATE ADJECTIVE: The answer was *good*.
OBJECTIVE COMPLEMENT: He made the answer *good*.

Adj 1   Comparison of Adjectives

In order to use adjectives correctly, one must know their three degrees of comparison: the *positive degree* (the simplest form), the *comparative degree* (used to compare two persons or things), and the *superlative degree* (used to compare more than two persons or things).

1. Some adjectives are compared by adding *er* and *est* to form the comparative and superlative degrees.

POSITIVE	COMPARATIVE	SUPERLATIVE
kind	kinder	kindest
plain	plainer	plainest

2. Some adjectives, especially those of more than two syllables, are compared by using the words *more* and *most* or *less* and *least* to form the comparative and superlative degrees.

POSITIVE	COMPARATIVE	SUPERLATIVE
beautiful	more beautiful	most beautiful
conscientious	less conscientious	least conscientious

3. Some adjectives of one and two syllables are compared both ways.

calm	calmer	calmest
calm	more calm	most calm

4. Some adjectives are irregular in comparison.

good	better	best
bad	worse	worst
much	more	most
many	more	most
little	less	least

EXERCISE 1. Write the degrees of comparison of each of the following:

1. ill	6. fine	11. many	16. difficult
2. happy	7. pretty	12. hungry	17. rapid
3. wonderful	8. famous	13. quick	18. intelligent
4. lively	9. charming	14. thin	19. fat
5. hasty	10. sturdy	15. few	20. sweet

EXERCISE 2. Write a sentence about each of the following, using the requested degree of an appropriate adjective:

1. a fire (comparative degree)
2. an assignment (superlative degree)
3. a sunset (superlative degree)
4. a friend (positive degree)
5. a career (comparative degree)

EXERCISE 3. Words like *perfect, straight, correct,* and *dead* cannot be compared. Name five other such adjectives.

47

ADVERBS

Adv   Definition

An <u>adverb</u> is a word that modifies a verb, an adjective, or another adverb.

An adverb also performs certain functions in a sentence. The principal ones are the following:

1. It tells time: *now, then, yesterday, soon.*
2. It tells place: *here, there, forward.*
3. It indicates manner: *quickly, pleasantly, well, thus.*
4. It indicates degree: *very, somewhat, just, rather.*
5. It introduces a question: *When* shall we leave? *Where* are you?
6. It says *yes* or *no: Yes,* it is. *No,* it isn't.

EXERCISE. List in two columns the adjectives and adverbs used in these sentences. Write the word that each modifies.

1. The dreadful ravages of the dust storms were still fresh in people's minds. 2. Suddenly another tragedy struck. 3. A long period of rainy weather brought the inevitable result — floods. 4. The very worst floods in American history occurred in 1937. 5. Five hundred thousand persons speedily left their homes. 6. Electric-light plants were soon submerged by the swirling water, and whole communities remained entirely in darkness. 7. Then many railroad tracks were washed away, and food supplies were promptly cut off. 8. People huddled miserably on housetops, and often the houses floated down the river. 9. The radio was often used effectively to direct rescue workers. 10. The muddy water seemed to be everywhere.

Adv 1   Conjunctive Adverbs

As its name indicates, a conjunctive adverb is a combination of a conjunction and an adverb.

48

A <u>conjunctive adverb</u> is a word that connects two independent clauses and at the same time acts as an adverbial modifier of the second clause.

Some conjunctive adverbs are *furthermore, also, however, besides, nevertheless, consequently, moreover, so, for example, on the other hand, at the same time.*

> The flood destroyed property; *moreover,* it took lives.
> The situation seemed hopeless; *however,* help was coming.

EXERCISE. Combine the sentences in these groups by using conjunctive adverbs. In the examples, notice the punctuation of sentences containing conjunctive adverbs.

1. Dust storms and floods were destroying American soil. They were destroying man's means of livelihood.
2. The Federal Government recognized the seriousness of the situation. A Soil Conservation Act was passed.
3. In CCC camps, young men were planting trees. They were building check dams.
4. New methods of farming were introduced. Farmers were taught the values of contour plowing and rotation of crops.
5. After the dust storms, the shifting sand created a problem. Even shifting sand can be checked by proper planting.

Adv 2   Comparison of Adverbs

Adverbs are compared in the same ways as adjectives. (See page 46.)

EXERCISE. Write each of the following adverbs in the three degrees of comparison:

1. near	6. pleasantly	11. loudly	16. well
2. far	7. late	12. often	17. quickly
3. slowly	8. soon	13. sadly	18. happily
4. slow	9. politely	14. wearily	19. softly
5. courteously	10. efficiently	15. badly	20. surely

Exercises in Supplying Adjectives and Adverbs

EXERCISE 1. Supply five interesting and colorful adjectives to modify the noun in each of these sentences:

1. The old man was –?–.   3. The sunset was –?–.
2. The –?– baby howled.   4. The –?– assignment exhausted me.

EXERCISE 2. Supply five interesting and colorful adjectives to modify the pronoun in each of these sentences:

1. The one with the scar is –?–.   3. This smells –?–.
2. She was –?–.   4. Mine tastes –?–.

EXERCISE 3. Supply five adverbs to modify the verb in each of these sentences:

1. He speaks –?–.   3. The dog barked –?–.
2. She smiles –?–   4. The child was spanked –?–.

EXERCISE 4. Supply five adverbs to modify the adjective in each of these sentences:

1. It was a –?– cold day.   3. The scene was –?– beautiful.
2. The illusion was –?– real.   4. His bank account was –?– low.

EXERCISE 5. Supply three adverbs to modify the adverb in each of the following:

   1. He spoke –?– haltingly.
   2. They shook hands –?– warmly.
   3. The pupils worked –?– diligently.
   4. She moaned –?– loudly.

PREPOSITIONS

Prep   Definition

A <u>preposition</u> is a word used to show the relationship between a noun or a pronoun and another word in the sentence.

Some of the most common prepositions are:

about	at	by	in	through
above	before	concerning	inside	to
across	behind	despite	into	toward
after	below	down	near	under
against	beneath	during	of	up
along	beside	except	off	upon
among	between	for	on	with
around	beyond	from	over	within

Some prepositions are made up of more than one word. They are called *phrasal prepositions*, or *compound prepositions*.

according to	for the sake of	in regard to
because of	in addition to	in spite of
by means of	in case of	instead of
by way of	in front of	on account of

Prep 1   Prepositional Phrase

A <u>prepositional phrase</u> is a group of words that includes the preposition, the noun or the pronoun that is its object, and any words that modify the noun or the pronoun.

During the Missouri floods *in* 1947, approximately 115,000,000 tons *of* topsoil *in* Iowa were washed away *by* the rain.

EXERCISE. List each preposition and its noun or pronoun object that you find in these sentences:

51

1. According to estimates, the loss of rich topsoil had cost Iowa one hundred thirty-four millions of dollars.   2. With the loss of topsoil comes a serious decrease in the fertility of the land.   3. This sort of loss can be measured in reduced production year after year.   4. By the statistics of one authority, virgin soils in Ohio once yielded a hundred bushels of corn to the acre; the average now is forty-two bushels to the acre.   5. Because of soil erosion, the land of plenty is rapidly going downhill.

Preposition or Adverb or Conjunction?

A number of words are used both as prepositions and as adverbs. It is the *use* of such words in the sentence that determines their part of speech.

PREPOSITION: Rich soil went *down* the river.

ADVERB: Stocks went *down*.

PREPOSITION: People stayed *inside* their houses.

ADVERB: People stayed *inside*.

A number of words may also be used both as prepositions and as conjunctions. Again, use in the sentence is the one determining factor.

PREPOSITION: Certain problems are set *before* us.
CONJUNCTION: They must be settled *before* it is too late.

PREPOSITION: Let's go to the movies *after* dinner.
CONJUNCTION: We left *after* they had arrived.

EXERCISE. What parts of speech are the italicized words in these sentences?

1. Great dams and reservoirs are being built *because of* the pressing need.   2. In many cases, the projects seem to have been undertaken "*after* the horse had been stolen."   3. Contour plowing has been introduced *because* it reduces erosion. 4. A farmer plows around a hill *for* obvious reasons. 5. Furrows

from top to bottom are bad, *for* they make direct channels *for* water.   6. *After* the plowing, the rapid flow of water is retarded. 7. Strip cropping helps to keep the water *in* the soil.   8. Water and topsoil may be washed *down* as far as the belt, or strip, of grass.   9. The water and topsoil are held there *by* the planted terrain.   10. It cannot easily flow *by*.

Prep 2   Uses of Prepositional Phrases

A prepositional phrase that modifies a noun or a pronoun is used as an adjective.

Devastations *of various kinds* had taught serious lessons.

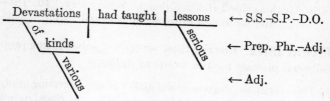

A prepositional phrase that modifies a verb, an adjective, or an adverb is used as an adverb.

MODIFIES VERB: History moved *in strange patterns*.

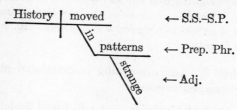

MODIFIES ADJECTIVE: The 1930's were hard *for many*.

MODIFIES ADVERB: Will you give your report tomorrow *in the afternoon?*

EXERCISE 1. List the prepositional phrases in these sentences. Write how each is used — as an adjective or as an adverb — and the word that it modifies.

1. The gloom of depression days was gradually lifting. 2. The suffering of the inhabitants of the Dust Bowl and of those in the flooded areas was not forgotten. 3. At the same time, the advent of happier days cheered everyone. 4. More automobiles could be seen on the roads. 5. The streamlined automobile was coming into vogue. 6. Americans gasped at their first sight of these strange cars. 7. With the next gasp, they reached into their pockets and bought. 8. Air conditioning was becoming popular in theaters and restaurants. 9. Air conditioning in the early days was wonderful in a damp, clammy way. 10. Times did look better for almost everyone in 1936 and 1937.

EXERCISE 2. Rewrite these sentences, substituting prepositional phrases for the words in italics:

1. *Transportation* progress in the 1930's is an interesting study. 2. Everything was being built *bigger* and *faster*. 3. *Speed* records were being set by ships and planes. 4. In 1936, the Douglas DC-3 had a *two-hundred-miles-an-hour* cruising speed. 5. People literally held their breath *excitedly*. 6. *The China Clipper's* successful flight to Manila created another *excited* stir. 7. *The Queen Mary's* construction was an *engineering* triumph. 8. *The Hindenburg's* flights reminded one of *Jules Verne's* imaginative stories. 9. Life was moving *fast and furiously*. 10. Much *past* gloom was forgotten.

EXERCISE 3. Add interesting prepositional phrases to these skeleton sentences:

1. The ghost shook his chains.
2. The old woman cried.
3. The sun rose.
4. The taffy had stuck.
5. Johnny lied.
6. I read the letter.
7. Girls frighten me.
8. Men bore me.
9. There was a valentine.
10. Gravy fell.

54

CONJUNCTIONS

Conj   Definition

A <u>conjunction</u> is a connective that links words, phrases, or clauses.

Since some conjunctions are used to link parts of equal value and others are used to link parts of unequal value, two kinds are necessary. The two kinds of conjunctions are *co-ordinate* and *subordinate*.

Conj 1   Co-ordinate

A <u>co-ordinate conjunction</u> joins words, phrases, or clauses of equal rank in meaning. The most common of these are *and, but,* and *or* (negative *nor*).

> LINKS WORDS: Candid cameras *and* boogie-woogie came into vogue in the 1930's.
> LINKS PHRASES: Inspired by Benny Goodman *and* by their own love of swing, young people became jitterbugs.
> LINKS CLAUSES: People were amused, *but* they were also impressed.

Certain co-ordinate conjunctions come in pairs. These are *correlative conjunctions* and include *either — or, neither — nor, both — and, not only — but also.* They are used chiefly for emphasis.

> *Neither* scorn *nor* criticism stopped the craze.
> *Both* boys *and* girls liked jam sessions.
> *Not only* dance rhythm *but also* vocabulary changed.

EXERCISE. How might the following paragraph be improved through the use of co-ordinate conjunctions?

In the early years of the depression, people were in no mood for "hot" music. They wanted sweet tunes. They wanted sentimental tunes to tear at their heartstrings. "Star Dust" was popular.

So was "Stormy Weather" in the early 1930's. Time passed. Tastes and interests changed. People still liked "sweet" music. There was an undeniable revival of interest in the jazz of the 1920's. Thus swing had its beginnings.

Conj 2   Subordinate

A <u>subordinate conjunction</u> joins a subordinate clause to a principal clause.

The most common subordinate conjunctions are listed on page 15.

> *Although* jazz probably had its origin in New Orleans, Europe influenced its development.

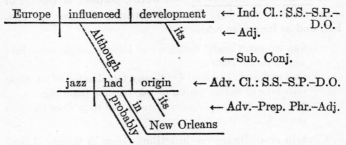

When England and France wanted "hot" music, Benny Goodman had the answer.

His first records were so good *that* the craze swept America.

EXERCISE 1.   Point out the subordinate conjunctions in the following sentences.   Point out, too, the subordinate clause which each introduces.

1. In 1937 and 1938, swing was so popular that it was almost a mania.   2. If we can believe accounts, Benny Goodman's appearance at the Paramount, a motion-picture theater in New York, caused a near riot.   3. Although the doors would not open until 8 A.M., three thousand boys and girls were waiting in the streets at six.   4. The crowd was so great that the fire

department was called in.   5. After the doors were finally
opened, thousands of disappointed "alligators" were left outside.
6. The concert itself sounded as if bedlam had broken loose.
7. If people thought the "Big Apple" and the "Charleston"
crazy exhibitions, they should have seen the audience at that
concert.   8. They were scornful possibly because they didn't
understand.   9. The audience was happily exhausted when the
concert ended.   10. The popularity of this new kind of music
continued until it reached tremendous proportions.

EXERCISE 2. List both the co-ordinate and the subordinate conjunctions in these sentences:

1. No doubt you have read or heard about the Carnival of Swing
in 1938.   2. It was held in New York, and twenty-five bands
played.   3. The bands played while 23,000 admiring fans listened.   4. The fans not only listened but also screamed their
admiration.   5. They listened for five hours and forty-five
minutes, but from all appearances they would have listened until
doomsday was called.

EXERCISE 3. Rewrite the following paragraph, and
improve it through the wise use of co-ordinate and subordinate conjunctions:

An upswing in interest in music could be seen in young people.
It could be noted also in adults. The jitterbugs had such favorites
as Benny Goodman. They liked Tommy Dorsey. They certainly liked Artie Shaw. They knew why they liked them. The
radio included programs of opera. There were symphonic programs, too. The American public's interest in good music had
been aroused. The upswing in interest was surely encouraging.

INTERJECTIONS

Int   Definition

An interjection is a word that shows surprise or strong feeling.
It has no grammatical relationship to the rest of the sentence.

An interjection that shows strong feeling is followed by
an exclamation point. The word after it begins with a
capital letter.

Horrors!   The house is on fire.

| Horrors | ← Interj. |
| house \| is | ← S.S.–S.P. |

← Adj.–Prep. Phr.

An interjection that shows only mild feeling is followed
by a comma. The word after it does not necessarily begin
with a capital letter.

Oh, this is the last straw.
Ah, I should say so.

Oaths and slang words also are regarded as interjections.

EXERCISE 1.   Write the following sentences correctly:

1. goodness we're ruined
2. well don't cry
3. my you take things calmly
4. horrors my house is burning
5. ah things are different
6. quick get a bucket
7. nonsense let it burn
8. help this is terrible
9. pshaw it's your imagination
10. hurrah we're saved

EXERCISE 2.   Use an interjection in a sentence concerning each of the following:

1. a thief
2. a touchdown
3. a toothache
4. a flower
5. a storm
6. a failure
7. a wound
8. Santa Claus
9. a cake
10. a worm
11. a scene
12. new shoes

EXERCISE 1, SUBJECTS AND PREDICATES. Copy these sentences on your paper. Draw one line under each complete subject and two lines under each complete predicate. Indicate each simple and compound subject and predicate by the appropriate initials: *S. S.*, *S. P.*, *C. S.*, *C. P.*

1. Among many could be seen an interest in realism. 2. Do you remember the "pretty" pictures in the early camera magazines? 3. Pretty rural scenes and chubby, dimpled babies were considered proper subjects. 4. Then the candid camera was developed, and a new craze struck America. 5. Candid shots did not flatter; they revealed the person as he was.

EXERCISE 2, KINDS OF SENTENCES. Write what kind of sentence each of these is — simple, compound, complex, compound-complex:

1. This craze had a healthful influence on photography. 2. People soon discovered that beauty is everywhere. 3. A face that is old and wrinkled can be beautiful. 4. People may be awed by a picture of a sunset, but they will stop to think at the sight of a picture of city slums. 5. Realism and romanticism are at opposite poles; but, as you will agree, each has its place.

EXERCISE 3, KINDS OF CLAUSES. Find the dependent clause in each of these sentences, and then write how it is used:

1. The picture magazines which appeared in the 1930's showed this new attitude toward art. 2. When one looks at *Life*, one sees realism in photography. 3. We recognize that these are pictures of everyday life. 4. The pictures are a record of what life actually is. 5. The realism which appeared in photography appeared also in other phases of art.

EXERCISE 4, DIAGRAMING. Diagram the five sentences in EXERCISE 2.

EXERCISE 5, PARTS OF SPEECH. Copy these sentences on your paper, and over each word identify its part of speech. Use abbreviations.

1. Artists like Benton and Wood and Curry were depicting life realistically and sometimes satirically. 2. Government artists were painting murals on post-office walls for the enjoyment of people like you and me. 3. Gracious! We must not forget the novelists and the playwrights. 4. Among these were many who did not see life through rose-colored glasses. 5. Erskine Caldwell and John Steinbeck gained fame for themselves everywhere for their realistic portrayals.

EXERCISE 6, USES OF WORDS. In the following sentences, explain the use of each word or group of words in italics:

1. *Showing* life as it is may result in *developing* a social conscience. 2. *To know* the truth, even though painful, is often an incentive *to do* something about it. 3. The American public, *reading* these unhappy records of American life, became an *awakened* public. 4. *There* were many forces at work. 5. New patterns of thinking were in the making; *moreover*, new patterns of living were also apparent.

EXERCISE 7, PREPOSITIONAL PHRASES. List the prepositional phrases in EXERCISE 5. Write how each is used — as an adjective or as an adverb.

EXERCISE 8, COMPARISON OF ADJECTIVES AND ADVERBS. Compare these adjectives and adverbs:

good	often	pretty
rapidly	little	intelligently
thin	beautiful	much

Gr T   Grammatical Terms

The following terms are used frequently in discussions of grammar. Turn to this list whenever you need a concise explanation.

Absolute Phrase. A group of words which stands as an independent element and consists of a noun or a pronoun and a modifying participle is called an *absolute phrase*. This construction is sometimes called a *nominative absolute*.

> *The years having passed,* we are prone to forget.

Adjective. An adjective is a word that modifies a noun or a pronoun: *tall* building, *ten* years. Adjectives derived from proper nouns are called *proper adjectives*. A proper adjective always begins with a capital letter: *American* people.

Adjective Clause. An adjective clause is a dependent clause that modifies a noun or a pronoun. Usually it is introduced by a relative pronoun (*who, whose, whom, which,* or *that*).

> Radio stars *who were popular* interest us.
> There are many *whom we still enjoy.*

Adjective Phrase. An adjective phrase is a group of words without a subject or a predicate that modifies a noun or a pronoun.

1. PREPOSITIONAL PHRASE USED AS ADJECTIVE: One *of them* is Lowell Thomas.
2. PARTICIPIAL PHRASE USED AS ADJECTIVE: The public, *listening to his broadcasts,* is informed.
3. INFINITIVE PHRASE USED AS ADJECTIVE: Another person *to gain fame* in the 1930's was Jack Benny.

61

Adverb. An adverb is a word that modifies a verb, an adjective, or another adverb: walks *quickly*, *very* kind, *almost* certainly.

Adverbial Clause. An adverbial clause is a dependent clause that modifies a verb, an adjective, or an adverb. It is usually introduced by a subordinate conjunction.

> The world listened *when it was Jack Benny time.*
> His humor was so amazing *that he became an institution.*

Adverbial Objective. An adverbial objective is a noun that is used as an adverb. Such words denote time, distance, weight, and value.

Adverbial Phrase. An adverbial phrase is a group of words without a subject or a predicate that modifies a verb, an adjective, or an adverb.

1. PREPOSITIONAL PHRASE USED AS ADVERB: Other honors went *to Fred Allen.*
2. INFINITIVE PHRASE USED AS ADVERB: Millions of fans waited *to hear George Burns and Gracie Allen.*

Antecedent. *Antecedent* is the term used to denote the word or group of words to which a pronoun refers.

> Then *Charlie McCarthy* revealed that *he* was a bad boy. (*Charlie McCarthy* is the antecedent of *he.*)
> *Edgar Bergen, who* sponsored Charlie, had *his* hands full. (*Edgar Bergen* is the antecedent of *who* and *his.*)

Appositive. An appositive is a noun or a pronoun placed near another noun or pronoun to explain it.

> Charlie McCarthy, an impudent little *block* of wood, caught the public's fancy. (The noun *block* is in apposition with *Charlie McCarthy.* The phrase, *an impudent little block of wood,* is spoken of as an *appositive phrase.*)

Articles. Articles are adjectives. The word *the* is a definite article; the words *a* and *an* are indefinite articles.

Auxiliary. An auxiliary is a helping verb; it helps to complete the verb phrase: *is* going, *has been* done, *might have been* finished.

Case. Case is one of the inflectional forms of a noun or a pronoun that indicates its relation to other words in the sentence. The three cases in the English language are *nominative, possessive,* and *objective.* The use of a noun or a pronoun in a sentence determines its case.

Clause. A clause is a part of a sentence that contains a subject and a verb. There are two kinds of clauses: *independent* (or principal) and *dependent* (or subordinate). An independent clause can stand alone as a simple sentence; a dependent clause depends upon another part of the sentence to give it meaning.

Ind. Cl.   Dep. Cl.
Bing Crosby initiated an era when crooners were heroes.

Comparison. Comparison is the change in an adjective or an adverb to denote a degree of quality, quantity, or relation. The three degrees are *positive, comparative,* and *superlative.* The positive degree gives the simplest form (*rapid, rapidly*); the comparative degree compares two persons or things (*more rapid, more rapidly* or *less rapid, less rapidly*); the superlative degree compares more than two persons or things (*most rapid, most rapidly* or *least rapid, least rapidly*).

Complex. The term *complex* refers to a kind of sentence that contains one independent clause and one or more dependent clauses.

Compound. The term *compound* refers to words, phrases, or clauses of equal value. It includes compound subjects, compound predicates, compound direct objects, compound phrases, and compound sentences.

Compound-complex. The term *compound-complex* refers to a kind of sentence that contains two or more independent clauses and one or more dependent clauses.

Conjugation. The conjugation of a verb shows all its forms in the proper order. See pages 29 to 31 for a complete conjugation of the verb *to drive*.

Conjunction. A conjunction links words, phrases, or clauses. The two kinds of conjunctions are *co-ordinate* and *subordinate*.

   1. A *co-ordinate conjunction* joins words, phrases, or clauses of equal rank in meaning. The most common co-ordinate conjunctions are *and, but,* and *or* (negative *nor*). *Correlative conjunctions* are co-ordinate conjunctions used in pairs. The most common of these are *either — or, neither — nor, both — and,* and *not only — but also.*
   2. A *subordinate conjunction* joins a subordinate clause to a principal clause. Some subordinate conjunctions are *after, although, as, because, if, since, so that, than, that, through, till, unless, until, when, where, whether,* and *while.*

Conjunctive Adverb. A conjunctive adverb is an adverb that connects two independent clauses and modifies the whole clause in which it appears. Some conjunctive adverbs are *moreover, however, therefore, nevertheless, hence, furthermore, consequently, accordingly.*

Co-ordinate. The term *co-ordinate* indicates equality of rank.

Correlative. See **Conjunction.**

Declension. See **Inflection.**

Direct Address. Direct address, sometimes known as a *noun of direct address*, is the name of a person spoken to or a word used instead of the name.

> *Henry,* do you like old movies?

Direct Object. A direct object follows a transitive verb and names the receiver of the action.

> You have probably seen a *number.*

Ellipsis. Ellipsis is the omission of a word or several words, clearly understood, from an expression.

> Although (they are) old, many are still excellent. Perhaps you have seen one more recently than I (have). When (you were) looking at it, did you think of its date?

Expletive. An expletive is a word used merely to intro- duce a certain order of parts of a sentence. It is not a special part of speech; and it is not independent, as are interjections. The words *there* and *it* are the chief expletives.

> *There* was a charming fantasy by Walt Disney.
> *It* is a pity you did not see it.

Gender. Gender distinguishes a noun or a pronoun ac- cording to sex. Nouns and pronouns can be classified according to three genders: *masculine, feminine,* and *neuter.* Nouns which refer to either masculine or fem- inine are said to be of *common gender* (*teacher, clerk, person*).

Gerund. A gerund is a verbal, ending in *ing,* that does the work of a noun.

1. SUBJECT: *Hearing* the song sung by everyone must have been thrilling.
2. DIRECT OBJECT: Children and adults began *whistling* "Heigh-ho."

Independent Elements. Certain words and groups of words are grammatically unrelated to the sentences of which they are a part. They are inserted to give emphasis, to add further information, and to inject variety. The most commonly used independent elements are *interjections, nouns of direct address, parenthetical expressions, expletives,* and *absolute phrases.*

1. INTERJECTION: *Oh,* I like that song.
2. NOUN OF DIRECT ADDRESS: *Sinatra,* sing it, please.
3. PARENTHETICAL EXPRESSION: The picture, *it seems to me,* inspired toymakers, too.
4. EXPLETIVE: *There* were amusing statuettes of the dwarfs.
5. ABSOLUTE PHRASE: *Walt Disney having captured public acclaim,* his future was assured.

Indirect Object. An indirect object noun or pronoun tells *to* or *for* whom something is done.

Walt Disney has given *us* Mickey Mouse, too.

Infinitive. An infinitive is a verbal that is usually introduced by the word *to.* It can be used as a noun, as an adjective, or as an adverb.

1. NOUN: *To judge* America by its movies is inadvisable.
2. ADJECTIVE: Does Hollywood see a need *to be* exact?
3. ADVERB: People wait eagerly *to see* certain pictures.

Inflection. Inflection means the alteration in the form of a word to indicate a change in relationship to other words. The change in verb forms is called *conjugation;* the change in adjectives and adverbs is called *comparison;* the change in nouns and pronouns is called *declension.* The declension of pronouns can be seen in the nominative, possessive, and objective forms (*I; my, mine; me*). The declension of nouns also can be seen: (*child, child's*).

Interjection. An interjection is a word that shows surprise or strong feeling.

> *Goodness!* These are startling facts.
> *Ah,* you are right.

Intransitive. The term refers to a verb that does not pass its action over to a receiver. An intransitive verb may be *complete* in itself; or it may *link* the subject with a noun, a pronoun, or an adjective in the predicate.

1. COMPLETE: The years *rolled* on.
2. LINKING: Momentous happenings *were* a part of the times.

Inverted Order. The term refers to that sentence structure in which the simple predicate precedes the simple subject.

Irregular Verb. A verb whose principal parts are formed in a variety of ways is spoken of as an irregular verb.

PRESENT	PAST	PAST PARTICIPLE
think	thought	thought
ring	rang	rung

Linking Verb. A linking verb (or *copulative verb*) shows the relationship between the subject and the predicate noun, the predicate adjective, or the predicate pronoun. The most common linking verbs are *be, seem, appear, become, look, feel, sound, taste, smell.*

> Chamberlain's umbrella *became* a symbol.

Modifier. A word or group of words that describes, limits, or qualifies another word or group of words is a modifier.

1. SINGLE-WORD MODIFIERS: Chamberlain carried *his black* umbrella.
2. PHRASE MODIFIER: Chamberlain carried his black umbrella *to Munich.*
3. CLAUSE MODIFIER: Chamberlain carried his black umbrella to Munich *when Czechoslovakia's fate was settled.*

67

Mood. The mood (or *mode*) of a verb indicates the point of view that can be taken toward its action. The three moods are *indicative, subjunctive,* and *imperative.*

1. The indicative mood gives a statement of fact.

2. The subjunctive mood expresses a condition that is contrary to fact, a doubt, or a wish.

3. The imperative mood gives a command.

See pages 29 to 31.

Nominative Absolute. See **Absolute Phrase.**

Nonrestrictive. The term refers to a phrase or a clause, used as an adjective, which merely adds further information about the noun or the pronoun it modifies. Because it is nonessential to the meaning, it is set off by commas.

> Joe Louis, *who was a rising young prize fighter,* knocked out Max Schmeling in 1938.

Noun. A noun is the name of a person, a place, or a thing: *fighter, victory, New York, Joe Louis.*

Nouns fall into two major classifications: *common nouns* and *proper nouns.*

1. A *common noun* is the name of any person, place, or thing. It never begins with a capital letter.

2. A *proper noun* is the name of a particular person, place, or thing. It always begins with a capital letter.

A *collective noun* may be either common or proper. This kind of noun refers to a group: *herd, group, class, jury, choir, team, Senate.*

Noun Clause. A noun clause is a dependent clause that is used as a noun.

SUBJECT: *That Hughes flew around the world* is known to all.
OBJECT: We know also *what his record was.*

Number. The term *number* is used to indicate whether a word refers to one or more than one. A word indicating *one* is *singular;* a word indicating *more than one* is *plural*.

Object. An object is a noun or a pronoun (or a phrase or a clause used as a noun) which receives the action of a transitive verb or verbal or which completes the meaning of a preposition.

1. DIRECT OBJECT: A noun or a pronoun that names the receiver of the action of the verb is a direct object.

   Hughes startled the *world*.

2. INDIRECT OBJECT: A noun or a pronoun that tells *to* or *for* whom something is done is an indirect object.

   He gave *aviation* a startling record.

3. OBJECT OF A PARTICIPLE: A noun or a pronoun that names the receiver of the action of a participle is called an object of a participle.

   Hughes, making the *flight* in three days, greatly influenced history.

4. OBJECT OF AN INFINITIVE: A noun or a pronoun that names the receiver of the action of an infinitive is called an object of an infinitive.

   "Wrong-way" Corrigan wanted to make a *record*, too.

5. OBJECT OF A GERUND: A noun or a pronoun that names the receiver of the action of a gerund is called an object of a gerund.

   Making a wrong-way *flight* was a good stunt.

6. OBJECT OF A PREPOSITION: A noun or a pronoun that is governed by a preposition is known as the object of a preposition.

   He landed in *Ireland* instead of in *California*.

69

Objective Complement. A noun or a pronoun that shows who or what the direct object becomes as a result of the verb, or an adjective that completes the meaning of the direct object, is an objective complement. Objective complements usually follow such verbs as *choose, call, name, elect, make.*

The people called him a great *hero.*

Parenthetical Expression. A word or a phrase added to a sentence that would be structurally complete without it is called a parenthetical expression. Some commonly used are *it seems to me, I repeat, as you know, however.*

The world generally, *to say the least,* seemed to be going in the "wrong direction."

Participle. A participle is a verb form used as an adjective. A participle and the words governed by it make up a *participial phrase.* Participles have three tenses:

1. *Present participle* ends in *ing: going, running.*
2. *Past participle* is the third principal part: *seen, done.*
3. *Perfect participle* consists of the word *having* plus the third principal part: *having swum, having known.*

Parts of Speech. Words are classified according to their uses in sentences. The eight classifications are *nouns, pronouns, verbs, adjectives, adverbs, prepositions, conjunctions,* and *interjections.*

Person. The term refers to changes in pronouns and verbs. The *first person* shows that the person is the speaker, the *second person* shows that the person is spoken to, and the *third person* shows that the person is spoken about.

FIRST PERSON: *I* enjoy history.
SECOND PERSON: *You* probably enjoy history, too.
THIRD PERSON: *He* makes it clear.

70

Phrase. A phrase is a group of words without a subject or a predicate used as a single part of speech.

1. PREPOSITIONAL PHRASE:
   The crisis *in Munich* was serious. (Adjective)
   It occurred *in 1938.* (Adverb)
2. PARTICIPIAL PHRASE:
   The world, *suffering from the jitters,* waited. (Adjective)
3. INFINITIVE PHRASE:
   They wanted *to forget,* if possible. (Noun)
4. GERUND PHRASE:
   Hearing a broadcast on October 30, 1938, made many forget. (Noun)
5. VERB PHRASES: *were listening, should have known*

Predicate. The predicate is the part of the sentence that tells something about the subject. The *simple predicate* (or *compound predicate*) is always a verb or a verb phrase. The *complete predicate* includes the simple predicate (or *compound predicate*) and all related words.

          s. s.   s. p.
The broadcast was called "The War of the Worlds."

Preposition. A preposition is a word used to show the relationship between a noun or a pronoun (its object) and another word in the sentence. Some commonly used prepositions are *in, of, by, from, under, without, to, through,* and *upon.*

Principal Parts. Verbs have three basic forms on which the tenses are built; these forms are called the *principal parts.* They are the *present,* the *past,* and the *past participle.*

PRESENT	PAST	PAST PARTICIPLE
eat	ate	eaten
take	took	taken

Pronoun. A pronoun is a word used in place of a noun to refer to it, or point it out.

1. PERSONAL PRONOUNS: *I, you, he, she, it, we, they*
2. RELATIVE PRONOUNS: *who, whose, whom, which, that*
3. INTERROGATIVE PRONOUNS: *who, whose, whom, which, what*
4. INDEFINITE PRONOUNS: *anyone, everybody, few, none*
5. DEMONSTRATIVE PRONOUNS: *this, that, these, those*
6. REFLEXIVE AND INTENSIVE PRONOUNS: *myself, himself, yourself, themselves*

Regular Verb. A verb whose second and third principal parts are made by simply adding *d* or *ed* to the first principal part is a regular verb.

PRESENT	PAST	PAST PARTICIPLE
work	worked	worked
dive	dived	dived

Restrictive. The term refers to a phrase or a clause, used as an adjective, which identifies the noun or the pronoun it modifies. Because it is essential to the meaning of the sentence, it is never set off by commas.

> The broadcast *which described the invasion of the men from Mars* frightened people out of their wits.

See also **Nonrestrictive.**

Sentence. A sentence is a group of words that expresses a complete thought. Sentences are classified according to meaning.

1. A *declarative sentence* makes a statement. (.)
2. An *interrogative sentence* asks a question. (?)
3. An *exclamatory sentence* expresses strong or sudden feeling. (!)
4. An *imperative sentence* makes a command. (. or !)

Sentences are classified also according to structure.

1. A *simple sentence* has one subject and one predicate, either or both of which may be compound.

2. A *compound sentence* is made up of two or more independent, or principal, clauses properly joined.

3. A *complex sentence* is made up of one independent, or principal, clause and one or more dependent, or subordinate, clauses.

4. A *compound-complex sentence* is made up of two or more independent clauses and one or more dependent clauses.

Simple. The term *simple* generally refers to sentence structure or to subjects or predicates. See **Sentence, Subject,** and **Predicate.**

Subject. The subject is the part of the sentence that tells what or whom the sentence is talking about. The *simple subject* is the most important noun or pronoun in the complete subject. The *complete subject* includes the simple subject and all words closely related.

<u>The portrayal of the invasion</u> <u>was very realistic.</u>
S. S.   S. P.

Subordinate Clause. A subordinate clause is one that cannot stand alone.

Substantive. *Substantive* is a term that refers to any word or group of words used as a noun. This classification includes nouns, pronouns, noun clauses, infinitives which are used as nouns, and gerunds.

Tense. The tense of a verb indicates the time of an action or of an occurrence. The six tenses are *present, past, future, present perfect, past perfect,* and *future perfect.* See page 25.

Transitive. The term *transitive* refers to a verb that passes its action over to a receiver. Sometimes a transitive verb takes a direct object, and sometimes it passes its action over to the subject of the sentence.

1. DIRECT OBJECT RECEIVER: Orson Welles *directed* the show.
2. SUBJECT RECEIVER: The show *was directed* by Orson Welles.

Verb. A verb expresses either action or a state of being. See also **Transitive** and **Intransitive.**

Verbal. A verbal is a verb form which is used as an adjective, an adverb, or a noun. See **Participle, Infinitive,** and **Gerund.**

Voice. The form of a transitive verb that shows whether the subject is acting or being acted upon is indicated by the term *voice.* The two voices are *active* and *passive.* The active voice shows the subject as the actor. The passive voice shows the subject as the receiver of the action.

1. ACTIVE: A world catastrophe *eclipsed* the Martian "invasion."
2. PASSIVE: The Martian "invasion" *was eclipsed* by a world catastrophe.

USAGE

AGREEMENT

Persons who say, "Bill and Ann *was* there," "Everybody turned in *their* papers," and "*These* kind of assignments are easy" are having trouble with agreement.

US 1   Kinds of Agreement

(1) Subject-verb, (2) Pronoun-antecedent, and (3) Adjective-noun

Subject-Verb Agreement

A verb must agree with its subject in person and number.

1. A singular subject takes a singular verb.

Each *decade reveals* interesting personalities.

2. A plural subject takes a plural verb.

Personalities are a part of history.

3. A compound subject joined by *and* takes a plural verb.

Even *you* and *I are* history makers.

4. A compound subject representing one person, thing, or idea takes a singular verb.

Ham and *eggs is* a good combination.
My *shield* and *guide is* you.

EXERCISE 1. Choose the correct verbs for these sentences:

Many kinds of persons (1. helps, help) in making history. The inventor and the scientist (2. is, are) contributors. The explorer who (3. charts, chart) the unknown (4. makes, make) his contribution. The musician and the painter and the actor (5. has, have) all helped to create life as people (6. knows, know) it today. Perhaps it (7. doesn't, don't) seem possible, but even John Q. Public (8. has, have) influenced the course of events. The Presidents and statesmen (9. is, are) certainly contributors to history, but history (10. don't, doesn't) depend on them alone.

5. A compound subject made up of two singular nouns or pronouns joined by *or, nor, either — or,* or *neither — nor* takes a singular verb.

RIGHT: Neither *business* nor *education is* exempt.

6. A compound subject made up of two plurals joined by *or, nor, either — or, neither — nor* takes a plural verb.

RIGHT: Neither *humorists* nor *philosophers are* excused.

7. A compound subject made up of a singular and a plural joined by *or, nor, either — or, neither — nor* takes a verb agreeing with the nearer subject.

RIGHT: Either *experience* or history *books give* proof.
RIGHT: Either history *books* or *experience gives* proof.

EXERCISE 2. Choose the correct verbs for the following sentences:

1. Neither the high nor the low (is, are) exempt from his part in the total pattern. 2. Either habit in thinking or actual mis-

teachings (has, have) placed too great an emphasis on persons in high positions. 3. A statesman or a general (doesn't, don't) necessarily sway history more than does a common citizen. 4. Perhaps neither you nor your teacher (is, are) able to name all the Presidents of the United States. 5. However, neither you nor your friends (is, are) ignorant of the contributions made by some of them. 6. Moreover, neither the reputation nor the specific events of the lives of such persons as Will Rogers, Richard E. Byrd, Amelia Earhart, and Babe Ruth (is, are) unknown. 7. Neither a high office nor a fat bank account (does, do) the trick. 8. Either leadership or acceptance of duties (is, are) more important. 9. Neither you nor I (is, are, am) exempt. 10. Either present days or future time (is, are) going to be the witness.

Special Problems in Subject-Verb Agreement

1. In sentences beginning with the words *there, here,* or *where,* the subject follows the verb. The words *there, here,* and *where* have nothing to do with the form of the verb and may be disregarded.

> WRONG: There is persons like Will Rogers to consider.
> RIGHT: There *are persons* like Will Rogers to consider.

2. In sentences in which the simple subject is followed by a phrase, the verb must agree with the subject, not with any word in the phrase.

> WRONG: One of Will Rogers's contributions were his wit.
> RIGHT: *One* of Will Rogers's contributions *was* his wit.

3. In sentences in which the simple subject is followed by words like *together with, in addition to, as well as,* select your verb without regard for such words.

> WRONG: His wit, together with his homely philosophy, were hailed by the people.
> RIGHT: His *wit,* together with his homely philosophy, *was hailed* by the people.

4. In sentences in which a predicate noun differs from the subject in number, the verb agrees with the subject, not with the predicate noun.

WRONG: His philosophy were truth and whimsicality neatly blended.

RIGHT: His *philosophy was* truth and whimsicality neatly blended.

5. When the subject is plural in appearance but actually singular in number, as in *news, mathematics, physics, economics,* a singular verb is used.

WRONG: The news of his death were a great shock.

RIGHT: The *news* of his death *was* a great shock.

6. When the subject specifies an amount, such as an amount of time, money, or space, a singular verb is used. Words stating an amount are generally singular.

RIGHT: *Two times two is* four.

RIGHT: Ten *days is* a short time.

7. When the subject is a title of a book, a singular verb is used. Even though the title is plural in form, it is considered singular.

RIGHT: *The Folks is* by Ruth Suckow.

8. When the subject is the name of a firm, a singular verb is used. Even though the name seems to be plural, it is considered singular.

RIGHT: *Smith Brothers is* open for business.

9. When the subject is an indefinite pronoun, it takes a verb that is either singular or plural, according to the number of the pronoun.

The following indefinite pronouns are singular:

each	anyone	no one	someone
everybody	anybody	nothing	either

The most common plural indefinite pronouns are:

several   both   few   many

WRONG: Everyone in the class were asked to give an opinion.
RIGHT: *Everyone* in the class *was asked* to give an opinion.
WRONG: A few of the group was not ready.
RIGHT: A *few* of the group *were* not ready.

The indefinite pronouns *some, all,* and *none* may be either singular or plural, according to their use in a sentence.

10. If the subject is a collective noun that refers to a group taken as a whole, it takes a singular verb. If the different members of the group are considered individually, the subject is plural and takes a plural verb.

RIGHT: The *class has* its assignment.
RIGHT: The *class have been discussing* among themselves Will Rogers's wit.

EXERCISE 1.   Select the correct verbs for these sentences:

The remarks of Herbert Hoover (1. is, are) indicative of Will Rogers's contribution. According to Hoover, Will's whimsicalities (2. was, were) a way by which the people (3. was, were) kept on an even keel. "There (4. was, were) no bitter stings," said Hoover. "There (5. was, were) kindly jokes." This talent, together with his keen understanding of life and events, (6. was, were) a boon. Everyone who heard him or who read his articles (7. was, were) made a little happier. Anyone who (8. thinks, think) that that (9. doesn't, don't) constitute a contribution (10. has, have) misjudged values.

EXERCISE 2.   Choose the correct verbs for these sentences:

Probably everybody in your class (1. has, have) read biographies of Will Rogers and (2. knows, know) all the details of his life. John Williams and Sons (3. is, are) advertising one now. *Will Rogers* by O'Brien (4. is, are) an excellent book. A group of my friends (5. has, have) agreed that there (6. is, are) no better stories about him anywhere. The news about their opinions (7. has, have) apparently leaked out because many in the class (8. has, have) been asking for this book. Five days (9. is, are) the time limit at the library, but there (10. is, are) few who will need that long.

EXERCISE 3. Make up sentences using each of these words or phrases with the present tense of a verb:

1. Three dollars
2. Mathematics
3. Either you or I
4. Bread and butter
5. There
6. *The Canterbury Tales*
7. The jury
8. Neither the twins nor their mother
9. Jane, together with,
10. Everybody
11. One of the men
12. Six and eleven

EXERCISE 4. Use your dictionary to determine the number (singular or plural) of each of these:

measles	mumps	statistics
scissors	whereabouts	acoustics
tactics	paints	politics

Pronoun-Antecedent Agreement

A pronoun must agree with its antecedent in number and gender.

1. A singular pronoun should be used to refer to a singular noun.

RIGHT: *Will Rogers* was proud of *his* Indian blood.

2. A plural pronoun should be used to refer to a plural noun.

RIGHT: *Persons* proud of *their* colonial ancestry were often surprised.

EXERCISE 1. Choose the correct pronouns for these sentences:

1. These persons often bragged about (his, their) ancestors who came over on the *Mayflower*. 2. Will Rogers in (his, their) slow drawl had the right answer for (him, them). 3. Will would say that (his, their) ancestors were on the shore waiting to meet (his, theirs). 4. His humor had no barbs; (it, they) had only kindliness. 5. People listened to his humor and found that (it, they) were never hurt by (it, them).

3. A singular pronoun should be used to refer to a singular indefinite pronoun.

> RIGHT: *Everybody* did *his* best.
> RIGHT: *Neither* would say that *he* was to blame.

If a sentence does not show the gender of an indefinite pronoun, use a masculine pronoun to refer to it.

4. A plural pronoun should be used to refer to a plural indefinite pronoun.

> RIGHT: *All* did *their* best.
> RIGHT: *Few* would say that *they* were to blame.

EXERCISE 2. Choose the correct pronouns for the following sentences:

1. Each in the class is doing (his, their) report on a famous American. 2. Some are doing (his, theirs) on the Presidents of the United States. 3. Others have chosen military men for (his, their) topics. 4. Of course everybody wants to write about someone (he, they) admires. 5. Anyone who does otherwise will find (himself, themselves) having a very dull time. 6. Both my best friends are doing (his, theirs) on explorers. 7. One is doing (his, their) report on Byrd; the other chose Amelia Earhart for (his, their) topic. 8. Nobody in the class seems to be unhappy in (his, their) choice. 9. Of course none can finish (his, their) report as fast as (he, they) would like. 10. Everyone is having trouble finding (his, their) source material.

5. A plural pronoun should be used to refer to two or more antecedents joined by *and*.

RIGHT: *Bob* and *Tom* have *their* reports organized.

6. A singular pronoun should be used to refer to two or more antecedents joined by *either — or* or *neither — nor* if both antecedents are singular.

RIGHT: Neither *Bob* nor *Tom* has finished *his* yet.

7. A plural pronoun should be used to refer to two or more antecedents joined by *either — or* or *neither — nor* if both antecedents are plural.

RIGHT: Neither *friends* nor *enemies* have dared offer *their* suggestions.

8. When one of the antecedents is singular and one is plural, the pronoun should agree with the closer one.

RIGHT: Neither *teacher* nor *students* have offered *their* ideas.
RIGHT: Neither *students* nor *teacher* has offered *his* ideas.

EXERCISE 3. Choose the correct words for these sentences:

1. Either Ann or Louise will tell you (she knows, they know) the secret.   2. Neither Bob nor Tom will admit that (he has, they have) told the girls.   3. Neither boys nor girls have shown (his, their) ability to keep a secret.   4. Either parents or a friend is sure to say that (he knows, they know).   5. Either your brother or your sisters point (his, their) fingers and say that (he knows, they know).   6. Bob and Tom have carried books in (his, their) brief cases.   7. My friends and I have used (my, our) eyes. 8. Neither Einstein nor Oppenheimer has written (his, their) theories on wit and humor.   9. So, either the boys or the little man who wasn't there must be doing (his, their) research on atomic energy.   10. Neither Bob nor Tom nor the other students look as though (he, they) could understand what (he, they) read.

EXERCISE 4. Each of the following sentences contains an error in pronoun-antecedent agreement. Make the necessary corrections.

1. Henry has chosen Will Rogers as the subject of their report.
2. Chuck, one of the Thomas twins, has chosen Walt Disney for theirs. 3. Neither Henry nor Chuck will have difficulty in finding material for their report. 4. Everybody must know that they need more than opinions for their report. 5. Some may make his reports dull by omitting pertinent anecdotes. 6. Nobody likes to find that they are reading a catalogue of facts.
7. Henry and Chuck have found that his reports included many colorful anecdotes. 8. All will be glad when he reads what the two have written.

Adjective-Noun Agreement

The demonstrative adjectives *this, that, these, those* must agree in number with the words they modify.

1. The adjectives *this* and *that* are singular and modify singular nouns and pronouns only.

> RIGHT: *This story* is a good one.
> RIGHT: *That one* is even better.

2. The adjectives *these* and *those* are plural and modify plural nouns and pronouns only.

> RIGHT: *These anecdotes* are interesting.
> RIGHT: *Those kinds* add punch.

Avoid such expressions as "these kind," "those sort," "these type" since *kind, sort,* and *type* are singular; *these* and *those* are plural.

EXERCISE 1. Which adjective — *this, that, these, those* — should be used in each of these sentences?

1. –?– story about Will Rogers's schooling interests us.
2. I like –?– kind of story.

3. –?– picture of Will Rogers that I am showing you is a good likeness.
4. –?– picture which I had last week did not show him smiling.
5. –?– lock of hair which hung down on his forehead was characteristic.
6. I like –?– kind of discussion which we are having.
7. Do you remember –?– story Miss Evans told us about him yesterday?
8. –?– quotation that I have here is a gem.
9. "I'm just an old country boy," he said to –?– persons who tried to flatter him.
10. –?– sentences are easy.

EXERCISE 2. Write five sentences of your own using the words *kind*, *sorts*, *type*, *kinds*, and *sort* plus one of the four adjectives.

PRONOUN USAGE

Problems related to case are responsible for our difficulties in pronoun usage. The most serious mistakes occur in the use of personal pronouns ("Me and him went fishing"); the next most serious, in the use of relative and interrogative pronouns ("I know who you mean," "Whom is it?").

US 2   Problems in Pronoun Usage

Case Forms of Personal Pronouns

On page 41 are listed the nominative, possessive, and objective case forms of the personal pronouns.

In the use of personal pronouns in the nominative case, two problems arise.

1. The subject of a sentence or of a dependent clause is in the nominative case.

WRONG: Chuck and me are reporting on Walt Disney.
RIGHT: Chuck and *I* are reporting on Walt Disney.

WRONG: The subject which him and me chose is fine.
RIGHT: The subject which *he* and *I* chose is fine.

2. A predicate pronoun is in the nominative case.

WRONG: A man with extraordinary ability is him.
RIGHT: A man with extraordinary ability is *he*.

The use of the pronoun after the infinitive *to be* is sometimes tricky. If the pronoun refers to a noun or a pronoun in the nominative case, it, too, is in the nominative case. If it refers to a noun or a pronoun in the objective case, it, too, is in the objective case.

RIGHT: The *man* with the shy manner is certain to be *he*.
RIGHT: I knew the *man* to be *him*.

EXERCISE 1. Choose the correct pronouns for these sentences:

The subject which Chuck and (1. I, me) chose has a wealth of material. (2. He, Him) and (3. I, me) have dug out old magazines. The librarian and (4. we, us) have been regular sleuths. It was (5. she, her) who found the best material on Disney. We knew Miss Larson to be (6. she, her) with the good ideas.

In the use of personal pronouns in the possessive case, only one problem gives difficulty.

3. The possessive form of the pronoun should always be used with a gerund.

> WRONG: We read of him creating Mickey Mouse.
> RIGHT: We read of *his* creating Mickey Mouse.

In the use of personal pronouns in the objective case, there are a number of problems.

4. The direct object of a verb is in the objective case.

> WRONG: Movie fans love he and Minnie Mouse.
> RIGHT: Movie fans love *him* and Minnie Mouse.

5. The indirect object is in the objective case.

> WRONG: Disney has given you and I two lovable characters.
> RIGHT: Disney has given *you* and *me* two lovable characters.

6. The object of a preposition is in the objective case.

> WRONG: He has depicted human characteristics in he and Minnie.
> RIGHT: He has depicted human characteristics in *him* and Minnie.

EXERCISE 2. Choose the correct possessive and objective forms for these sentences:

Between you and (1. I, me), the personal characteristics which Disney has given to Mickey and (2. she, her) have made (3. they, them) very appealing. Disney has given Minnie and (4. he, him) cheerful dispositions. We find (5. he, him) and (6. she, her) plucky at all times. For other movie fans and (7. we, us), Mickey and Minnie are admirable little creatures. Many of (8. we, us) human beings might very wisely imitate (9. them, their) diligent working and planning. Furthermore, I object to (10. you, your) saying, "Are you a man or a mouse?"

Difficulty sometimes arises in sentences containing an incomplete clause introduced by *than* or *as*. Always use the form you would use if the clause were complete.

> WRONG: Perhaps Mickey is braver than her.
> RIGHT: Perhaps Mickey is braver than *she* (is).

> WRONG: Probably more people are fonder of him than she.
> RIGHT: Probably more people are fonder of him than (they are of) *her*.

EXERCISE 3. Choose the correct pronoun forms for these sentences, and be able to give your reasons:

You and (1. I, me) know that Disney found Mickey in his old garage-studio. (2. He, Him) and Mickey became great friends. Disney has told you and (3. I, me) that Mickey's original name was Mortimer. Between you and (4. I, me), Mortimer is a big name for a little mouse like (5. he, him). Donald Duck is another character whom other movie-goers and (6. we, us) dote upon. (7. He, Him) and Mickey make a fine pair. We enjoy (8. them, their) getting into scrapes and out of them. If Mickey is more cheerful than (9. he, him), certainly Donald is (10. he, him) who is testier than all the other characters put together.

Case Forms of Relative and Interrogative Pronouns

The words *who, whose, whom, which,* and *that* can be used to introduce dependent clauses.

The words *who, whose, whom, which,* and *what* can be used to introduce questions.

Only the use of the nominative form (*who*) and of the objective form (*whom*) causes any great difficulty.

1. Always use *who* when a subject form is needed.

RIGHT: Walt Disney is the one *who* creates the characters.
Subj.

RIGHT: Everyone knows *who* he is.
Pred. N.

RIGHT: There are others *who*, so I am told, help in making the thousands of pictures. (Disregard parenthetical expressions; they do not affect the structure of the clause.)
Subj.

2. Always use *whom* when an object form is needed.

RIGHT: His helpers are persons *whom* he has trained.
D. O.

RIGHT: He chooses persons *whom* cartooning appeals to.
Obj. of Prep.

RIGHT: Apparently he knows *whom* to pick. (*Whom* is in the objective form because it is the subject of the infinitive *to pick*.)

EXERCISE 1. Choose the correct pronouns for the following sentences:

1. Fourteen thousand pictures are required of those (who, whom) do the filling in.   2. Movie audiences, (who, whom) a ten-minute short amuses, are usually unaware of the vast amount of labor.   3. Walt Disney, to (who, whom) several "Oscars" have been awarded, amazed all (who, whom) listened when he suggested a full-length feature cartoon.   4. Those (who, whom) Disney argued with should have given in at once.   5. Disney is a man (who, whom), I am told, has a dogged determination.

EXERCISE 2. Now choose the pronouns for these:

1. You and I know (who, whom) produced *Snow White and the Seven Dwarfs.*   2. Everyone (who, whom) saw it loved it.   3. Certainly there couldn't be anyone (who, whom) it didn't appeal to.   4. Approximately 140,000 drawings were done by the staff (who, whom) saw it through to completion.   5. If I were asked (who, whom) to choose as my favorite character in the movie, it would be Dopey.

VERB USAGE

The child who wrote to his teacher, "I have wrote *have gone* a hundred times and I have went home," is one of thousands who have heard the wrong forms for so long that they sound right. In addition to writing the answers to the following exercises, plan to do them orally so that the *sound* of the correct forms is emphasized.

US 3   Verb Demons

1. Master the *lie* and *lay* verbs.

The *lie-lay-lain* verb means "to recline" or "to stretch out." It is usually intransitive and therefore does not take an object.

The *lay-laid-laid* verb means "to place" or "to put." It is usually transitive and takes an object.

LIE-LAY-LAIN	LAY-LAID-LAID
I lie down now.	I lay the book down now.
I lay down yesterday.	I laid the book down yesterday.
I have lain down often.	I have laid it down often.

EXERCISE 1. Choose the verbs for these sentences:

1. Yesterday someone (lay, laid) *I Married Adventure* on my desk. 2. It (lay, laid) there for some time before I (lay, laid) my eyes on it. 3. I did not know that in it (lay, laid) all kinds of fascinating adventure. 4. After it had (laid, lain) on my desk for some time, I (lay, laid) my other work aside and began to read. 5. I simply (lay, laid) back in my chair and read. 6. Earlier I had read that from the very beginning adventure (lay, laid) before Martin Johnson. 7. He (lay, laid) plans to see the far corners of the globe. 8. Others have (lain, laid) the same sort of plans, but those plans have (lain, laid) unfulfilled. 9. Then in 1896 an Eastman Kodak salesman (lay, laid) opportunity on his doorstep. 10. Opportunity did not have to (lie, lay) there long for Martin to recognize it.

2. Master the *sit* and *set* verbs.

The *sit-sat-sat* verb means "to occupy a seat." It is generally intransitive and does not take an object.

The *set-set-set* verb means "to put" or "to place." It is generally transitive and takes an object.

SIT–SAT–SAT	SET–SET–SET
I sit down now.	I set the dish down now.
I sat down an hour ago.	I set the dish down an hour ago.
I have sat down to rest.	I have set the dish down for you.

EXERCISE 2. Choose the correct verbs for these sentences:

1. The Kodak salesman (sat, set) a Kodak on the counter of Martin Johnson's father's store.   2. Probably Martin (set, sat) and looked at it.   3. We know that it (set, sat) him to thinking. 4. Photography had not yet (set, sat) its mark.   5. But Martin did not (set, sit) there dreaming.   6. He (set, sat) himself to learning about photography.   7. He (set, sat) by the hour taking the camera apart.   8. Martin had (set, sat) goals for himself; and his father (set, sat) happily by, offering encouragement. 9. Finally at fifteen, Martin (set, sat) himself to the job of taking pictures.   10. After his "victims" had (set, sat) for their pictures, Martin extracted ten cents from them for a dozen portraits.

3. Master the *rise* and *raise* verbs.

The *rise-rose-risen* verb is usually intransitive and does not take an object.

The *raise-raised-raised* verb is usually transitive and takes an object.

RISE–ROSE–RISEN	RAISE–RAISED–RAISED
I rise now.	I raise the window blind now.
I rose early this morning.	I raised the blind yesterday.
I have risen reluctantly.	I have raised the blind each day.

EXERCISE 3. Choose the proper verb forms for these sentences:

1. Martin Johnson did not (rise, raise) much money on his first expedition. 2. Although he (rose, raised) early and worked hard, he could not (rise, raise) funds sufficient for his needs. 3. Finally, he went home; but his ambition never ceased (raising, rising). 4. Very shortly he (rose, raised) a dreadful disturbance at school through some faked pictures of the faculty. 5. The faculty members (raised, rose) in righteous indignation. 6. Martin's stock had lowered, not (raised, risen). 7. He then (rose, raised) enough money to go to Chicago. 8. His stock in adventure, if not in education, had (raised, risen). 9. One day he (rose, raised) $4.25 and bet a friend he could go to London and back on that amount. 10. When he returned, he had twenty-five cents and a love of adventure that was to continue to (raise, rise).

A Number of Troublesome Verbs

The many times that we hear "I seen," "we done," and "they have went" testify to the fact that there are other verbs, too, which give difficulty.

EXERCISE 1. On your paper write the three principal parts of each of these verbs:

see	do	come	go
know	throw	eat	run
think	ring	swim	dive
freeze	wear	drink	choose
give	dwell	wring	swing
slay	steal	dream	sting
fly	shine	draw	get
tear	write	take	shrink
break	flow	grow	begin
catch	swear	burst	forbid

91

EXERCISE 2. Write the correct forms of the verbs for these sentences:

You probably have (1. hear) about the time Martin Johnson (2. take) a trip with Jack London. Martin (3. swear) that he was a good cook, and London (4. take) him as a member of the crew. On this trip Martin (5. see) many of the islands in the South Seas. He (6. steal) every opportunity to use his camera and (7. take) many pictures. When he (8. come) home, he (9. show) his pictures to the wondering citizens of his Kansas home town. Martin Johnson had decided where his future (10. lie).

EXERCISE 3. Choose the correct verbs for these sentences:

Before long, Martin Johnson was (1. drew, drawn) back to the South Seas. This time his bride (2. went, gone) with him. Enough had been (3. wrote, written) of the fearful island of Malekula to have (4. drove, driven) them in the opposite direction. But that was the place they had (5. chose, chosen) to visit. There they were (6. catched, caught) by some cannibals and would have been (7. ate, eaten) had not a lucky break saved them. Their fame (8. raised, rose) rapidly because of the excellent pictures which they (9. took, taken). Some time later Carl Akeley (10. saw, seen) some of their pictures and asked them to specialize in pictures of wild animals.

EXERCISE 4. Write the correct verb forms for these sentences:

Today the Johnsons are (1. know) especially for their pictures of animals. They have (2. give) Americans exact knowledge of the animals of the jungle. The jungle (3. come) to be the Johnsons' home. They (4. speak) on lecture tours and then (5. flee) back to the jungle to the work they loved best.

ADJECTIVE AND ADVERB USAGE

There are only a few points to remember in the use of adjectives and adverbs, but they are crucial points. The chief question concerning a modifier is: "How is it used in the sentence?"

US 4   Single-word Modifiers

An <u>adjective</u> modifies a noun or a pronoun.

An <u>adverb</u> modifies a verb, an adjective, or another adverb.

Adj.   Adv.   Adv.   Adj.

Many persons very freely contributed their share.

The adverb form frequently ends in *ly*.

ADJECTIVES	ADVERBS
free	freely
cheerful	cheerfully

Since many adverbs do end in *ly*, it is easy to spot mistakes like the following:

WRONG: They do their work easy.
RIGHT: They do their work *easily*. (*Easily* modifies *do*.)

WRONG: I should sure like to go.
RIGHT: I should *surely* like to go. (*Surely* modifies *should like*.)

WRONG: It was real warm.
RIGHT: It was *really* warm. (*Really* modifies *warm*.)

EXERCISE. Choose the correct words for the following sentences. When in doubt, ask what the word modifies.

Another American who is (1. sure, surely) remembered (2. vivid, vividly) for his (3. extraordinary, extraordinarily) contributions to American life is Richard E. Byrd. (4. Certain, Certainly) it is difficult to list them (5. quick, quickly). A

(6. rapid, rapidly) survey reveals (7. immediate, immediately) his (8. dangerous, dangerously) trips to the North and South poles. The list has (9. mere, merely) begun, as everyone (10. sure, surely) knows.

Some Special Problems

There are certain combinations of adjectives and adverbs (not ending in *ly*) which give difficulty.

1. *Good* and *well*

   Good is always an adjective: *good* job, *good* idea.
   Well may be used as either an adjective or an adverb.

   As an adjective, *well* means:

   1. Fortunate, satisfactory, suitable
       RIGHT: All is *well*.

   2. Not sick
       RIGHT: I am *well*. I feel *well*.

   3. In satisfactory conditions or circumstances
       RIGHT: He is *well* where he is.

   As an adverb, *well* means "satisfactorily."
       RIGHT: He did his work *well*.

2. *Bad* and *badly*

   Bad is always an adjective: *bad* results, *bad* behavior.
   Badly is always an adverb: played *badly*, acted *badly*.

   WRONG: The game ended bad for us.
   RIGHT: The game ended *badly* for us.

3. *Most* and *almost*

   Most is generally an adjective: *most* persons, *most* things.
   Almost is always an adverb: *almost* all, *almost* finished.

   WRONG: The crowd is most gone.
   RIGHT: The crowd is *almost* gone.

4. *Slow* and *slowly*

Slow may be used as either an adjective or an adverb: *slow* movie, go *slow*.

Slowly is an adverb: drive *slowly*, go *slowly*.

Although *slow* can be an adverb, the other adverbial form, *slowly*, is generally used with all verbs except *drive* and *go*. Probably the frequent use of *slow* in traffic signs has helped to standardize the usage.

EXERCISE. Choose the correct words for these sentences:

(1. Most, Almost) persons know that Byrd flew (2. slow, slowly) around the world in three minutes. He could do it very (3. good, well) because he was at the North Pole. It seems (4. most, almost) impossible. As the plane went (5. slow, slowly) around the North Pole, Byrd made observations as (6. good, well) as he could. The plane was behaving very (7. good, well). On the trip north, Byrd and his pilot Bennett had noticed, (8. most, almost) at the same time, that the oil leaked (9. bad, badly). That was a (10. bad, badly) moment for both of them.

Two Special Uses of Adjectives

1. An adjective is generally used after a verb like *smell*, *taste*, *feel*, *sound*, and *seem*.

> WRONG: Success tasted sweetly.
> RIGHT: Success tasted *sweet*. (Sweet modifies *success*.)

> WRONG: No one felt badly.
> RIGHT: No one felt *bad*. (*Bad* modifies *no one*.)

Both *good* and *well* may be used with the verb *feel* but with different meanings.

> RIGHT: I feel *good*. (High spirits are indicated.)
> RIGHT: I feel *well*. (Good health is indicated.)

95

2. When the word order of a sentence is subject-verb-object-modifier, an adjective should be used to modify the object. An adverb should be used to modify the action of the verb.

RIGHT: He made the house *safe* for occupancy.

RIGHT: He made the house *safely* before it began to rain.

EXERCISE.   Choose the right modifiers for these sentences:

1. The engine sounded (good, well). 2. Byrd's face looked (happy, happily). 3. Success made Byrd and Bennett feel (good, well). 4. Bennett held the stick (tight, tightly). 5. Byrd made his calculations (accurate, accurately).

Problems of Comparison

1. The comparative degree of an adjective or an adverb should be used in comparing two persons or things.

RIGHT: Which is *more reliable*, a sextant or a compass?

2. The superlative degree of an adjective or an adverb should be used in comparing more than two persons or things.

RIGHT: The *best* compass in the world is disturbed by the magnetic pole.

3. Be careful to avoid double comparisons.

WRONG: No one was more surer of that than Byrd.

RIGHT: No one was *surer* of that than Byrd.

4. In making comparisons of this sort, always exclude from the group the person or thing being compared.

WRONG: Bob knows more about compasses than anyone in his class.

RIGHT: Bob knows more about compasses than *anyone else* (or than *any other person*) in his class.

EXERCISE. Complete these sentences with the correct words or groups of words:

Bob is (1. surer, surest) of his subject than (2. any of us, any of the rest of us). He can state (3. more quickly, most quickly) than I that the true pole lies a thousand miles beyond the magnetic pole. He is certainly the (4. smarter, smartest) one in the class; but of course we're (5. more smarter, smartest, smarter) than he is in some other things. Bob can use a sun compass (6. more accurately, most accurately) than (7. anyone, any other person) I ever saw. But any one of us can read a sundial (8. faster, fastest) than he. Everyone likes to be (9. better, best) in some things. However, some persons work (10. more diligently, most diligently) than others.

Turn to page 231 for work on the correct placement of modifying words, phrases, and clauses.

PREPOSITION AND CONJUNCTION USAGE

US 5   Two Special Problems

Only two groups of words seem to give difficulty.

1. *Like — as — as if*

   Use *like* as a preposition.
   Use *as* and *as if* as conjunctions to introduce clauses.

   Obj. of Prep.
   RIGHT: We work *like beavers.*
   Clause
   RIGHT: We work *as beavers work.* (not "like beavers work")
   Clause
   RIGHT: We work *as if we were beavers.* (not "like we were beavers")

2. *Without — unless*

   Use *without* as a preposition.
   Use *unless* as a conjunction to introduce a clause.

   Obj. of Prep.
   RIGHT: We cannot work *without guidance.*
   Clause
   RIGHT: We cannot work *unless we have guidance.*

EXERCISE. Choose the correct words for these sentences:

(1. Without, Unless) one knows of Byrd's contribution to blind flying, one is (2. without, unless) full information. He worked (3. like, as) mad. (4. Like, As, As if) you may know, he produced a good wind-drift indicator. (5. Like, As, As if) this were not enough, he recognized the value of flares to determine the direction of the wind.

Review Exercise

EXERCISE, Usage. Fifteen of the following sentences contain a variety of errors in usage. Make the necessary corrections as you copy them.

1. The present, like you and me knows it, has came about slow.
2. There is many persons whom I know have contributed to it.
3. Presidents have not necessarily did more than anyone.
4. Explorers, painters, musicians, novelists have all contributed their share.
5. Neither one person nor another are more essential.
6. Each of these persons has done something good.
7. Like you know, things must sure be good for something.
8. A person whom I wish to emphasize lives like a hermit may write the most beautifullest symphony.
9. If no one hear it, it is of little value.
10. Once a man talked with three workmen.
11. Each of them were asked what they were doing.
12. One of the men were making ten dollars a day.
13. The second whom was questioned was lying bricks.
14. The man was sure not doing very good in his questioning.
15. He spoke exceedingly fearfully to the third workman.
16. The third said that he was helping to build a cathedral.
17. There was a man who had sat himself a goal.
18. He was doing a good job good.
19. Everyone can sure make their contribution to society.
20. Neither child nor adult are exempt.

CAPITALIZATION

REASON FOR USE

Capitalization is an aid to communication. Capital letters are signals designed to help the reader to interpret the thought of the writer. They indicate the point at which one thought is ending and another is beginning. They are helpful in calling certain words to the reader's particular attention. For practical purposes, then, they are worthy of notice. If you want your written communication easily understood by others, you will master the following rules:

Cap   Rules for Capitalization

Capitalization is one of the least standardized aspects of written English. In general, the trend seems to be toward fewer capital letters, but,

> Be not the first by whom the new is tried,
> Nor yet the last to lay the old aside.

You will be reasonably safe if you observe certain definite rules that govern the most necessary uses of capital letters.

Cap 1   Capitalize the first word of every sentence.

I was sitting in the living room reading the newspaper.
What a thud I heard!

Cap 2   Capitalize the first word of a direct quotation.

Beginning with the sentence, "These are the times that try
men's souls," Thomas Paine challenged the disheartened
patriots to sterner efforts.

If only a fragment of a sentence is quoted, no capital
letter is used.

Looking at the large book, he asked if I had "taken up reading for exercise."

Cap 3   Capitalize the first word of every line of poetry.

Laugh and the world laughs with you;
Weep and you weep alone.
ELLA WHEELER WILCOX

Cap 4   Capitalize the first word of each division or subdivision of an outline. Use capital letters to set off the major subtopics.

LEARNING TO STUDY
I. When to study
    A. At school
    B. At home
II. Where to study
III. How to study

Cap 5   Capitalize the first word of a formal resolution.

100

Resolved, that Poe contributed more to American literature than did Hawthorne.

Cap 6   Capitalize the first word after a strong interjection.

Help! The books are falling.

Cap 7   Capitalize the first word and all important words in a title.

The opening section of *The New Yorker* is called "The Talk of the Town."

I saw *Life with Father*.

"The Glamour of Punctuation" is the title of one of the chapters in *The Art of Plain Talk*.

Articles, prepositions, and conjunctions appearing in titles are considered unworthy of capitalization.

EXERCISE. Copy these sentences on your paper, using capital letters wherever needed. Be prepared to give a reason for each of your decisions.

1. hawthorne's novel, *the house of the seven gables*, was published in 1851. 2. miss Long said in class yesterday, "his reputation had previously been established by *mosses from an old manse* in 1846 and *the scarlet letter* in 1850." 3. the first chapter of *the house of the seven gables* is titled "the old pynchon family." 4. the name Pyncheon reappears in four later chapter titles, "the pyncheon of today," "the pyncheon garden," "alice pyncheon," and "governor pyncheon." 5. horrors! the story seems to be about the Pyncheons. 6. resolved, that the book should be read. 7. this poem by Holmes may be appropriate:

> deal gently with us, ye who read.
> our largest hope is unfulfilled —
> the promise still outruns the deed —
> the tower, but not the spire, we build.

Cap 8   Capitalize all proper nouns.

This rule includes the names of the following:

1. **Days, months, holidays:** Tuesday, May, Christmas
2. **Persons and pets:** John Smith, Rover
3. **Schools, colleges, and universities:** Central High School, Harvard University
4. **School subjects which are language studies or which name specific classes:** English, Spanish, Algebra II
5. **Towns and cities:** Jamestown, Raleigh
6. **States:** Arkansas, Pennsylvania
7. **Countries and continents:** England, North America
8. **Streets:** Main Street, Avenue of the Americas
9. **Points of the compass when they represent a section of the country, but not directions:** They live in the East; they went east last year.
10. **Rivers, oceans, mountains, and other geographical locations:** Ohio River, Atlantic Ocean, Adirondack Mountains, Sahara, Gulf of Mexico
11. **Political parties:** Republican, Democrat
12. **Churches and religious denominations:** Baptist Church, Universalist, Protestant, Catholic
13. **The Deity, the Bible and its books:** God, the Bible, the Psalms
14. **Languages and nationalities:** Latin, English
15. **Races of people:** Oriental, Caucasian
16. **Firms:** American Book Company
17. **Organizations and institutions:** United Nations, Carnegie Endowment for International Peace
18. **Special products:** Wearlong Shirts
19. **Buildings:** Empire State Building
20. **Departments of government:** Department of the Interior, Congress, Senate, House of Representatives
21. **Historical documents:** Declaration of Independence

22. **The President of the United States**
23. **Wars:** Revolutionary War, War of 1812
24. **Things personified:** The spirit of Liberty lives on.
25. **Ships, automobiles, railways, trains, air lines, airplanes:** *Queen Mary, The Hiawatha, Spirit of St. Louis*

EXERCISE. Copy these sentences, inserting capital letters where necessary. Give a reason for each decision.

1. samuel clemens (mark twain) was a widely traveled author.
2. although he grew up in the middle west on the west bank of the mississippi, he came to know the south, the west, and the east.
3. as a young man he worked as a printer in new york, philadelphia, washington, keokuk, and cincinnati. 4. setting out in 1857 in search of quick wealth in south america, he fell in with a mississippi river pilot, horace bixby, and decided to learn his profession. 5. in clemens's three years on the river, he saw all types of humanity: small merchants, poor whites, wealthy planters, slaves, creoles, easterners, europeans. 6. when the war between the states broke out, the steamboat traffic collapsed. 7. after brief service in the Confederate Army, samuel and his brother orion made the long overland journey by wells fargo stagecoaches to the new nevada territory. 8. sam was a reporter for a time on the virginia city *enterprise*, then moved on to san francisco, and from there to hawaii. 9. in 1867 he went east, where he sailed on the *quaker city* to southern europe and the near east. 10. after his return to america, he lectured, published *the innocents abroad*, took a fling at owning and editing a buffalo newspaper, and married olivia langdon of elmira, new york.

Cap 9   Capitalize titles used with proper names and the titles of the highest government officers appearing without their names.

Major Lee   Principal Ashby   the Attorney General

Titles are not capitalized if they follow *my, a,* or *the:* my aunt Mary, a captain, the lawyer.

Titles are not capitalized when they are used in place of names: the colonel, the principal, the freshman counselor.

Cap 10   Capitalize *Father* and *Mother* and other such nouns when they take the place of a name or are used with a name.

I told him to ask Mother.
The new priest is Father Kelly.

Cap 11   Capitalize the pronoun *I*.

He told me that I had passed the test.

Cap 12   Capitalize initials.

K. J. Lewis   Henry W. Longfellow

Cap 13   Capitalize proper adjectives.

English poetry   American history

Cap 14   Capitalize a noun, or an abbreviation of a noun, followed by a numeral.

Room 101   No. 9   Article VI

Cap 15   Capitalize the first word and all nouns in the salutation of a letter and the first word in the closing.

Dear Mr. Blake: Yours truly,
My dear Suzie,   Cordially yours,

Cap 16   Capitalize abbreviations of the following:

1. A title that is written as part of a person's name and a degree following a name:

Dr. F. C. Hill   Walter F. Taylor, Ph.D.   Jack Thomas, Jr.

104

2. Names of months, states, countries, points of the compass, and words like _Street_:

    Jan.   Nebr.   U.S.A.   NE   Newport Ave.

3. Periods of time:

    A.M.   P.M.   B.C.   A.D.

According to Webster, A.M. and P.M. can also be written in lower case. See page 377 for additional information.

Review Exercises

EXERCISE 1. Copy these sentences, using capital letters wherever needed. Give a reason for each decision.

1. at an early age, willa cather moved with her father and mother from virginia to nebraska. 2. during her adolescence near red cloud, nebraska, she absorbed impressions that loomed large in her later work. 3. after her first novel, _alexander's bridge_, she turned for materials to the primitive west of her youth and produced _o pioneers_. 4. this was the story, i am told, of the conquest of a stubborn soil by the first generation of immigrant farmers, and especially by a strong young swedish woman, alexandra bergson. 5. at the end of the book the swedish woman says, "we come and go, but the land is always here. 6. and the people who love it and understand it are the people who own it — for a little while." 7. antonia shimerda, the heroine of miss cather's next novel, was "a rich mine of life, like the founders of early races." 8. _the song of the lark_ is about a methodist minister's daughter who becomes an internationally famous opera singer. 9. you may be told in english class that thea kronborg is remarkable for the fact that she develops as the story progresses. 10. miss cather's next book, _the professor's house_, might provide a topic for a debate class: resolved, that success is harmful to happiness.

EXERCISE 2. Copy these sentences on your paper, using capital letters wherever needed:

1. after _the professor's house_ miss cather turned to historical novels to show the influence on primitive america of a humane

and disciplinary force, the roman catholic church. 2. *death comes for the archbishop* is a story of the church in the old southwest. 3. miss cather's next book, *shadows on the rock*, is laid on the banks of the st. lawrence river in old quebec, in the days when frontenac was sent out by louis XIV. 4. miss cather gave a clear picture of the non-british races — german, bohemian, scandinavian, and french — on the american frontier. 5. she portrayed these people in a friendly spirit of democracy which emphasizes their essential humanity rather than their nationalities. 6. not the least attraction of miss cather's historical novels lies in the unassuming courage with which her people go about setting up a civilized state in the wilderness. 7. the courage she pictures is seldom of the kind required in conquering reluctant nature or in facing hostile indians. 8. "her kind of courage," said miss townsend in american literature class on monday, "shows how an individual can maintain the decencies of civilization in the midst of a barren life." 9. thea kronborg in the opera, godfrey st. peter in his study, and alexandra on her farm, all unite in this — that their lives gained fulfillment through creative activity directed toward worthy goals. 10. thus we might outline miss cather's contribution to american literature as follows:

  I. quantity — small
 II. quality — high
    a. worthy goals
    b. genuine characterizations

EXERCISE 3. Write the proper nouns in this list:

1. aunt nellie 2. yazoo river 3. pikes peak 4. "the daring young man on the flying trapeze" 5. my sister's birthday 6. junior high school 7. the city of new york 8. the south 9. bok tower 10. mathematics 11. australia 12. socialist party 13. french 14. university of wisconsin 15. book-of-the-month club 16. the state department of the united states 17. mayflower pact 18. diesel engine 19. rocket planes 20. the president of the first national bank 21. john g. whittier 22. pan-american relations 23. no. 6 24. the new testament

PUNCTUATION

REASON FOR USE

Punctuation, like capitalization, is a mechanical aid to communication. It will be easier for people to understand what you mean if you follow the standard rules. As you have probably discovered, a change in punctuation may completely alter the meaning of a sentence. There is a legend that Bismarck helped bring on the Franco-Prussian War by changing a few commas in a telegram. Your use of punctuation and capitalization may not be disastrous, but a misuse may confuse your readers.

Punc   Rules for Punctuation

Here are the principal uses of the various marks of punctuation:

Punc 1   The Period

1. **Use a period after a declarative sentence.**

"Snow-Bound" is one of Whittier's best poems.

2. Use a period after an imperative sentence that does not exclaim.

Hand me that book, please.

3. Use a period after an indirect question.

I wonder whether you have read Hawthorne's stories.

4. Use a period after a request even though, for the sake of courtesy, it is worded as a question.

Will you kindly sign and return the enclosed card.

5. Use periods after initials and most abbreviations.

F. D. Brown   Mr.   Dr.   M.D.   B.C.   etc.   i.e.

Do *not* use a period after a contraction.

isn't   nat'l   o'clock   who's

Do *not* use periods in an alphabetical combination which has become accepted as a word in common speech.

TVA   FHA   FM   AFL   CIO

6. Use a period after a numeral or a letter that sets off a heading in an outline.

> I. Poetry
> A. Lyric
> B. Epic
> II. Prose

Do *not* use a period after the title of a theme.

Do *not* use a period after a page number within a sentence.

Punc 2   The Question Mark

1. Use a question mark after a direct question.

Do you know who wrote *Moby Dick?*

2. Use a question mark after each item of a series of elliptical phrases or clauses which constitute a single sentence.

The reporter always asks: Who? What? When? Where? Why? How?

What do you know about Europe? about South America? about Australia?

3. Use a question mark, within parentheses, after a word or a statement the accuracy of which is questionable.

John Smith was born in 1580 (?) and died in 1631.

Do *not* use a question mark to indicate humor or sarcasm.

Punc 3   The Exclamation Point

1. Use an exclamation point after a sentence that expresses surprise or strong feeling.

What a good book this is!

2. Use an exclamation point after a strong interjection.

Horrors! The man is insane.

Do *not* use an exclamation point merely for the sake of emphasis. Overuse weakens its effectiveness. Never use more than one exclamation point after a single exclamation.

EXERCISE 1. Copy the following sentences, inserting the appropriate marks of punctuation:

1. I wonder whether you are familiar with the short stories of Bret Harte 2. Do you happen to know them 3. Goodness You do have something to anticipate 4. How earthy his stories always are 5. My friend, Mrs R L Erskine, says that Harte is a very important figure in the development of regional literature 6. Do you know the characteristics of Harte's style his choice of

characters his vocabulary his locale .7. With great skill he combined this picturesqueness with Western humor 8. What a drawling Western method of understatement he used 9. He wrote poems, too; did you know that 10. The next time you are in the library look up Harte in the card catalogue

EXERCISE 2. Copy these sentences, inserting the necessary punctuation:

1. John's history instructor, F D Nelson, assigned an outline for the next day 2. He said, "Please develop the main divisions of my outline" 3.

        I The Puritan way of life
        .   A Spirit of the age
             B Puritan humanism
             C Essential issues
        II Puritan writings

4. Didn't John find a book on American literature by Walter F Taylor, Ph D, that helped him 5. In another book, *The Puritans*, by Perry Miller and Thomas H Johnson he found some useful quotations 6. Gracious How smart he is going to be 7. He asked if John would be correct to write that Jonathan Edwards died in 1758 (uncertain date) 8. Did John check with the encyclopedia with a biography with other reference books 9. We know positively that Edwards died in 1758 10. What a valuable contribution Edwards made to Puritan theology and literature

Punc 4   The Comma

A comma indicates a partial stop. It is valuable in that it shows the reader the relationship of subordinate parts to principal parts. Moreover, it sets off parts which might be read together and thus cause confusion. A comma in written communication takes the place of a slight drop in voice, which distinguishes similar parts in oral communication.

However, one of the most common errors on student themes is the superfluous use of commas. Use a comma only when it is specifically called for by one of the following rules:

1. Use a comma to separate the principal clauses of a compound or a compound-complex sentence joined by *and, but, or, nor*.

> To estimate the historical achievement of Poe is easy, but to judge his ultimate worth is difficult.

Note that the comma comes *before* the conjunction.

Do not confuse principal clauses with parts of a compound predicate or other compound elements that may be joined by co-ordinate conjunctions.

> PRINCIPAL CLAUSES JOINED BY CO-ORDINATE CONJUNCTION: Bret Harte wrote about the California miners, and George W. Cable wrote about the Southern Creoles.
>
> COMPOUND ELEMENTS JOINED BY CO-ORDINATE CONJUNCTION: Harte and Cable wrote about special groups of people and set their stories in particular regions.

EXERCISE. Copy the following sentences, inserting commas where needed. Be sure to distinguish between principal clauses and compound elements.

1. Nathaniel Hawthorne's family had lived in New England since 1630 and this background is apparent in his writings. 2. One of his ancestors had been a judge in the Salem witchcraft trials and others had gone to sea from Salem. 3. The Puritan past weighed heavily upon Hawthorne and this can be seen in his writings. 4. Few men knew better than he the pages of Puritan history and none knew so well the Puritan character. 5. Within Salem lingered the grimmest Puritan memories and at near-by Boston was the seat of the Puritans' struggle against royal authority. 6. Puritan ideas were warp and woof in the cultural pattern which Hawthorne inherited and out of these somber materials his art was compelled to take form. 7. This restricted background may have had its disadvantages but out of it came *The Scarlet Letter*. 8. The story turns upon the struggle between

natural impulse and conscience and it reveals the consequences of that struggle in an individual.   9. Merely to tell a story of guilty love was not Hawthorne's aim but he follows the history of four people to bring forth the inevitable fruits of sin.   10. *The Scarlet Letter* won Hawthorne a secure place in American literature but he went on to write another great book.

2. Use a comma to set off an introductory adverbial clause and certain introductory phrases.

(a) Use a comma when you begin a sentence with an adverbial clause.

After he had organized his notes, he began to write.
If you read widely, you will learn much.

(b) Use a comma after an introductory participial phrase.

Pausing outside the house, Wakefield sighed.
Pushing his books aside, John got up.

(c) Use a comma after an introductory absolute phrase.

The composition having been completed, John checked it for errors.
The errors being corrected, John returned his paper to his instructor.

(d) Use a comma after an introductory prepositional phrase when a comma makes the meaning clearer.

Through the intercession of the President, Robinson was appointed to the position.

3. Use a comma after transitional words and phrases like *in the first place, moreover, in addition.*

Furthermore, he succeeded excellently.

EXERCISE. Copy the following sentences, inserting the necessary commas. Be prepared to cite the rule for each of your decisions. In your own written work pay particular attention to the application of these principles.

1. While his contemporaries were busy with creative work James Russell Lowell developed into a discerning critic. 2. Although Lowell's criticism is important a reader's first impression is likely to be disappointing. 3. Wandering through digression after digression the reader is painfully aware of Lowell's lack of constructive ability. 4. Borrowing one of Lowell's comments on Emerson one may say that Lowell himself apparently shuffled his paragraphs like a deck of cards. 5. In his interpretation of literature Lowell was the first American critic to bring to his task a real historical perspective. 6. Consequently although his organization is haphazard Lowell judged literary merit by well-defined standards. 7. Holding to these standards Lowell declared that the primary aim of literature is pleasure. 8. Moreover with characteristic idealism he insisted that literature should elevate as well as please. 9. "If God made poets for anything it was to keep alive the traditions of the pure, the holy, and the beautiful." 10. According to Norman Foerster Lowell developed "the sanest and most comprehensive conception of literature formed in America prior to the twentieth century."

4. Use commas to set off words and phrases which add to or explain the meaning.

To *set off* means to use commas both before and after the element, unless, of course, it comes at the beginning or at the end of the sentence.

(a) Appositives

An appositive, or a word in apposition, limits or qualifies the meaning of another word, adds to its meaning, or emphasizes it. Most appositives are set off by commas.

SET OFF: Do you like Edna St. Vincent Millay, *the modern American poet?*

NOT SET OFF: My brother *Bob* says she is his favorite poet.

(b) Addresses and dates

Vachel Lindsay's early home was in Springfield, Illinois, a city with many memories of Lincoln.

His "General William Booth Enters into Heaven" appeared in the January, 1913, issue of *Poetry*.

(c) Words of direct address, introductory words, mild interjections, and other conversational elements

WORDS OF DIRECT ADDRESS: "Listen, my children, and you shall hear . . . ."

"YES" AND "NO" AT THE BEGINNING OF A SENTENCE: Yes, I'll be glad to help.

MILD INTERJECTIONS: "Oh, give me a home where the buffalo roam. . . ."

(d) Explanatory words in direct quotations

He said, "_____."
"_____," she answered.
"_____," I muttered, "_____."

(e) Parenthetical words and phrases

Some people, so I am told, prefer Longfellow to Whittier.

EXERCISE. Copy the following sentences on your paper, inserting commas as needed:

1. Sarah Orne Jewett was a native of the quiet village of South Berwick Maine.   2. Daughter of a country doctor she went often with her father on his professional calls.   3. In this way so it seems she came to know people intimately.   4. One of Mrs. Stowe's novels *The Pearl of Orr's Island* awakened Miss Jewett to the beauty of New England.   5. "I wanted the world to know their grand simple lives" she said, explaining her own stories.   6. It was a world of subdued colors to be sure that Miss Jewett chose to portray.   7. Well she could make it interesting.   8. Her stories as it turned out have much the charm of Whittier's best-loved poem "Snow-Bound."   9. With two other short-story writers Harte and Cable Miss Jewett established regionalism

in our literature.   10. Yes she made a place for herself midway perhaps between romance and realism.

5. Use commas to set off nonrestrictive clauses.

A subordinate clause is *nonrestrictive* if it can be omitted without changing the meaning of the principal clause. A subordinate clause is *restrictive* if it limits the principal clause and if its omission would prove detrimental to the meaning.

Sometimes the meaning the writer wishes to convey determines whether a clause is restrictive or nonrestrictive.

> NONRESTRICTIVE: The most characteristic theme of Miss Millay's poetry, whatever may be her actual subject, is the love of life.
> *The King's Henchman*, which is a romantic drama of old Saxon England, was published in 1927.
> RESTRICTIVE: For Irving the ideal existence is that of the gentleman who is content to pass his time in the quiet and purity of the country.
> RESTRICTIVE OR NONRESTRICTIVE, DEPENDING UPON MEANING: His picture, which hung in the hall, was thought to have something supernatural about it. (There is only one picture; its location is additional information. Remove the commas and we have several pictures of the man, but only one has something supernatural about it.)

6. Use commas to set off nonrestrictive participial phrases.

> NONRESTRICTIVE: Irving, writing of such characters as Rip Van Winkle and Ichabod Crane, achieved fame.
> RESTRICTIVE: Characters revealing subtle traits of human nature live forever.

EXERCISE. Copy the following sentences, setting off with commas all nonrestrictive clauses and phrases:

1. Sidney Lanier maturing in the desolate South of the reconstruction was never able to give more than a fraction of his time

to poetry.   2. Lanier being determined to build a new life returned to the South which he had served bravely during the War between the States.   3. Lanier who lived several years in Georgia finally settled in Baltimore which was to be his home for the rest of his life.   4. He supported his family by playing in the Peabody Symphony Orchestra which he loved and by writing advertising copy for railroads.   5. Later he was appointed lecturer at Johns Hopkins University which had newly been founded.   6. This teaching experience which was valuable in several ways yielded a number of poems bearing the stamp of genius.   7. The fundamental thing which should be said of Lanier is that he had an artist's imagination.   8. "The Song of the Chattahoochee" and "Marsh Song — At Sunset" are lyrics which are among Lanier's best.   9. "The Marshes of Glynn" is a poem which reveals him as the master of a new orchestral style in verse.   10. Lanier writing of nature shows plainly that he is of that distinguished line which begins with Burns and extends through Shelley and Whitman down into our own time.

7. Use a comma to separate words, phrases, or clauses in a series.

Vachel Lindsay's poetry is designed for oral reading, chanting, or singing.

Lindsay's poems are delightful in their freshness, in their wealth of imagery, and in their vitality.

You will want to read Lindsay's poems because his jingling couplets are novel, because he is a spokesman for our older folkways, and because he is one of the most popular twentieth-century poets.

Many of our best writers do not use a comma before the *and* in a series. This usage is entirely correct. The comma should be used, however, if needed for clarity.

NOT CLEAR: He wrote short stories, novels, character sketches and essays. (Four types of writing, or were the last two a combination?)

116

8. Use commas to separate co-ordinate adjectives modifying the same noun.

O. Henry wrote humorous, swift-moving, ingenious stories.

If the last adjective is thought of as part of the noun (*short story*, for example), treat it as a noun and do not place a comma before it. The meaning is the deciding factor.

Gertrude Stein was an active old woman. (*Old woman* has the force of a single noun, like *postman; active* modifies *old woman.*)

EXERCISE. Copy the following sentences, inserting commas wherever needed:

1. Hawthorne's personality is as many-sided as baffling as mysterious as that of Poe.   2. Hawthorne was a New England Irving an idler a lover of life a connoisseur of refined beauties of sensation.   3. He was keenly alive to the taste of good food the exhilaration of a plunge in Walden Pond or the opulent beauties of nature.   4. His enjoyment of nature was affected by lights clouds shadows and reflections.   5. He took delight also in the noisy jostling life in city village and highway.   6. Hawthorne was a keen observer of people and manners a mirthful companion a lover of life a potential vagabond.   7. This was not Hawthorne's predominant phase since he was essentially serious thoughtful and introspective.   8. He never freed himself from a certain deep underlying gravity.   9. Tirelessly he probed human nature the well-springs of action the interplay of deep moral forces.   10. Hawthorne studied man's unsuspected weaknesses his unlooked-for strength of soul in crucial moments.

9. Use a comma to show the omission of a verb in a compound sentence.

Main-Travelled Roads was written by Hamlin Garland; *Main Street*, by Sinclair Lewis.

10. Use a comma after explanatory words like *namely* and *for example*.

> The two authors have a quality in common; namely, their realism.

Notice that the explanatory word is preceded by a semi-colon. (See page 122.)

11. Use a comma after a conjunctive adverb.

The common conjunctive adverbs are *so, hence, thus, then, still, accordingly, also, besides, however, moreover, otherwise, therefore, nevertheless*. Notice that a semicolon precedes the conjunctive adverb.

> John thought he had enough notes; still, it was better to be sure.

12. Use a comma to set off a title or a degree following a proper name.

> James Mason, Jr., spoke first.
> Chief historian of American journalism is Frank Luther Mott, Ph.D.

13. Use a comma after a surname when it precedes a first name.

> Look for a book catalogued under the name of Mott, Frank Luther.

14. Use a comma before *A, An,* or *The* when it follows a title.

> Perhaps you will find also *Course in Journalistic Writing, A* by Hyde.

15. Use a comma after the salutation of a friendly letter and after the complimentary close of any kind of letter.

> Dear Chuck,   Your friend,
> Dear Peggy,   Sincerely yours,

16. Use a comma between sentence elements that might incorrectly be read together.

> To John, Smith was always kind.
> Who it was, was not known.

EXERCISE 1. Copy the following letter, inserting commas wherever needed:

> 19 Madison Avenue
> Omaha 6, Nebraska
> November 28, 19—

Dear Chuck

I saw Jack Lewis Jr. last night. He was home from Nebraska University for the week end; I from State Teachers College. Jack asked me the title of that humorous book you mentioned in English class last spring. I couldn't recall it but promised that I would find out; accordingly I am dashing off this letter.

I am enjoying my college English. My professor seems human in spite of being listed in the catalogue as V. Royce North B.A., M.A., Ph.D., Litt.D. Jack is worried about his English grades. If he could just be induced to study Jack would do very well.

Let me know please how you are doing; also send me the title of that book.

> Your pal
> *David*

EXERCISE 2. Copy these sentences, inserting commas wherever necessary:

1. The letter from Chuck David found very interesting.
2. David thought he remembered the book; however he checked with the card catalogue.
3. There it was listed: *Early Worm The* by Benchley Robert.
4. David prefers Leacock; Chuck Benchley.
5. My favorite is still another; namely John Mason Brown.

119

Review Exercises

EXERCISE 1.   Copy the following sentences, inserting all necessary commas. Be prepared to cite a rule for each of your decisions.

1. William Dean Howells was born March 1 1837 at Martin's Ferry Ohio.   2. Since his father was a country printer his training in journalism began early.   3. While working as a reporter on a Columbus Ohio newspaper Howells wrote a campaign biography of Abraham Lincoln.   4. Lincoln being elected Howells was appointed consul to Venice.   5. After he had spent four years in Europe Howells returned to become assistant editor and later editor of *The Atlantic Monthly*.   6. Those years in Boston it may be caused Howells's realism to be less daring than that of Mark Twain for example.   7. However Howells was by temperament inclined to urbanity to self-restraint to observance of the Victorian decencies.   8. Howells's voluminous production included poems travel books plays novels and criticism.   9. In both the novel and the critical essay which represent his best work Howells became known as a leader of the realistic movement.   10. A realistic author however can render only those phases of life which he is equipped to observe.

EXERCISE 2.   Copy the following sentences, inserting all necessary commas. Can you cite the rule that applies to each one?

1. Howells's vision of human nature included comedy ethics and economics.   2. In the polite circles in which he moved Howells discovered material admirably suited to the subtle realistic comedy of manners.   3. The New England conscience whose vagaries continually interested and sometimes amazed the western-born Howells provided motivation for his characters.   4. An excellent example of his comedy of manners although not his strongest novel is *The Lady of the Aroostook*.   5. Lydia Blood a simple country girl proves to be the only woman on board the *Aroostook* on a voyage to Trieste.   6. Two Bostonians Dunham and Staniford ridiculously discuss their scruples about making

friends with Lydia. 7. Staniford falls in love with Lydia but he feels he cannot tell her until she is under the "protection" of her aunt in Venice. 8. When Lydia is safely in Venice the comedy becomes even more amusing because Lydia and her aunt Mrs. Erwin cannot understand each other's social code. 9. Mrs. Erwin is shocked at Lydia's attending church without a chaperon and Lydia is equally shocked at her aunt's attending the opera instead of church on Sunday evening. 10. Here evidently Howells has created a comedy of manners which plays amusingly over the surface of life and exposes some of the less serious more entertaining follies that flesh is heir to.

EXERCISE 3. Copy the following sentences, inserting commas wherever necessary:

1. *The Rise of Silas Lapham* Howells's most popular novel established in fiction a character peculiarly American the self-made businessman. 2. Through exploiting a paint mine found on his father's farm Lapham has become a millionaire. 3. When the son of an old Boston family falls in love with his daughter Lapham finds that wealth brings problems as well as advantages. 4. Meanwhile in another field Lapham's character is subjected to test after test. 5. His new house burns uninsured his wife temporarily loses confidence in him he makes an unfortunate loan to a former partner and his business finally fails. 6. Nevertheless when tempted to recoup himself by dishonesty Lapham manfully "rises" resists gives up his business and on the verge of old age starts life anew on his ancestral farm. 7. In his acumen his kindliness and his rugged honesty Lapham stands for the best in the old-fashioned individualistic businessman. 8. *Silas Lapham* is a problem novel and it portrays human nature facing difficult questions of ethics. 9. Was Lapham's failure retribution for his having dealt ungenerously with his partner or was this conviction only another vagary of the unaccountable New England conscience? 10. Howells as usual does not commit himself in regard to the ethical problem which he has posed.

Punc 5   The Semicolon

The semicolon is a halfway mark between the comma and the period. The pause it indicates is more pronounced than that shown by the comma but less so than that signified by the period. You may often choose between the semicolon and the period, depending upon the shade of meaning you have in mind. The semicolon implies greater logical unity between the clauses than the period would show. Unless this logical unity is evident, use a period.

1. Use a semicolon between independent clauses of a compound sentence when they are *not* joined by a co-ordinate conjunction.

Vachel Lindsay was not only for the people; he was of the people.

John reported on *The Gilded Age;* Susan, on *The House of Mirth.*

2. Use a semicolon between independent clauses of a compound or a compound-complex sentence when one of the clauses contains one or more commas.

Edith Wharton regarded Henry James as the chief master of English fiction; and he, in turn, considered her his most proficient follower.

3. Use a semicolon between independent clauses joined by a conjunctive adverb.

A semicolon precedes a conjunctive adverb; and, as you saw on page 118, a comma follows it.

Both Mrs. Wharton and Henry James lived abroad during their last years; nevertheless, they are claimed by American literature.

4. Use a semicolon to set off such explanatory words and phrases as *namely, for example, in fact, that is.*

Choose a narrow subject for your report; for example, a single author.

5. Use a semicolon to separate elements in a series if the elements themselves require commas.

Among the writers studied were Poe, the short-story writer; Whitman, the poet; Mark Twain, the novelist; and Eugene O'Neill, the dramatist.

As a reformer, Hamlin Garland wrote a vigorous piece of propaganda in *Jason Edwards;* as a critic, the plea for truthfulness in *Crumbling Idols;* as an objective realist, *Rose of Dutcher's Coolly;* as a biographer, *Ulysses S. Grant;* and as a local colorist, the vivid romance titled *Hesper.*

EXERCISE. Copy the following sentences, inserting semicolons wherever needed. In some sentences, commas also will have to be inserted.

1. Stephen Crane was a pioneer naturalist and his novel *Maggie* is our first important piece of naturalistic fiction. 2. In *The Red Badge of Courage* Crane applied naturalism to the War between the States moreover he even introduced impressionism. 3. The novel carries us from the beginning to the end of a battle we see the battle only as it appears to a young Northern private, Henry Fleming. 4. Fleming goes on marches the purpose of which he cannot understand he fires at enemies he cannot see and finally he marches off without knowing whether his army has lost or won. 5. *The Red Badge of Courage* debunks the picture of war offered by the romancers and what is more it offers an experience that is sufficiently valuable to establish the book as a classic. 6. The authenticity of *The Red Badge* is not the result of personal experience indeed when Crane wrote the book he had never smelled powder. 7. Crane had the accounts of veterans to go by he had the model of Tolstoy's *War and Peace.* 8. Later Crane became a war correspondent henceforth most of his work lapsed into newspaper writing. 9. Through Howells Crane came into contact with the poems of Emily Dickinson and these poems together with Whitman's may have prompted him to break into verse. 10. Like Whitman Crane employed free verse but his lines are tuned to a brevity comparable to Emily Dickinson's.

Punc 6   The Colon

The colon is a rather formal mark of punctuation, one that does not appear often in ordinary writing.

1. Use a colon to introduce a long or formal statement.

John Dickinson (1732–1808), firmly believing in the preservation of liberty, even by force of arms, stated:

"Honor, justice, and humanity call upon us to hold and to transmit to our posterity, that liberty which we received from our ancestors. It is not our duty to leave wealth to our children, but it is our duty to leave liberty to them."

2. Use a colon to introduce a list.

You may choose a novel by one of the following authors: Mark Twain, Henry James, William Dean Howells, Hamlin Garland, Edith Wharton.

3. Use a colon to introduce a series that is used as an appositive.

If Edna St. Vincent Millay has dealt with few themes, she has dealt with those that are most intensely poetic: the loveliness and joy of life and the transitoriness of happiness.

4. Use a colon to separate two main clauses when the second clause explains the first.

We need not make loud claims for American literature: we need only study it.

5. Use a colon between the hour and minute figures of clock time, between the title and the subtitle of a book when the subtitle explains the title, and in Biblical references.

10:30 P.M.   *New England: Indian Summer*
Matthew 13:7

6. Use a colon after the salutation in a business letter.

Dear Sir: Dear Mr. Marston:

EXERCISE 1. Copy the following letter, inserting colons wherever needed:

> 506 Broad Street
> Pittsburgh 6, Pennsylvania
> November 28, 19—

Library of Congress
Washington, D. C.

Gentlemen

I am preparing a report on the sources of the following poems by Robert Frost "The Bearer of Evil Tidings," "Mending Wall," and "Birches." I shall appreciate your sending me any information that will be helpful.

Can you help me also to locate the painting "The Bearer of Evil Tidings," which Frost says inspired his poem of the same title? I should appreciate your giving me the following information place where I can purchase a small reproduction, price, and name and address of the owner of the original.

> Yours very sincerely,
> *Robert Talcott*

EXERCISE 2. Punctuate these sentences correctly as you copy them:

1. At 9 35 last evening I finished reading *Behemoth The Story of Power*. 2. Listen to this interesting statement made by Paine "These are the times that try men's souls. The summer soldier and the sunshine patriot will, in this crisis, shrink from the service of his country; but he that stands it *now*, deserves the love and thanks of man and woman." 3. The truth is evident he was not sufficiently ambitious to succeed. 4. The day was full of cheer the carols, the mistletoe, and the lovely aroma of roasting turkey. 5. John 3 16 is one of my favorite verses.

EXERCISE 3. Write an original sentence that will clearly illustrate each of the rules covering the use of the colon.

Punc 7   Quotation Marks

1. Use double quotation marks to enclose a direct quotation.

"Nothing gives an author so much pleasure as to find his works respectfully quoted by other learned authors," Benjamin Franklin once stated.

Emerson says in one of his essays, "The only gift is a portion of thyself."

"For a long time," Thoreau remarked dryly, "I was reporter to a journal of no very wide circulation."

"I was all alive and inhabited my body with inexpressible satisfaction," Thoreau wrote; "both its weariness and its refreshment were sweet to me."

Notice that quotation marks come in pairs. Do not make the common mistake of leaving out one set. If a quotation consists of several sentences, place the quotation marks at the beginning and at the end of the entire quotation.

When a quotation is several paragraphs in length, begin each paragraph with quotation marks but place them at the end of the last paragraph only. This rule applies only to a continued speech by one person.

In writing dialogue, use a separate paragraph and separate quotation marks for every change of speaker.

Never place quotation marks around indirect quotations.

2. Use double quotation marks to enclose borrowed material.

Mark Twain aptly described the reconstruction period as the "gilded" age.

3. Use double quotation marks to enclose slang expressions and nicknames used in formal writing.

Huck Finn's "pap" is a naturalistic piece of characterization.

4. Use double quotation marks to enclose words used in a particular way.

Although desperately in love with Lydia, Staniford thought it would be ungentlemanly to propose until she was placed under the "protection" of her aunt.

5. Use double quotation marks to enclose the titles of short stories, booklets, poems, and songs.

Walt Whitman figures in Edith Wharton's short story "The Spark."

"O Captain! My Captain!" is a lament for Lincoln's death.

Julia Ward Howe wrote the words for "The Battle Hymn of the Republic."

Do *not* use quotation marks to enclose the following:

a. Titles of books, magazines, and newspapers
b. Titles of themes when such titles are written at the top of your paper
c. Slogans or proverbs
d. Common nicknames generally accepted: Babe Ruth, Buffalo Bill
e. Any nicknames in informal writing
f. Slang in informal writing
g. Any parts which you think are clever or humorous

It is important that you learn to place the quotation marks properly in relation to other marks of punctuation. Place the quotation marks *after* the period and the comma.

"Mark Twain had a drawling kind of humor," said Mr. Conway, "and it pervades most of his stories."

Place the quotation marks before the colon and the semicolon.

His age was "gilded"; it was also exciting.

Place the question mark, the exclamation point, and the dash *before* the quotation marks when they apply to the quoted matter. Place these marks *after* the quotation marks when they apply to the sentence as a whole.

Ellen exclaimed, "What a wonderful character Huck Finn is!"
Did Ellen say, "Huck is better than Tom Sawyer"?

6. Use single quotation marks to enclose a quotation within a quotation.

This is the only use for single quotation marks.

"Recent observation has led me to believe that all people fall into two classifications," John stated. "The idea was first suggested to me by the following line of Robert Frost's: 'The world is full of willing people; some willing to work, and the rest willing to let them.'"

In the rare event of quoting material within a quotation that is itself quoted, use double quotation marks within the single quotation marks.

EXERCISE. Copy the following sentences, making new paragraphs and placing quotation marks where necessary:

Have you read O. Henry's A Municipal Report? John asked Sue as they came out of the drugstore. No, I haven't, she replied, but I've read some of his other stories. I really like them. I have a collection of Bret Harte stories. So far I've read only Tennessee's Partner. Do you know any of these stories? she asked, showing John the table of contents. We read The Outcasts of Poker Flat in class, he said. We are studying poetry and short stories at the same time, he added. Isn't that confusing? Sue asked. Not at all, John rejoined; we're looking for parallels. I'm looking for a good short story about Lincoln. I've found some fine poems about him. I don't know whether I prefer O Captain! My Captain! or Abraham Lincoln Walks at Midnight. Oh, Sue said, our teacher read us Lindsay's poem. She reads beautifully. This morning she said, Students, let's use the record player today.

Punc 8   The Apostrophe

Three of the four uses of the apostrophe are discussed elsewhere in this handbook. Review them before doing the exercise below.

1. **Use an apostrophe to indicate possession.** (See page 36.)

2. **Use an apostrophe to indicate a contraction.** (See page 204.)

3. **Use an apostrophe to indicate the plural of a letter, a number, a sign, or a word referred to as such.** (See page 203.)

4. **Use an apostrophe to indicate the omission of letters in words in dialect.**

> "Fur," said the Deacon, "'t's mighty plain
> Thut the weakes' place mus' stan' the strain;
> 'N' the way t' fix it, uz I maintain,
>   Is only jest
> T' make that place uz strong uz the rest."

OLIVER WENDELL HOLMES

EXERCISE 1. Copy each of these sentences, punctuating it correctly:

1. Its pleasant to read Oliver Wendell Holmess poetry. 2. Hes a poet whos easy and comfortable to read. 3. Ive always enjoyed "Old Ironsides." 4. Mothers favorite is "The Last Leaf," and my brothers say that "To an Insect" is theirs. 5. Im hoping that they wont find this verse by Lowell:

> To say why gals acts so or so,
>   Or dont, ould be presumin;
> Mebby to mean *yes* an say *no*
>   Comes nateral to women.

EXERCISE 2. Write the singular and plural possessives of each of the following: (1) ox, (2) child, (3) witch, (4) mother, (5) alumnus, (6) Jack and Jill — joint possession, (7) boys and girls — individual possession.

Punc 9   The Hyphen

Turn to pages 205 to 207 for a full discussion of the use of the hyphen in hyphenated words.

In addition to the problem of writing hyphenated words correctly, there is the problem of syllables. Frequently it is necessary to break a word at the end of a line. Determine first exactly where it is permissible to make the separation, and then use a hyphen to indicate it. See page 379 for additional information on syllabication.

EXERCISE. Use hyphens to show the syllabication of each of these words:

duration	monopolize	November	scenery
package	nonresistant	levity	recommend
immortal	hollyhock	follow	escort
counterfeit	conclusion	bankruptcy	approval
protestation	ubiquitous	vulnerable	transference

Punc 10   The Dash

Although frequent use of the dash is a tiresome mannerism, there are occasions when the dash will give a shade of meaning that no other mark of punctuation provides.

1. Use a dash to indicate a sudden break in thought or sentence structure.

Gentlemen may cry peace, peace — but there is no peace.
PATRICK HENRY

Hint everything — assert nothing.
    EDGAR ALLAN POE

I can't praise him enough — but what do you think?

2. Use dashes to set off interrupting words, phrases, or clauses which are emphatic or which are themselves split by commas.

Mrs. Wharton has endowed *Ethan Frome* with "that imponderable something more" — to quote her own words — "which causes life to circulate in it and preserve it a little from decay."

They wanted to publish a perfect paper — there is no such thing — but didn't succeed.

3. Use a dash to indicate speech that is broken or faltering.

"I — I'm not sure exactly where I — I left my paper," I stammered.

4. Use a short dash between numbers in a page reference.

pages 3–17   pp. 8–20

EXERCISE. Copy these sentences, inserting dashes wherever they seem desirable. Be able to defend each use.

1. William Gilmore Simms you must have heard of him was more realistic in his treatment of the Indian than Cooper ever was. 2. Simms was a prolific producer thirty-five novels of the type popularized by Scott and Cooper. 3. There is some good material on Simms on pages 216 218 of *A History of American Letters*. 4. Simms you know he was a poor Southerner made his way with difficulty into a gentleman's profession, the law. 5. Although he was disregarded by the aristocracy, he remained loyal one wonders why to the plantation class.

Punc 11   Parentheses

1. Use parentheses to enclose additional information that does not disturb the construction of the sentence. Dashes are sometimes used for the same purpose.

Harte portrays the West as a curious onlooker, or (to change the figure) he takes the role of a circus barker.

2. Use parentheses to confirm dates or figures in letters.

I am enclosing three dollars ($3.00), which will cover the order.

3. Use parentheses to enclose words or statements the accuracy of which is questionable. (See page 109.)

The main part of a sentence which contains a parenthetical insertion is punctuated exactly as it would be if the parenthetical matter were not there. Any punctuation mark used at the point where the parenthetical material is inserted follows the second parenthesis.

Punc 12   Brackets

Use brackets to enclose explanatory words or phrases in a quotation.

The brackets separate your words from those of the person you are quoting.

In typewritten copy, the brackets must be drawn in, since the standard typewriter keyboard does not provide brackets.

> According to the historian Parrington, "He [Thomas Paine] was probably the greatest pamphleteer that the English race has produced, and one of the great idealists."

EXERCISE.   Copy the following sentences.   Insert parentheses and brackets in accordance with the rules you have just studied.

1. He quoted the head librarian it was Miss Conrad in his report.   2. Miss Conrad said, "Franklin's *Autobiography* covers his life up to 1775."   The correct date is 1757.   3. Franklin's printing business and other activities the clerkship of the Pennsylvania Assembly and the postmastership of Philadelphia enabled him to retire in 1748.   4. His prudential teachings "Beware of little expenses; a small leak will sink a great ship," is an example were published in *The Way to Wealth*.   5. Its emphasis on individual enterprise everyone was interested in the penny-saved-is-a-penny-earned philosophy made the book a best seller.

Punc 13   Dots

Use dots to indicate an omission from a quotation.

To indicate an omission at the beginning of a sentence or within a sentence, use three dots. To indicate an omission at the end of a declarative sentence, use four dots. The last dot is the normal end mark.

> In Boston, England, Hawthorne was served by "an exceedingly grim waiter . . ., apparently a genuine descendant of the old Puritans. . . ."

Punc 14   Underlining, or Italics

For a full discussion of this topic, turn to pages 381 and 382.

Review Exercises

EXERCISE 1.   Copy the following sentences, inserting the proper end marks:

1. Please let me know your decision as soon as possible
2. Why didn't you tell me you were coming
3. Don't go
4. Have you read John Hersey's *Hiroshima*
5. He asked me whether I had read it
6. You may enjoy reading Max Miller's *I Cover the Waterfront*
7. Have you read *Where Are They Now*
8. She exclaimed over the fruit: Oranges Apples Bananas
9. She asked the group, "Has anyone seen my notebook"
10. Where are they all: Johnny Bill Tom Frank
11. They had wondered whether they would be missed
12. I cried out, "Help! I'm falling"
13. Did anyone pay any attention
14. Will you please sign on the dotted line
15. She asked whether I knew his address

EXERCISE 2. Copy the following sentences, inserting commas wherever needed:

1. Poe developed the form of the short story but Irving is more important historically.
2. Irving's sketches may be classified as short stories but they have much of the essay about them.
3. With its vivid description serving as a background "The Stout Gentleman" is a masterpiece of short fiction.
4. Poe saw the possibilities of the short fiction pieces with which his contemporaries Irving and Hawthorne were working.
5. Poe developed the impressionistic story in which a single effect is the aim with incidents characters setting and style all contributing.
6. In writing of Hawthorne's tales which he admired Poe said "Every word *tells* and there is not a word which does not *tell*."
7. Although the plot is of some importance in a short story of local color the chief interest lies in the oddity of the place and people.
8. Bret Harte wrote of the Far West; George Washington Cable of the Old South.
9. Mary E. Wilkins Freeman's short story "A New England Nun" is chiefly a character study but the New England setting provides a plausible background.
10. John said "I like short stories because I can finish one at a sitting"; but his sister exclaimed "Nonsense! You just don't like to sit very long."

EXERCISE 3. Copy the following sentences, inserting semicolons and commas wherever necessary:

1. The fields of the short story and the novel overlap: short-story writers like Jack London wrote successful novels novelists like Edith Wharton wrote excellent short stories.
2. Hamlin Garland wrote with reforming zeal at the beginning of the twentieth century Sinclair Lewis is following in his footsteps today.

134

3. The romantic novel is still with us however the present-day novel is predominantly realistic.

4. Booth Tarkington first achieved popularity with romantic fiction nevertheless he gradually turned toward a realistic presentation of American life.

5. Wealthy herself one might have expected Edith Wharton to write best of the socially elite on the contrary she achieved her greatest success with a story of bleak impoverished rural life.

EXERCISE 4. Copy the following sentences, inserting colons wherever needed:

1. Pearl Buck followed a Chinese family through three novels *The Good Earth, Sons, A House Divided*.

2. The twentieth century has produced many outstanding novelists we need not fear comparison with earlier periods.

3. The library opened at 830 A.M.; it was 831 when he looked in the card catalogue for *Word Magic Tested Answers to 100 Everyday Situations*.

4. Above the statue of Lincoln are carved these words

With malice toward none, with charity for all. . . .

5. Dear Mr. Wellsford

Please send me copies of the following books Cather's *Song of the Lark*, Lewis's *Arrowsmith*, London's *Call of the Wild*.

Sincerely,
Thomas Ryan

EXERCISE 5. Copy the following sentences, inserting quotation marks, apostrophes, dashes, parentheses, or brackets as needed:

1. My favorite poet is Emily Dickinson, she said. I particularly like the poem that begins, I never saw a moor. . . .

2. Poes famous poem Annabel Lee has a lilting quality in such lines as, The moon never beams, without bringing me dreams.

3. Bob quoted lines from Whittiers Telling the Bees:

> Since we parted, a month had passed
> To love, a year.

4. The reason for Bobs choice of lines isnt hard to guess I said to myself.

5. *Merci beaucoup*, the young woman said. That is French for Thank you. I am most grateful for your directions, she added in English.

EXERCISE 6. Copy these sentences on your paper, punctuating them correctly:

1. Could you make a list of the best stories the best poems the best essays
2. As you know there are many Best Books Clubs in America and they are doing much to stimulate reading
3. When we make our own list of best books we probably include those which have especially influenced us that is only natural
4. Certain books have wielded an influence for many years consequently theyre generally considered classics
5. We have seen how clothes songs slang amusements quickly go out of style said Miss Townsend yesterday we can appreciate therefore the importance of an authors work that lives on for centuries

EXERCISE 7. Write sentences of your own in which you illustrate the use of the following:

1. A colon to introduce a list
2. A comma to set off a series
3. A semicolon in a compound sentence
4. Single quotation marks to indicate a quotation within a quotation
5. Dots to indicate an omission from a quotation

DICTION

WORDS

Although communication started with signals, we could never have advanced without words. They are the real basis of our whole civilization. The possession of a rich and exact vocabulary, consequently, is of the utmost importance. But mere possession is not enough; ability to use that vocabulary effectively and correctly is essential.

First we need to increase our vocabulary and then to refine it. Let us parody Herrick's advice,

> Gather ye rosebuds while ye may:
> Old Time is still a-flying.

Let us gather words! Close acquaintanceship with the dictionary is one way to achieve that end.

Dic   Use of the Dictionary

The dictionary is an exceedingly useful tool. In the introductory section of *Webster's New International Dictionary, Second Edition*, for instance, you will find a brief history of the English language, a guide to pronunciation, explanatory notes, and a section listing new words that have recently come into the language. On the pages in the back of the book, you will find abbreviations, signs and symbols, a pronouncing gazetteer, and a pronouncing biographical dictionary.

In addition to spelling and pronunciation of words, the dictionary provides information about grammar, derivation, and meaning, as well as synonyms and idiomatic phrases.

The status of some words is indicated by such labels as *Colloq.* (Colloquial), *Dial.* (Dialectal), *Obs.* (Obsolete), *Tech.* (Technical), *Slang.* You will find that a word may be acceptable in some usages but not in others; the labels are the guide. *Dope* is listed in the dictionary as a verb, but Webster labels three of its four meanings as *Slang.* *Ritzy* also appears in the dictionary, but Webster labels all its meanings as *Slang.*

Under *punk*, Webster marks two of the meanings *Slang* and one *Obsolete.* Meanings not so branded are in good use. Under *phony*, all meanings are labeled *Slang.* Under *pinch* used as a noun, one meaning is marked *Dialectal;* one, *Obsolete;* one, *Slang;* and one, *Rare.*

Dictionaries are of various sizes and degrees of value. The most comprehensive treatment of words will be found in an unabridged dictionary. You will surely refer to an unabridged dictionary countless times during your life, but you may never own one. Ownership of one of the smaller dictionaries is almost a necessity. In choosing any dictionary, one should satisfy oneself on two scores: (1) Is the dictionary of recent date? (2) Has the dictionary been published by a recognized authority in the field?

The following dictionaries you will find to be thoroughly trustworthy:

Unabridged Dictionaries

A New English Dictionary (also titled *The Oxford English Dictionary*), The Macmillan Company

The New Standard Dictionary of the English Language, Funk & Wagnalls Company

Webster's New International Dictionary of the English Language, Second Edition, G. & C. Merriam Company

Abridged Dictionaries

Thorndike Century Senior Dictionary, Scott, Foresman Company

Webster's Collegiate Dictionary, G. & C. Merriam Company

Winston *Simplified Dictionary*, The John C. Winston Company

EXERCISE 1. Use an unabridged dictionary to find the answers to the following:

1. How many meanings has *run* as a noun? as a verb?
2. What parts of speech are the following words: *alter, invite, suspicion, but, principal?*
3. At what age did the following authors die: Edgar Allan Poe, John Greenleaf Whittier, Henry Wadsworth Longfellow, Herman Melville, William Cullen Bryant?
4. What is the literary meaning of each of these words: *novel, elegy, melodrama, lyric, essay?*
5. What is the preferred pronunciation of each of the following: *Ave Maria, garage, Chopin, coupon, chauffeur, cello?*

EXERCISE 2. What is the source and original meaning of each of the following words: *curfew, boycott, echo, guerrilla, delicatessen?*

EXERCISE 3. Use an abridged dictionary to answer these questions:

1. What are the plurals of the following nouns: *stratum, datum, sheep, tomato, lynx?*
2. Are the following verbs transitive, intransitive, or both: *sing, bite, contest, confuse, pass?*

Dic 1   Enunciation and Pronunciation

Try at all times to speak clearly and distinctly.

Most Americans speak too rapidly. Slow down enough to give all sounds their correct value. Do not omit or slur sounds; do not confuse or blur them. Your listener would like to have a chance to understand you.

Try at all times to give letters in words the correct sounds and to accent the right syllables.

Study the key to pronunciation given at the bottom of dictionary pages, and learn to interpret the diacritical marks. In distinguishing accent marks, you will find that the primary stress is indicated by a heavy mark and the secondary stress by a light mark.

Clear and Correct Vowel Sounds

The following are the major problems related to the enunciation and pronunciation of vowels:

1. **Sound long vowels exactly.**

   ā: *A* d*a*y m*a*de the st*a*te f*a*mous.
   ē: H*e* gave m*e* a k*e*y.
   ī: *I* f*i*nd the pr*i*ces h*i*gh.
   ō: *O*h, n*o*, th*o*se are l*o*w.
   ū: Can you *u*se these c*u*bes?

EXERCISE. How should each of these words be pronounced? Whenever you are in doubt, check with the dictionary.

abdomen	culinary	leisure	sacrilegious
apparatus	data	oral	solace
aviator	duke	penalize	status
biography	grimy	pugilist	stupid
condolence	isolate	radiator	zoology

2. Sound short vowels exactly.

ă: The advertisement can absolutely prove it.

ĕ: The end of the epic was excellent.

ĭ: It was interesting.

ŏ: There was considerable knowledge of the conspiracy.

ŭ: Bud dug his heels into the rug.

EXERCISE. Say each of these words correctly:

adept	docile	italic	respite
admirable	fragile	juvenile	tepid
bade	genuine	piano	winsome
deaf	horrible	recipe	wish
dirigible	Italian	rinse	zealous

3. Do not drop a necessary vowel sound.

By dropping a necessary vowel, cruel becomes "crule"; regular becomes "reglar"; poem becomes "pome."

EXERCISE. Practice saying these words. The vowels frequently omitted are printed in italics.

boundary	generally	medieval	probably
chocolate	geography	memory	really
environment	geometry	naturally	separate
factory	history	Niagara	sophomore
finally	laboratory	occasionally	vegetable

4. Do not add a vowel sound.

Athletics sometimes becomes "athaletics," and film becomes "fillum." Avoid these errors.

EXERCISE. Practice saying these words correctly:

barbarous	grievous	mischievous
convenience	helm	remembrance
disastrous	hindrance	suffrage
elm	lightning	ticklish
foundry	maintenance	umbrella

141

Review Exercise

EXERCISE. Practice saying the following words correctly and clearly. Each contains at least one crucial vowel sound.

again	culinary	mathematics	suite
alias	experiment	precedence	toward
amateur	federal	quinine	vagary
automobile	hiatus	roof	vaudeville
burglar	literature	squalor	yacht

Clear and Correct Consonant Sounds

The following are some of the problems related to the enunciation and pronunciation of consonants:

1. Sound *th* clearly. Do not give it the sound of *d* or *t*.

EXERCISE. Can you sound the words in each pair so clearly that a listener can distinguish between them?

bread	breadth	tanks	thanks
doze	those	tick	thick
hundred	hundredth	trust	thrust
tan	than	wit	with

2. Sound *wh* clearly.

Words like *when, where, which,* and *why* were originally spelled *hwen, hwere, hwich,* and *hwy.* Those old spellings, by the way, indicate the correct pronunciations.

EXERCISE. Say the words in each of these pairs so clearly that a listener can distinguish between them:

watt	what	wig	Whig
wear	where	wile	while
weather	whether	wit	whit
wen	when	witch	which
wet	whet	world	whirled

3. Sound the consonants *f* and *v* clearly. Do not use them interchangeably.

EXERCISE. Say each of these words correctly:

fail	vail	file	vile
fast	vast	fine	vine
fat	vat	fur	Virginia
feign	vein	knife	knives

4. Sound the consonants *s* and *z* correctly.

The *s* in some words sounds like *z*.

EXERCISE. Say each of these words correctly:

absolutely	Diesel	muzzle	suggest
absurd	horizon	oaths	vice versa
because	jeopardize	paradise	zeal
chastisement	muscle	seal	zero

5. Sound the consonants *d* and *t* distinctly.

EXERCISE. Practice saying the following words:

bold	cold	panted	told
bolt	colt	partner	tottered
bottle	detracted	patron	twittered
butter	fiddle	potatoes	welded
cattle	little	riddle	welt

6. Do not drop a necessary consonant sound.

The dropping of necessary consonant sounds changes words like *awkward* to "awkard" and *arctic* to "artic."

EXERCISE. Practice saying these words, making certain not to drop any necessary consonants:

abrupt	February	kept	recognize
crept	gentleman	length	sixths
district	government	library	slept
entertaining	hundredths	lists	stalwart
facts	interesting	pumpkin	suggest

7. Do not add a consonant sound.

Avoid adding sounds as in these words: *attacked* (not "attackeded"), *once* (not "oncet"), *drowned* (not "drownded"), *overalls* (not "overhalls").

8. Do not sound silent letters.

EXERCISE. How should each of these words be pronounced? Consult your dictionary whenever you are in doubt.

almond	glisten	salmon	toward
bouquet	herb	silhouette	viscount
column	indict	soften	Wednesday
corps	mortgage	subtle	wry
debris	often	sword	yacht

9. Do not transpose sounds.

The transposition of sounds turns words like *perspiration* into "prespiration," *modern* into "modren," and *apron* into "apern." See page 191 for a list of such words.

Review Exercise

EXERCISE. The following words are frequently mispronounced because of a variety of errors in consonant sounds. Can you pronounce each correctly?

cello	diphtheria	longevity	schism
chaos	epoch	orgy	spigot
chic	flaccid	postpone	strength
clique	forsythia	psalm	xylophone
depot	indictment	qualm	yolk

Accent the Proper Syllable

In the dictionary, a heavy mark (′) indicates the syllable on which primary stress is given; a lighter mark (′) indicates secondary stress.

The words in this list are stressed on the *first* syllable:

ab'solutely	ex'quisite	im'potent	pref'erable
ad'mirably	gon'dola	in'teresting	rec'ipe
ap'plicable	har'ass	mis'chievous	res'pite
com'parable	hos'pitable	pos'itively	tres'pass
des'picable	il'lustrate	prec'edent	ve'hement

The words in this list are accented on the *second* syllable:

abdo'men	condo'lence	inex'plicable	romance'
accli'mate	deco'rum	inhos'pitable	secre'tive
adult'	epit'ome	inquir'y	super'fluous
bouquet'	grimace'	preced'ence	tarpau'lin
calli'ope	incom'parable	research'	vagar'y

The words in this list are accented on the *third* syllable:

acciden'tally	importune'	pertina'cious
bombardier'	indefat'igable	ultima'tum
cigarette'	irreduc'ible	unfrequent'ed

EXERCISE 1. Use your dictionary to find the preferred pronunciation of each of these words:

adult	decadence	Hindu	rebound
confiscate	exchequer	illustrative	rodeo
coyote	exemplary	irrefutable	separative

EXERCISE 2. Copy these words, accenting the proper syllable. Practice saying the words aloud.

acumen	contemplate	genuine	maintenance
address	conversant	harass	memorable
advertisement	detail	herculean	municipal
alias	dictionary	hotel	preferable
apropos	disputable	illustrate	reinforce
automobile	éclair	impious	revolt
bayonet	equitable	implicit	robust
clandestine	exigency	incognito	telegraphy
coincidence	finance	indisputable	theater
commandant	formidable	infamous	usurp

Review Exercise

EXERCISE. Read the following story,[1] pronouncing each word correctly:

"Form a posse!" shouted the robust sheriff. "A most formidable brigand is at large."

"Is where?" asked the comptroller, lying on an exquisite divan. He was enjoying a respite from the worries of finance.

"You chimpanzee," replied the sheriff, gnashing his teeth, "your ignorance is lamentable — and grievous, and —"

"Irremediable," supplied his incomparable deputy, who hated the comptroller for divers causes. With an admirable twist to his mustache, he continued, "Unless I err, the gibbet, an elephantine tripod, is ready, sheriff. Let's end this longevity of our barbarous brigand."

"He means levity," roared the comptroller. But they had left, carrying with great travail a tarpaulin and a tepee.

After passing a commandant and his corps, who offered means of condign punishment — but no help or victuals — they halted their excursion, for culinary purposes, albeit they had only one vegetable, some pecans, a salmon, and little venison.

"We must wrestle with this further," bade the sheriff in his address.

"Aye," responded a mischievous adult, chewing in bestial fashion, "although genuine venison would be preferable. In zoology, I remember, viscera were not —"

"I reckon," calmly interrupted the incomparable deputy, gnawing, "we'd better reconnoiter. Our infamous, despicable combatant —"

"Competent," corrected the agile comptroller, who, completing his chores, had arrived. "Your orthoëpy is —"

"Admirable," finished the sheriff, all roiled. "Let's cross this bayou."

"Chaos and mortgages!" shouted the comptroller, scratching himself as they forded the creek. The water had rinsed off his medicinal preparation for eczema.

[1] By permission. From "The Sheriff's Dilemma," copyright, 1940, by G. & C. Merriam Co.

"The curse of the brigand!" was the cry, and they seized him. An epistle and a coupon disclosed his cognomen. Mounting a natural dais near a crevasse, he gave, somewhat awry, his version of his biography.

While erecting the caryatids on the façade of a cathedral, he fell into the slough of despond because of conjugal difficulties. His courtierlike attitude was short-lived, and he married a geisha who had a penchant for buying perukes all the livelong day.

"Impious," muttered the sheriff, looking askance at him, "but explicable. And your conversion to a life of heinous crime is sequacious. Now, an autopsy will —"

"No alibi," went on the brigand, now docile enough, "will condone my debut into crime. Hospitable, subtle, I could have been —" He daubed his eyes. The incomparable deputy, discomfited, plucked a gladiolus and burst into ribald song. Becoming anecdotal, the brigand told of a gala orgy in an occult chasm, the story almost causing a schism in the group.

Failing to soften the jury, he was indicted as a sleek villain, as the epitome of all criminal debris. To his valet he bequeathed his broken, though reparable, yacht. Deaf to all, he drank naphtha to cure his ague and diphtheria. Finally, bitten by remorse, already clad in cerements, he contracted rabies, and, muttering diphthongs, burst his jugular vein. With great clangor, his demise was announced. A psalm was sung as a requiem by the posse, which made up the cortege.

Dic 2   Vocabulary Enrichment

Language is an ever-growing, ever-changing tool of communication. Each year we need new words to express new ideas. Sometimes entirely new words are coined to take care of the need; other times old words are modified or given new meanings. The discovery of certain drugs has given us words like *sulfa*, *streptomycin*, and *penicillin*. World War II gave us such words as *blitzkrieg*, *Roger*, *landing strip*. Once an *alligator* was merely a member of the crocodile family; now it is also a machine with jaws like an alligator. Words like *swing, liquidate, jam session, foxhole* have all had an interesting evolution of meanings. To be an intelligent listener and reader, one needs a broad and ever-increasing vocabulary.

Ways to Build a Vocabulary

How can you improve your stock of words?

1. You can begin by looking up unfamiliar words in the dictionary. This is a good practice, but it has some limitations. For example, if you are reading while on your vacation, you may not have a dictionary at hand. Even if you have, the story may be so exciting that you will not want to take time to thumb through a dictionary.

2. If the book or magazine you are reading happens to be your own, you can read with a pencil in hand. As your eye catches an unfamiliar word, you can check, underline, or circle it. When you have finished reading, turn to the dictionary and begin your word hunt. We use the dictionary when we can, but acquiring a vocabulary consists of much more than looking up the meanings of words.

3. To learn words, we must depend primarily on experience. As Emerson said, "Every new relation is a new word." When we learn about anything that is new, we concurrently learn words with which to talk about it.

An English textbook cannot provide many experiences, but it can suggest some fundamental facts about words.

1. Intelligent Guessing, or Understanding by Context

Besides using the dictionary, you may increase your vocabulary by attempting to guess the meanings of strange words.

Suppose you are reading Washington Irving's "Rip Van Winkle" and you come across this sentence: "The great error in Rip's composition was an *aversion* to all

kinds of profitable labor." What do you do if you do not
know the word *aversion?* If you are like most readers, you
probably skip over it. In this sentence, because of all that
is said about Rip, you can reasonably conclude that he is
unwilling to work, that he dislikes work. Synonyms for
aversion are, in fact, *dislike* and *unwillingness.*

Sometimes we fail to guess the meaning of a word because we don't bother to look at it carefully. Have you
ever stopped to think that a first-year student in high
school or college is called a *freshman* because he is *newly
arrived,* or that a *broadcast* is *widely thrown out?*

EXERCISE 1. The following words contain numbers
from one to ten. Can you identify them without consulting a dictionary?

1. bicycle	6. quartet
2. September	7. December
3. November	8. sextant
4. octopus	9. trivial
5. pentagon	10. unique

EXERCISE 2. Be your own dictionary. Try to guess the
meanings of the italicized words in the following sentences
taken from the first chapter of *The House of the Seven
Gables.* Then look up the words to find how well you have
done.

1. Half-way down a *by-street* of one of our New England towns
stands a rusty wooden house, with seven *acutely* peaked *gables,*
facing toward various points of the compass, and a huge, *clustered*
chimney in the midst. 2. The street is Pyncheon Street; the
house is the old Pyncheon House; and an elm-tree, of wide *circum-
ference,* rooted before the door, is familiar to every town-born
child by the title of the Pyncheon Elm. 3. The aspect of the
venerable mansion has always affected me like a human *counte-
nance,* bearing the traces not merely of outward storm and sun-

shine, but expressive, also, of the long *lapse* of mortal life, and accompanying *vicissitudes* that have passed within. 4. Were these to be *worthily* recounted, they would form a *narrative* of no small interest and instruction. 5. But the story would include a *chain of events* extending over the *better part* of two centuries, and, written out with reasonable *amplitude*, would fill a bigger volume than could *prudently* be *appropriated* to the *annals* of all New England during a similar period.

2. Specialized Vocabularies

Most of us have not one but many vocabularies. We use one vocabulary when we discuss sports with a friend, and another when we talk vocational preparation with a counselor. Each field has a particular vocabulary.

The following lists represent some specialized vocabularies. Do you know the meaning of each word, and can you use each in a sentence?

BUSINESS VOCABULARY

qualifications	bona fide	affidavit	liquidate
expansion	revolutionize	inventory	factor
injunction	fraudulent	insolvent	fiscal
appraise	depreciate	defray	dividend
aggregate	accrue	expedite	budget

VOCABULARY OF LITERATURE

sonnet	paradox	subtle	autobiography
ballad	metaphor	crisis	denouement
epic	allegory	antagonist	imagery
lyric	meter	protagonist	romantic
satire	subplots	connotation	realistic

VOCABULARY OF ART

bas-relief	Byzantine	gargoyle	Gothic
etching	futurism	impressionism	cubism
primitive	Renaissance	caricature	representation

VOCABULARY OF MUSIC

opera	aria	symphony	concerto
overture	cadence	requiem	staccato
wind instruments	a cappella	andante	tempo

NEWSPAPER VOCABULARY

agenda	columnist	bureaucrats	tribunal
incognito	syndicated	regime	filibustering
corroborate	laud	propaganda	raze
indicted	rebuttal	divulge	larceny
aspirant	plebiscite	broach	parley

VOCABULARY OF THE RESTAURANT

| table d'hôte | hors d'oeuvre | entree | meringue |
| glacé | napoleon | éclair | pie à la mode |

3. New Words

New words come into being constantly. Have you noticed how dictionaries keep up-to-date? Sometimes a "New Words" section is added to tide them over to a new edition.

EXERCISE. See whether these words in their current meanings are in the latest dictionary you have available:

amphibious	ferry	Link trainer	prefabricated
blood bank	guinea pig	motel	sharecropper
by-pass	hostel	pixilated	stooge
beam	jam session	microfilm	swing shift
dither	laminate	polio	telecast

4. Specific Words

A visitor to this country once claimed that he could manage very well with three English words: *swell*, *lousy*, and *okay*. Those are three general words used to cover thousands of situations. Actually they are so general and so overused that they have little meaning.

151

If you want to convey exact ideas, you must have exact words at your command. There is little meaning in such statements as: "She is a *beautiful* girl." "We had a *wonderful* time." "He *went* down the street." "A *man* knocked at the door." Specific details or specific words are needed to give exactness to each sentence.

One way to increase your vocabulary is to discard the first general term that comes to mind. Search for the specific word that more nearly conveys your meaning.

Each of these four lists of words shows specific meanings for the general words heading the lists. What other words can you add to each list?

GO	WORKED	GOOD LOOKING	TAKE
trudge	cleaned	stunning	accept
stagger	dug	handsome	seize
strut	plowed	glamorous	steal
stride	studied	petite	conquer
saunter	polished	attractive	carry

Writing in generalities is a common fault in themes. If you overcome this habit, you will have gone far toward improving your compositions. Notice the following:

GENERAL AND VAGUE: Ethan went up the hill.

EXACT: Ethan trudged up the hill.

GENERAL: "The Monkey's Paw" is a good story.

EXACT: "The Monkey's Paw" is a terrifying story of horror.

GENERAL: Ted did his assignment in literature.

EXACT: Ted read "The Gold Bug" by Poe and memorized "Annabel Lee."

GENERAL: Junior is a bad baby.

EXACT: Junior howls night and day.

GENERAL: Painting was his profession, and he made a valuable contribution along that line.

EXACT: Thomas Hart Benton painted the mural of John Brown in the Kansas State Capitol.

152

EXERCISE 1. Find ten or more specific substitutes for each of the following words:

1. good   3. swell
2. said   4. thing

EXERCISE 2. What specific words can you substitute for the italicized words in the following sentences?

1. Mark Twain tells many *interesting* frontier stories. 2. One of the *best* is about a *well-known* outlaw named Slade. 3. Once Slade was *taken* by a party of men who intended to *do away* with him. 4. They disarmed him, *put* him in a strong long-house, and placed a guard over him. 5. Slade *asked* his captors to send for his wife so that he might *see* her. 6. Mrs. Slade was a *brave, sweet, intelligent* woman. 7. She *got on* her horse and rode *quickly* to her husband. 8. When she *got there*, they let her in without searching her. 9. Before the door could be closed, she *brought out* a couple of *guns*, and she and *Mr. Slade came out.* 10. Then, under a brisk fire, they mounted double and *rode* away unharmed.

5. Concrete and Vivid Words

Make a general or abstract idea easy to grasp by stating it in concrete words.

Try to visualize as you write. When you use words that have real meaning for you, they are more likely to have real meaning for the reader. Charles Dickens gave good advice when he said, "Don't say the old lady has a bad temper. Lead her in and let her howl."

VAGUE: He worked hard at his typing.

CONCRETE: He typed ten letters after dinner.

PICTURESQUE: He beat the heart out of his typewriter.

COLORLESS: She assumed an air of culture.

PICTURESQUE: Her air of culture was as convincing as a Halloween mask.

DRY: He has no future.

COLORFUL: He's been where he's going.

EXERCISE 1. Collect from magazines or books ten concrete expressions that give you a clear mental picture. Analyze them to find out what gives them life — strong verbs, colorful nouns, or imagery by other means.

EXERCISE 2. Improve the following sentences:

1. The man said, "Good morning."
2. There was plenty of food at the picnic.
3. Jane had on a new outfit.
4. He looked awful as he walked down the street.
5. The Joneses bought a car.

Review Exercises

EXERCISE 1. Can you correct the following vocabulary "boners"?

1. His I.Q. test showed him to be a maroon.
2. Mother had candid sweet potatoes for dinner.
3. The diseased was buried after a short funeral service.
4. Having only one wife or husband is monotony.
5. A blizzard is one of the gibets.
6. He couldn't make himself heard because of the noisome class.
7. A parabola is an arbor or trellis in a garden.
8. Señorita Gonzalez was taking her afternoon fiesta.
9. They had reached a stalagmite in their argument.
10. An auricle is a person or thing who is supposed to give divinely inspired answers to questions.

EXERCISE 2. The following are statements made on a college board examination. Make the necessary corrections.

1. Macbeth was incorporated as king.
2. Love is stronger than any profession.
3. He listened to the prosophy of the witches.
4. Hamlet watched the upheaval of Yorick's skull.
5. Sweet are the uses of conversity.

6. Because of his stature and his preoccupied air, Napoleon was domineered.

7. Silver minds have been discovered in Athens.

8. When a man's wife dies, his life may be dismantled for a while.

9. The constant nagging of Lady Macbeth slowly boiled Macbeth into a frenzy.

10. Henry VIII enjoyed all charnel joys to the fullest.

11. Dimmesdale preached to his perish.

12. Edward VIII was carefree of the advice of his counselors.

13. Silas Marner was rapidly becoming unhappy, morose, and obsolete.

14. Shakespeare's *Hamlet* is a delightful example of revenge.

15. Irene Forsyte was a concretion of beauty.

EXERCISE 3. Answer each of these questions:

1. If a *monsoon* is a rainy season, what is a *lampoon?*

2. If *minor* means "inferior in bulk," what does *miner* mean?

3. If a *biographer* is one who writes the history of a person's life, what does a *lexicographer* do?

4. If a *flamingo* is a bird, what is a *fandango?*

5. If a *grandmother* is a relative, what is a *grampus?*

6. If a *wreath* is a garland of flowers, what is a *wraith?*

7. If *flotsam* is wreckage of a ship found floating on the sea, what is *jetsam?*

8. If a *zither* is a musical instrument, what is a *zephyr?*

9. If *raucous* means "harsh" and "shrill," what does *caucus* mean?

10. If a *corsage* is a bouquet, what is a *cortege?*

EXERCISE 4. List several synonyms for each of these badly overworked words:

1. awful	6. glad	11. nice
2. clever	7. hard	12. pretty
3. cute	8. interesting	13. quickly
4. end	9. mad	14. scared
5. get	10. mean	15. smart

EXERCISE 5. Rewrite this flowery paragraph, putting it into good, straightforward prose:

It was a beauteous evening. When I looked at the maiden sitting beside me on the park bench, I noticed that she had golden tresses, orbs of cerulean blue, a swanlike neck, a brow of alabaster, and teeth of pearls. She was utterly adorable and utterly divine. So I inquired whether she would tread the flowery path with me. There we were, under the twinkling heavens, listening to the twittering of our feathered friends. But alas and alack, 'twas then that I discovered that her brow was really alabaster — solid.

EXERCISE 6. Supply the necessary antonym for each of these sentences:

1. Grandfather was not parsimonious; he was –?–.
2. Let us establish good policies; let us not –?– them.
3. The diamond is genuine, not –?–.
4. They lived in harmony, not –?–.
5. The farmers found the yield was scarce; they had hoped it would be –?–.
6. You could tell that the group was friendly, not –?–.
7. The horse was restive, not –?–.
8. Once he was obscure; now he is –?–.

EXERCISE 7. Since many initials have become part of our vocabulary, it is important to know the principal ones. For what do the following stand?

1. TVA	5. F.B.I.	9. USSR	13. A.W.O.L.
2. A.B.	6. M.D.	10. C.P.A.	14. R.N.
3. A.A.A.	7. AFL	11. FHA	15. P.T.A.
4. S.P.C.A.	8. CIO	12. R.S.V.P.	16. TNT

Dic 3   Figures of Speech

Figures of speech are always thought of immediately in relation to poetry; they are also excellent devices to add color and concreteness to prose.

The chief danger in the use of figures of speech lies in the acceptance of those which through overuse have become clichés. A figure of speech is successful when it is fresh and when it gives the reader or listener an honest picture.

The following are the kinds of figures of speech most frequently used:

Simile: A simile is an expressed comparison between two objects of unlike nature. The comparison is made through some common point of resemblance, and the word *like* or *as* is used.

Do not confuse the simile with a literal comparison. If you say that one girl reminds you of another, you are making a literal comparison. But when Robert Burns says that his girl is like a red, red rose and again that she is like a melody, he is using similes.

Scoops of sand and gravel from the colt's hoofs hit the fence with a sound *like shot.*

MARY O'HARA

There is no frigate *like a book*
To take us lands away.

EMILY DICKINSON

Some gather life *like faggots* in a wood.

LIZETTE WOODWORTH REESE

Metaphor: A metaphor is a comparison in which one thing is compared with another by speaking of it as if it were that other. The words *like* and *as* are not used in this kind of comparison.

The moon was a ghostly *galleon.*

ALFRED NOYES

When you are the *anvil*, bear —
When you are the *hammer*, strike.

EDWIN MARKHAM

157

Personification: Personification is a figure of speech that credits things, ideas, or qualities with personalities or with the attributes of man.

> The adjective is the *enemy* of the noun.
>
> UNKNOWN

> Admiration is the *daughter* of ignorance.
>
> BENJAMIN FRANKLIN

Apostrophe: An apostrophe occurs when one that is absent is addressed as though he were present.

> Thou, too, sail on, *O Ship of State*.
>
> HENRY WADSWORTH LONGFELLOW

> O powerful western fallen *star!* [Lincoln]
>
> WALT WHITMAN

Hyperbole: A hyperbole is an overstatement or an intentional exaggeration.

> The emptiness of ages in his face,
> And on his back the burden of the world.
>
> EDWIN MARKHAM

> Why, man, he doth bestride the narrow world
> Like a Colossus.
>
> WILLIAM SHAKESPEARE

Irony: Irony occurs when a person says one thing and means another.

> Does it matter? — losing your leg? —
> For people will always be kind.
>
> SIEGFRIED SASSOON

Allegory: An allegory is a prolonged metaphor.

Allegory sets forth one subject in the guise of another. The parables in the Bible and Aesop's fables are examples of short allegories; Bunyan's *Pilgrim's Progress* and Spenser's *Faerie Queene* are examples of long allegories.

Metonymy: Metonymy is the use of one word for another which it suggests.

The effect may be substituted for the cause, the cause for the effect, the container for the thing contained, and so on.

> Mother sets a good table.

> Carrying a corpse to where it shall rest in the grave,
> Night and day journeys a coffin.
>
> WALT WHITMAN

Avoid mixed imagery.

Unintentionally humorous results can occur if one shifts from one simile or metaphor to another.

> BAD: Swapping horses in the middle of a stream may land
> one in a sea of difficulty.
>
> BETTER: Swapping horses in the middle of a stream may be
> disastrous.

EXERCISE 1. Collect in your notebook interesting and effective figures of speech that you encounter.

EXERCISE 2. Find and name the figures of speech in the following quotations:

1. The fog comes on little cat feet.

CARL SANDBURG

2. Let me go quickly, like a candle light
   Snuffed out just at the heyday of its glow.

JOHN NEIHARDT

3. I asked the heaven of stars
   What I should give my love.

SARA TEASDALE

4. The innocent, sweet Day is dead,
   Dark Night hath slain her in her bed.
   SIDNEY LANIER

5. Stick close to your desk and never go to sea,
   And you *all* may be Rulers of the Queen's Navee!
   W. S. GILBERT

6. The dice of God are always loaded.
   RALPH WALDO EMERSON

7. Washington's fame is like the rock which bounds the ocean,
   and at whose feet its billows are destined to break harm-
   lessly forever.
   DANIEL WEBSTER

8. Crime and punishment grow out of one stem.
   RALPH WALDO EMERSON

9. My vigor is a new-minted penny,
   Which I cast at your feet.
   AMY LOWELL

10. O ye dead Poets, who are living still
    Immortal in your verse, though life be fled.
    HENRY WADSWORTH LONGFELLOW

EXERCISE 3. Using a figure of speech, write a one-sentence description of each of the following: (1) a book, (2) a cloud, (3) a highway, (4) life, (5) a lone pine tree.

Dic 4   Idioms and Colloquialisms

An idiom is an expression that as a whole conveys a meaning different from the one that might be assumed from the sum of the individual words.

When we say, "How do you do?" to a person, we don't mean that literally. Idioms are a vital part of our language, and it is important that they be used correctly.

1. Use the correct preposition in idiomatic phrases.

In many idioms the meaning is controlled by a preposition. Be sure you have the right preposition. Certain words require different prepositions to express different meanings. Here are some examples:

a. We are angry:

with a person   *at* a situation

b. We differ:

with a person   *about* a matter

c. We are impatient:

with a person   *at* a situation

d. We wait:

for someone   *on* someone
(appointment)   (service)

2. Do not omit part of an idiom.

WRONG: Judith cannot listen or sympathize with her cousin.
RIGHT: Judith cannot listen to or sympathize with her cousin.

3. Do not omit necessary articles or introduce unnecessary ones.

WRONG: Ted waited for a half an hour.
RIGHT: Ted waited for half an hour.
WRONG: He came to United States thirty years ago.
RIGHT: He came to the United States thirty years ago.

EXERCISE 1. Use correct prepositions with the following verbs:

accused	collide	engage	listen
center	conform	initiate	part

EXERCISE 2. Use correct prepositions with the following:

ambitious	independent	sick
according	obedient	sympathy
careful	prior	unequal
free	prodigal	unmindful
hatred	sensitive	worthy

EXERCISE 3. Correct each of these faulty idioms, and use the correct idiom in a sentence:

all the farther	kind of a
different than	off of
in back of	out loud
in search for	stay to home
independent from	try and

Dic 5   Slang

There is no doubt that slang is a part of our language. It is used freely in informal conversation, and some of it works its way eventually into accepted usage.

Although slang may add color and vigor in informal communication, it should be avoided in formal writing and speaking. The following indicates two dangers of slang:

1. Slang frequently is a substitute for individual thinking. It is easier to repeat a popular catchall phrase, such as "lousy," than to think of a word of your own.

2. Slang may obscure the thought. Good English must be as understandable to your grandmother in Kentucky as to your cousin in Idaho.

EXERCISE. Write ten sentences containing slang expressions popular at the present time. Then translate each sentence into recognized English.

    SLANG: Reading this heavy stuff gets me down.

    TRANSLATION: Reading Dreiser's long, badly constructed sentences bores me.

Dic 6 Triteness

Avoid clichés, or trite expressions. A cliché, or trite expression, is an expression that is stale.

Any expression, no matter how good it may be, becomes worn out after it has been used again and again. The first person who said that a girl had eyes like stars must have made a profound impression. However, since then so many girls have had eyes like stars that no one cares. In trite phraseology, brooks are always *gurgling;* embers are always *dying;* ideas are always *bigger and better.*

Clichés are frequently used because they save the writer the trouble of thinking through exactly what he means. Their use results in writing which is stale and ineffective.

EXERCISE 1. Make a list of clichés that you hear or read in the course of several days.

EXERCISE 2. Rewrite the following sentences, omitting the clichés. When you have finished, reread your sentences. If you have done a good job, they will sound more honest and sincere than the original ones.

1. Edgar Lee Masters bids fair to make a name for himself as a poet of one volume. 2. Not until he had reached the shady side of forty did Masters show signs of budding genius. 3. Masters saw the light of day in Kansas, was reared in Illinois, and became the proud possessor of a good legal practice in Chicago. 4. In 1914 and 1915, out of a clear sky, he produced the sketches of the *Spoon River Anthology.* 5. Overnight the book became a best seller, created a nation-wide furor, and established itself as a modern classic. 6. The *Spoon River Anthology* is made up of character portraits of the apparently poor but honest people who live their simple lives in a small town in the heart of the nation. 7. In form, it is a series of dramatic monologues in free verse, each one spoken by some specimen of humanity

buried in the village memorial park.   8. Masters's word picture of the inhabitants of the main street is only in part true to life. 9. More often than not, his characterizations are more or less controlled by a philosophy hostile to the materialism and morality of the Middle West.   10. This philosophy, infused with deep feeling, accounts largely for the bitterness with which Masters pierces the respectable surface of village life, revealing an ugly welter of greed, petty jealousy, hypocrisy, and maladjustment in that walk of life.   11. Rushing in where angels fear to tread, Masters anticipated Sinclair Lewis by five years in the attack on middle-class smugness.

Dic 7   Wordiness

Be concise.

Very obviously, when several words are used to express an idea that could be expressed in a single, strong word, the effectiveness of the writing is weakened. Hamlet's remark concerning "words, words, words" should be remembered whenever there is a temptation to pad.

Most authorities consider wordiness as falling into two classifications: *prolixity* and *redundancy*.

1. Prolixity

Prolixity is caused by the piling up of unnecessary details. Each sentence presumably expresses a unified idea. Certainly if too many details are added, the principal idea of the sentence will be obscured.

> She was killed when she slipped on the mountain path, in the new shoes she had told us the night before while we were sitting around the fireplace were such a bargain.

The sentence is wordy and unemphatic. Omit the unnecessary details, and the sentence becomes effective.

EXERCISE 1. Condense the following sentences by removing unnecessary words, phrases, or clauses, or by

substituting briefer constructions. Be sure that you do
not alter the meaning.

1. Joseph Hergesheimer's years of apprenticeship as a writer
of novels were unusually long and are said to have been unusually
difficult, for not until he had reached the age of thirty-four did
he succeed in having published his first volume, which was entitled *The Lay Anthony* (1914), which was the story of a boy's
efforts in seeking for purity. 2. It was three years later when
there appeared one of Hergesheimer's strongest novels, *The Three
Black Pennys*, a novel which was a study of the outcropping of
ancestral traits through three members of five generations in a
family of Pennsylvania ironmasters. 3. Carefully constructed
and wrought as is this second novel, *The Three Black Pennys*,
it was not until 1919, when he published another novel, *Java Head*,
that Hergesheimer can be said to have arrived at unquestioned
mastery in his field of writing. 4. The scene of *Java Head* is laid
in the port of Salem as it existed in the 1840's. 5. The story,
apart from some subsidiary episodes, deals with the effort,
eventually unsuccessful, of two people to preserve something
of clarity, integrity, and distinction within the slowly tightening
coils of hostile circumstances. 6. In the next novel, *Linda Condon*, also published in 1919, Hergesheimer treats, in a wholly different setting, the same theme as that which he employs in *Java
Head* — a woman's effort to render life orderly and beautiful,
notwithstanding the opposing odds of a confused, and in this case
vulgar, environment. 7. In *Balisand* (1924) Hergesheimer's central character, in this case a man, is again a person who is devoted
to the same effort to clear a straight path through a chaotic existence, although in this case the novel is given a setting in tidewater
Virginia at the time of the decline of the Federalist party. 8. In
such novels as those mentioned, *Java Head*, *Linda Condon*, and
Balisand, Hergesheimer succeeds in what must be considered the
difficult task of adapting romanticism in literature to an era or age
which is characterized by disillusionment. 9. His best characters continually search for, as has been pointed out, and often at-
tain in their own lives, the qualities of clarity, artistic form, and

distinction which they seek.   10. Their attainment, however, is
individual, not social; and life at large, which is either indifferent
to or hostile to their laboriously acquired graces, remorselessly
tramples down what may be described as the fragile flower of
loveliness; and hence arises the tragic tone which is characteristic
of Hergesheimer's romances, as we have said.

EXERCISE 2. Look up in an unabridged dictionary the
following words:

brevity	loquacity	succinctness
circumlocution	periphrasis	tautology
curtness	pleonasm	terseness
diffuseness	redundancy	verbiage
excision	sententiousness	verbosity

2. Redundancy

Avoid the useless repetition of an idea in different words.
This fault is called redundancy.

John thought the use of the amazing device of the electric
eye to open the doors of a garage was a new and novel innovation. (*New*, *novel*, and *innovation* all mean the same thing.
It is like saying *free gratis* or the *autobiography of my life*.)

Notice the following redundant expressions:

abundant wealth	many in number
ascend up	mental thought
assembled together	necessary requisite
big in size	new creation
cheap bargain	meet up with
circular in form	perfectly correct
circulated around	repeat again
entire monopoly	return back
fellow playmates	rectangular in shape
final result	this here
green in color	timeless eternity
important essentials	unexpected surprise

EXERCISE. Rewrite the following sentences, removing the redundancies:

1. Emerson called or titled Henry David Thoreau a "bachelor of thought and Nature"; but Thoreau's enjoyment of, or pleasure in, nature was not always invariably thoughtful. 2. He could abandon or give himself unreservedly, as few New Englanders could, to the spontaneous, unpremeditated enjoyment of the senses. 3. Thoreau could also, when he elected and chose, observe nature with the strict accuracy of a scientist. 4. It should be repeated again that he was interested less in the fact or reality than in or with the truth behind it; less in the actual material world than in that spiritual world of which he considered or held that nature was but the apparent, visible garment or clothing. 5. Like Wordsworth, Thoreau offers and gives us not nature herself, but nature as passed through or influenced and colored by his own personality. 6. His determination to liberate and free life from its enslavement to the business and tasks of earning a living led him to undertake a remarkable experiment in living. 7. The final result of his interest led Thoreau to live in a log cabin or hut, which he built himself, on the shore or edge of Walden Pond, near Concord. 8. To evade and escape the tyranny of "things" he deliberately and on purpose embraced poverty, choosing to prefer the freedom of old clothes and corncake to the comfortable and easy slavery endured by his fellow townsmen. 9. Thoreau tells the story of the good benefits of this experience and the end conclusions he drew from it in the book, *Walden*, which was published in 1854. 10. Really to read the biography of his life carefully is inevitably to grow in powers and abilities of observation; the visible world becomes rich in previously and formerly unnoticed beauties; and the face of nature takes on a strange and unfamiliar freshness, life, and vitality.

Dic 8   Euphony

Work for pleasant combinations of sound.

Read aloud what you write, and *listen* to the *sound* of your words and your sentences. Some words and some combinations of words seem to have a pleasant sound. Read aloud, too, selections of good prose. You will notice that good authors work very definitely for euphony.

You can achieve euphony in your prose writing by avoiding the following:

1. Alliteration (several words beginning with the same letter)

2. Rhyme

3. Inappropriate rhythm. Slow action should not be expressed in short, staccato sentences; neither should rapid action be expressed in long, ponderous sentences.

4. Excessive use of modifiers. If every noun and every verb are given one or more modifiers, the style becomes not only wordy but also unpleasant in sound.

EXERCISE 1. Improve the following sentences:

1. The simplest system is to segregate the secretaries.
2. He was conscientious and entirely conscious of his contract.
3. Time will tell whether we shall learn to spell.
4. The charming and beautiful girl spoke softly to the small, mischievous boy as he played with his old and broken toys.
5. Constant concentration conquers careless habits of carriage.

EXERCISE 2. Collect from books or magazines five prose passages wherein rhythms vary pleasantly.

EXERCISE 3. Make a list of words that you think are noticeably lacking in euphony. Then make a list of words that you think are pleasant to the ear.

Review Exercises

EXERCISE 1. Using an unabridged dictionary, follow these directions:

1. Find an antonym for each of these words: *confusion, conceal, deny, often, vigorous.*

2. Give the *military* meaning of the following: *casualty, blitz-krieg, line, logistics, rank.*
3. Divide these words into syllables: *duodecimal, geranium, repetition, separate, utilitarian.*
4. List the parts of speech represented by each of these words: *draw, fast, iron, minute, well.*
5. Find the origin of each of the following words: *alphabet, auto-graph, Machiavellian, monologue, travel.*

EXERCISE 2. What is the correct pronunciation of each of the following words? Be prepared to use each word in an oral sentence.

1. accompanist	6. circuitous	11. posthumous
2. address	7. clique	12. preferable
3. alias	8. culinary	13. route
4. applicable	9. demonstrative	14. toward
5. buoy	10. obese	15. zoology

EXERCISE 3. Write your guess as to the meaning of each of these words. Then look up the dictionary meaning.

1. autobiography	6. monomania
2. bipartisan	7. postgraduate
3. biweekly	8. preview
4. breakfast	9. referee
5. manuscript	10. reorganize

EXERCISE 4. What new meaning has each of the following words taken in recent years?

1. alligator	6. overtime
2. beam	7. panel
3. blackout	8. profile
4. draft	9. transcription
5. fifth column	10. wings

EXERCISE 5. Find five specific words to replace each of the following general words: *fix, hold, good, vehicle, very.*

169

EXERCISE 6. Rewrite the following statements, giving such concrete details that the reader will *see a picture:*

1. I was tired.
2. The food was all right.
3. I got wet.
4. The gymnasium was crowded.
5. The game was exciting.
6. The desk was untidy.
7. The assignment was hard.
8. Her clothes were conspicuous.
9. The sun was setting.
10. He liked the book.

EXERCISE 7. Substitute an original expression for each of these clichés. Use each in an oral sentence.

CLICHÉ	ORIGINAL EXPRESSION
He kept abreast of the times.	*He listened to six newscasts a day.*

1. nipped in the bud
2. more or less
3. did justice to the dinner
4. riot of color
5. feathered songsters
6. with bated breath
7. when all is said and done
8. launched into eternity
9. out of a clear sky
10. one in a million
11. green as grass
12. Grim Reaper
13. busy as a bee
14. poor but honest
15. skeleton in the closet
16. last but not least
17. bigger and better
18. few and far between
19. wish you were here
20. gone but not forgotten

EXERCISE 8. The following paragraph suffers from wordiness. Rewrite it, making sure that you remove only words, phrases, or clauses that are *unnecessary to the meaning.*

1. From 1900 to 1915 a group of men who were competent playwrights, including such men as Clyde Fitch, Augustus Thomas, and Percy MacKaye, attempted to help to bring to the commer-

cial theater some values other than the values of mere entertainment. 2. It turned out, as it happened, however, that the best American play of the early twentieth century was produced by a man who was not a professional playwright and who was only casually associated with the professional playwrights — William Vaughn Moody. 3. In his play *The Great Divide*, Moody dramatized, or portrayed, powerfully a conflict or struggle of ideals which he felt to exist between the West and New England. 4. One of the women characters, Ruth Jordan, a New England girl living on the Western ranch of her brother, marries a Westerner, Stephen Ghent, under circumstances that make her feel she has been bought rather than married for love only. 5. In solving or finding an answer to the psychological problems resulting from this marriage, Moody produced a drama or play whose solid and substantial dramatic worth has been very little impaired or damaged by four decades of rapid change in the theater and its activities.

EXERCISE 9. Improve the *sound* of the following sentences:

1. He said he would meet Leta on Sixteenth Street.
2. When he drove up in front of the old faded frame house, he saw suddenly that thick black smoke was pouring from the wide windows in the front.
3. There was one thing she demanded: she demanded that the child should be reprimanded.
4. As it grew late, the embers in the grate burned low.
5. John and his son saw the sun set on the seashore.
6. Miss Barrett says she wants new books for you who need review.
7. She sat there with a blank face, staring into space.
8. Mrs. Rippey ripped the seams of the old shirt.
9. The speaker said one should shun sibilant sounds.
10. As she sat, her dream shattered.

Dic 9   Faulty Diction

The following glossary contains words and expressions often misused. The list is not exhaustive, but it contains many of the most common violations of good usage.

Ability, capacity.   *Ability*, which is usually followed by the word *to*, means "skill or competence." *Capacity* means "power of receiving, containing, or absorbing."

> Her *ability* to speak was recognized.
> His *capacity* for work amazed us.

Accept, except.   *Accept* means "to receive with consent." *Except* means "to take or leave out."

Affect, effect.   *Affect* is never a noun in common usage. *Effect* as a noun means "result." As verbs, *affect* means "to influence"; *effect* means "to bring about."

> The colors *affected* the patients beneficially.
> The doctor *effected* a cure.

Affect means also "to make an impression or to pretend."

> He *affected* ignorance of the fight.

Aggravate, irritate.   *Irritate* means "to excite to momentary impatience." *Aggravate* means "to make worse or more severe."

> The noise *aggravated* his headache.
> A whimpering voice *irritates* me.

Ain't.   The expression is illiterate. Say *I'm not, you (we, they) aren't, he (she, it) isn't.*

All of.   Use *of* with pronouns but not with nouns.

> *All of them* had read *Moby Dick.*
> *All the books* had blue covers.

All the farther, all the faster.   Use *as far as, as fast as.*

> Three hundred miles is *as far as* I care to drive today.

172

Allusion, illusion. An *allusion* is an "indirect reference." An *illusion* is a "deception or false impression."

> *Moby Dick* contains many *allusions* to the Bible.
> The appearance of water on the pavement was an optical *illusion*.

Almost, most. Except to form the superlative degree, do not use *most* to modify an adjective.

> *Almost* all boys like football.
> *Most* boys like football.

Already, all ready. *Already* means "before some stated time; previously." *All ready* means "entirely prepared."

> She has *already* read this book.
> We are *all ready* to begin class.

Alright. Not correct. Say *all right*, although this is an overused substitute for *very well.*

Altogether, all together. *Altogether* means "wholly, thoroughly"; *all together* means "in a group."

> The poet was *altogether* unhappy.
> They went *all together* to the theater.

Alumnus, alumna. *Alumnus* means "a male graduate"; *alumni* is the plural. *Alumna* means "a female graduate"; *alumnae* is the plural. *Alumni* is used to refer to a mixed group.

Among, between. *Among* is used when referring to more than two persons or things; *between* applies to only two persons or things.

> Evangeline wandered *among* the trees.
> The heroine had to choose *between* money and position.

Any place, every place, no place, some place. Do not use. Say instead *anywhere, everywhere, nowhere, somewhere.*

As. Do not use *as* in place of *whether.*

> I don't know *whether* I should go.

As — as are correlatives. Do not replace the second *as* with *than.*

> WRONG: John is as quick, if not quicker, than Henry.
> RIGHT: John is as quick as Henry, if not quicker.

As, so. According to many authorities, *as—as* is used to make a positive comparison; *so—as* is used to make a negative comparison.

> Ellen is *as* clever *as* Anne.
> Ellen is not *so* clever *as* Anne.

Awful. Means "filling with awe." Do not use in the sense of *very bad* or *very great* except in informal writing.

Balance. Refers to equality; do not use for *remainder,* except in financial statements.

Because. Never use *because* to introduce a noun clause. Say, "The fact that . . ."

Beside, besides. *Beside* is a preposition meaning "at the side of." *Besides,* usually an adverb, means "in addition, moreover."

> He sat *beside* me.
> We had a dinner and a concert *besides.*

Blame on. Should not be used for *blame* or *blame for.*

Bunch. Means "a number of things of the same kind"; it should not be used to refer to people.

> He brought home a *bunch* of carrots.

Burst. The past tense and the present tense are the same. Do not make the mistake of saying "bust, busted, or bursted."

But, hardly, only, scarcely. All these words are negatives. Do not use them with other negatives.

But what, but that. Use simply the word *that*.

> There is no doubt *that* Whitman was a great poet.

Calculate. Used colloquially for *plan*, *think*, or *expect*.

Can, may. *Can* means "to be able to." *May* refers to opportunity, permission, or wish.

> Tomorrow I *can* bring my copy of the book.
> You *may* borrow it.

Cannot help but. A double negative. Use *cannot help*.

Can't seem to. Say *seem unable to*.

Common, mutual. A thing in which two or more share equally is *common*. A thing which is reciprocally given is *mutual*.

Complected. The correct word is *complexioned*.

Considerable. Use as an adjective, not as an adverb.

Continual, continuous. *Continual* means "occurring in steady, but not unbroken, succession." *Continuous* means "without interruption."

Could of. An illiterate expression. Say *could have*.

Couple. A pair, or "two of the same kind joined together." Do not substitute for the number *two*.

Credible, creditable, credulous. *Credible* means "believable"; *creditable* means "praiseworthy"; *credulous* means "easily deceived."

> The report was *credible*.
> He made a *creditable* record.
> Fortune tellers recognize that people are *credulous*.

Cute. Colloquial and overused.

Data. *Data* is the plural form and should be used with a plural verb.

> The *datum is* incomplete.
> The *data are* incomplete.

Different than. Say *different from*.

Disremember. Should not be used for *forget*.

Done. Correct only as the past participle of the verb *to do*. *Done* should never be used instead of the past tense *did* or as an auxiliary verb, "I done bought a new suit."

Don't. A contraction for *do not*. It is illiterate to use *don't* for *does not*. The correct contraction for *does not* is *doesn't*.

Drownded. Do not use for *drowned*.

Due to. May be used only when it is part of a phrase that refers to a noun.

> Absence *due to* illness is excused.

Each, either. *Each* means "every one of two or more considered individually." *Either* means "the one or the other."

Either, neither. When used as pronouns, these words take singular verbs. *Or* is the correlative of *either; nor*, of *neither*.

Elude, allude. *To elude* means "to avoid or escape." *To allude* means "to refer indirectly." *Elusive* and *allusive* are the adjectives.

Enthuse. Colloquial for "to make or to become enthusiastic."

Et. Do not use for *eaten*.

Etc. An abbreviation for the Latin *et cetera*, meaning "and other things." *Et* means "and"; it is therefore redundant to say "and etc." *Etc.* should always be set off by commas.

Expect. Means "to look forward to." *Expect* should never be used for *suppose*.

Farther, further. *Farther* is generally preferred for spatial distance; *further*, to indicate distance in time or degree. *Further* also means "additional."

> The Woodburys live *farther* down the street.
> We got no *further* with the discussion that night.
> *Further* work will be assigned tomorrow.

Fewer, less. *Fewer* indicates a smaller number. *Less* refers to a decrease in amount, degree, or value.

> *Fewer* persons were present.
> We had *less* time to spend.

Fine. Do not overuse as an adjective, and never use as an adverb.

Folks. Do not use to mean "relatives."

Formally, formerly. *Formally* means "conventionally." *Formerly* means "in time past."

> We dressed *formally*.
> *Formerly* we would have gone in slacks.

Former, latter. *Former* indicates the first of two named; *latter* refers to the second.

Funny. Means "laughable or humorous." Colloquially used for *strange* or *queer*.

Gent. Vulgar, shortened form of *gentleman*.

177

Good. Use only as an adjective.

Got. Past participle of *get*. Do not use to mean *must* or *ought*. Redundant in such expressions as "I've got a headache."

Gotten. Both *gotten* and *got* are past participles of *get*. Although *gotten* is considered archaic in England, it is correct in the United States.

Guess. Means "to form an opinion either without evidence or without sufficient evidence." Should not be used to mean *believe, think, expect.*

Had of. Omit the preposition.

> I wish I had known.

Had ought, hadn't ought. Illiterate.

Hadn't but. Do not use for *had only*.

> WRONG: He hadn't but a dime.
> RIGHT: He *had only* a dime.

Hardly. See **But, hardly, only, scarcely.**

Healthy, healthful. *Healthy* means "being sound and well"; *healthful* means "serving to promote health of body or mind."

> The boy is *healthy.*
> Some people find a dry climate *healthful.*

Hisself, theirselves. Do not use for *himself* and *themselves.*

How come? A vulgarism. Use *Why?*

Hygienic, sanitary. Both words pertain to health. *Hygienic* refers to the matter of personal habits; *sanitary* refers to matters of environment, such as water supply and sewage disposal.

If, whether. Some authorities believe that *whether* is preferable after the verbs *see, say, ask, learn, know, understand*.

> Do you know *whether* he is present?

In, into. *In* refers to a location within something. *Into* indicates motion toward the inside.

> He was *in* the garden.
> He fell *into* the pool.

In back of. Do not use in place of *behind*.

In regards to. Should never be used for *in regard to*.

Incredible, incredulous. *Incredible* means "too improbable to admit of belief." *Incredulous* means "skeptical."

> The excuse he gave was *incredible*.
> Our smiles showed that we were *incredulous*.

Ingenious, ingenuous. *Ingenious* means "shrewd, resourceful." *Ingenuous* means "frank, candid."

Instance, instant. An *instance* is "an example or case." An *instant* is "a very small portion of time."

Its, it's. The former shows possession. The form with the apostrophe is the contraction for *it is*.

Just. Do not use to mean *simply* or *quite*.

Kind, sort. Both these words are singular and require singular adjectives.

> I prefer *this kind* of paper.

Kind of. Do not use to mean *somewhat*. *Kind of* is correct when followed by a noun. Avoid "kind of a."

> It was *somewhat* dark.
> It was not that *kind of* work.

Later, latter. *Later* is the comparative of *late; latter* means "of two things, being the one mentioned second." *Latter* is used in conjunction with *former.*

Learn, teach. *Learn* means "to gain knowledge." *Teach* means "to give instruction."

>He *learns* quickly what I *teach* him.

Leave, let. *Leave* means "to go away" or "to allow to remain." *Let* means "to permit."

Liable, likely, apt. *Likely* indicates probability. *Liable* expresses obligation and implies also exposure to something harmful. *Apt* implies natural fitness in persons and suggests, too, habitual tendency.

>It is *likely* that we shall go to the circus.
>The parent is *liable* for damage done by his children.
>He is an *apt* pupil.

Lie, lay. *Lie* is an intransitive verb meaning "to recline"; the past tense is *lay. Lay* is the infinitive form of the transitive verb meaning "to put or set down."

>I *lie* down to read.　　　　I *lay* the book on the table.
>I *lay* down yesterday.　　　I *laid* it there yesterday.
>I *have lain* down often.　　I *have laid* it there often.

Like, as, as if. *Like* is a preposition requiring an object; *as* and *as if* are conjunctions used to introduce clauses.

>They play tennis *like* professionals.
>They play tennis *as* professionals do.
>They play tennis *as if* they were professionals.

Literally. Means "truly, accurately, not in an exaggerated manner." Do *not* make such statements as, "I was literally burned up."

Locate. Colloquial for *settle.*

Lose, loose. *Lose* means "to miss from one's possession or from its usual place." *Loose* as a verb means "to untie or to free." *Loose* as an adjective means "not fastened; unattached."

Lose out. Omit the *out*.

Lots, lots of. Do not overuse.

Luxuriant, luxurious. *Luxuriant* means "growing abundantly." *Luxurious* pertains to the possession of an abundance of material things.

> The flowers were *luxuriant*.
> The apartment was *luxurious*.

May, can. See **Can, may.**

May be, maybe. *May be* is a verb form. *Maybe* is an adverb meaning "perhaps."

Mighty. Colloquial for *very* or *extremely*.

Muchly. Use *much* or *greatly*.

Myself. *Myself* should not be used as the subject of a sentence or of a dependent clause.

> WRONG: Jack and myself went to the movies.
> RIGHT: Jack and *I* went to the movies.

Nice. Means "pleasing, agreeable, fastidious." Colloquial when used to indicate general approval.

Nohow. Do not use for *anyhow* or *anyway*.

None. Either singular or plural.

> *None are* ready for the test.
> *None* of the boys *has completed* his assignment.

Notorious. Indicates someone or something well known in an unfavorable sense. Do not use for *famous* or *noted*.

Nowhere near. Colloquial; use *not nearly.*

Nowheres. The correct form is *nowhere.*

O, oh. *O* is used with a noun in direct address; it is always capitalized and is not separated from the noun by any mark of punctuation. The interjection *oh* is not capitalized unless it is the first word in the sentence; it is followed by a comma or an exclamation point.

Off of. Omit the *of.*

> He fell off the horse.

O.K. For informal use only.

On. Do not use after such words as *later, plan, continue.*

One another, each other. Generally it is preferable to use *each other* when referring to only two, *one another* when referring to more than two.

Only. Be careful to put *only* where there can be no question about the word it modifies. Do not use *only* as a substitute for *but.*

Oral, verbal. *Oral* means "using speech"; *verbal* means "expressed in words" (either oral or written).

Ought to of. Do not use for *ought to have.*

Out. Do not insert after such verbs as *start, win, lose, miss.*

Out loud. Informal or colloquial for *aloud, loud, loudly.*

Outside of. Omit *of.*

> He stood *outside* the window.

> *Outside of* should not be used as a synonym for *except.*

> No one went with him *except* Harry.

Over with. Omit *with*.

Party, person. *Party* refers to a group of persons; *person* refers to a single individual.

Pass out. Slang in the sense of *faint*.

Pep. Slang.

Plenty. Correctly used as a noun only.

Practical, practicable. *Practical* means "useful; inclined to action rather than speculation." *Practicable* means "capable of being put into practice."

> Homer is a *practical* boy.
> The new road plans are highly *practicable*.

Pretty. Means "good-looking, attractive." Incorrectly used to mean "considerable" or "somewhat."

Principal, principle. The noun *principal* refers to a sum of money or to a leader or chief; the adjective *principal* means "highest in rank; main." *Principle* is a noun meaning "a fundamental truth or law."

Proof, evidence. *Proof* is information sufficient to establish the truth of something. *Evidence* is any information that is brought forward in an attempt to establish proof.

Proposition. Means "a statement, usually a sentence, proposed for consideration." Improperly used to mean *transaction, venture, difficulty, doctrine*.

Proven. Most good writers prefer *proved*.

Quiet, quite. *Quiet* is an adjective meaning "still or peaceful." *Quite* is an adverb meaning "completely." Do not substitute *quite* for *rather*.

183

Quite a few, quite a little. Colloquial. Say *a good many.*

Raise, rear. In the sense of "helping to grow," *rear* refers to children, *raise* refers to animals or crops.

> She *reared* her children on the income from the cattle she *raised.*

Real. Do not use for *very* or *really.*

Reckon. Means "to compute or to calculate." Do not use for *think* or *suppose.*

Recollect, remember. *Recollect* suggests a conscious effort to bring something back to mind. *Remember* suggests recall without planned effort.

Respectfully, respectively. *Respectfully* means "showing deference or regard." *Respectively* means "each in the order given."

> He spoke *respectfully* to his grandmother.
> John, Ellen, and Ted answered *respectively.*

Right. Do not use in the sense of *very.*

> WRONG: She is right clever.
> RIGHT: She is *very* clever.

Right away, right off. Do not use for *immediately* or *at once.*

Rise, raise. *Rise* is intransitive and means "to move upward." *Raise* is transitive and means "to cause to rise."

> I *rise* early every morning.   I *raise* dahlias.
> I *rose* early yesterday.   I *raised* dahlias last summer.
> I *have risen* early often.   I *have raised* dahlias for many years.

Say. Means "to utter." Incorrectly used to mean "give orders." Do not use *says* when the correct meaning calls for *said.*

> The officer told us (*not* said) to wait.

Seldom ever. Do not use for *rarely*.

Shape. Means "form or appearance." Do not use for *condition* or *manner*.

> He is in a serious *condition*.

Show. Means "exhibition or display." Incorrectly used as a synonym for *play, opera, motion picture,* or *radio program*.

Show up. Colloquial in the sense of "come" or "expose."

Sit, set. *Sit* is intransitive and means "to occupy a seat." *Set* is transitive and means "to put or fix in any place."

I *sit* here often.	I *set* the vase on the table.
I *sat* here yesterday.	I *set* the vase there yesterday.
I *have sat* here before.	I *have set* the vase there before.

So. Not incorrect, but vague and usually unnecessary. *So* should be followed by *that* in a purpose clause.

> He went to bed early *so that* he would be rested for the trip.

Some. Slang when used in the sense of *fine* or *remarkable*.

> WRONG: It was some party.
> RIGHT: It was a *delightful* party.

Some better. Say *somewhat better*.

Species. Is the same for both singular and plural.

> He developed a new *species* of dahlias.

Stationary, stationery. *Stationary* is an adjective meaning "fixed in a certain place." *Stationery* is a noun referring to writing paper and envelopes.

Such. Avoid the indefinite use of *such*. Don't say, "We had such a good time."
If *such* is followed by a relative clause, use *as* with it.

> The teacher gave *such* assignments *as* he thought best.

If *such* is followed by a result clause, use *that* with it.

There was *such* a long line *that* we decided not to wait.

Sure. *Sure* is slang when it is used for the adverb *certainly*.

Suspicion. A noun. The verb is *suspect*.

Swell. Slang when used to mean *first-rate*.

Take. Avoid colloquial and slang uses of this verb. Do *not* say *take up with, take in the movies, take on, take Whitman,* etc. Avoid also expressions like "I taken him home."

Tend, attend. When it means "to take care of," *tend* takes a direct object.

Phoebe *tended* the shop for her cousin.

Attend is followed by *to*.

I shall *attend to* your request at once.

Them. Do not use as an adjective. Use *these* or *those*.

This here, that there. Omit *here* and *there*.

I enjoyed *this* book.

Through. Incorrectly used to mean "completed."

Try and. The correct form is *try to*.

Unique. Means "being without a like or equal." *Unique* cannot be modified.

United States. Should always be preceded by *the*.

Up. Omit after such verbs as *end, rest, settle, open, polish*.

Used to could. Vulgarism. Say *used to be able*, or *once could*.

186

Very. Greatly overused. *Very* should be followed by *much* when used with the past participle.

Doris was *very much* pleased with her gift.

Want for. Omit the word *for* from the expression.

WRONG: Jack wants for me to go.

RIGHT: Jack wants me to go.

Want in or out. Use the complete expression *want to come in (out)* or *want to get in (out)*.

Way, ways. Do not use *way* for *away*.

He was *away* below passing.

Do not use *ways* for *way*.

Don planned to go only a little *way*.

Where. Cannot be substituted for *that*.

WRONG: I read where they had agreed to arbitrate.

RIGHT: I read *that* they had agreed to arbitrate.

Where at. Illiterate. Omit the *at*.

Whip cream. Say *whipped cream*.

Worst way. Do not use for *badly*.

Would have. Use *had* rather than *would have* in *if* clauses.

If you *had* (*not* would have) seen the letter sooner, you could have broken the appointment.

Would of. Illiterate. Say *would have*.

You all. Colloquial in the South for the plural *you*.

You was. Illiterate. *You were* is correct in both singular and plural.

187

Review Exercises

EXERCISE 1. Copy the following sentences, correcting the errors in diction. Notice that some of the sentences contain more than one error.

1. She was aggravated that Betty had not excepted her idea.
2. All of the assignments required written work.
3. Let us keep this information between us four girls.
4. I couldn't help but notice how dark complected he was.
5. I expect I live further from school than you do.
6. I guess he hadn't ought to have got that low a grade.
7. I literally exploded when he refused to learn me how to dive.
8. All three of them were devoted to each other.

EXERCISE 2. Copy the following sentences, correcting all the errors in diction:

1. Quite a few of the crowd wanted to leave right away.
2. Mary was mad because they didn't show up at the show.
3. You ought to tend to that there cold of yours.
4. Jim had a dog who used to could walk on his hind legs.
5. She came home with an effected accent.
6. She was all ready an alumni of Vassar.
7. She couldn't find the balance of her notes laying any place.
8. There is no doubt but what he is different than his brother.

EXERCISE 3. Copy the following sentences, correcting all the errors in diction:

1. The horse flicked it's tail kind of suddenly.
2. Leave your instructor learn you some diction.
3. I don't advise you to lay there; its apt to rain.
4. He lost out on lots of opportunities by being absent.
5. May be later on they would of had a nice time at the party.
6. Outside of John everyone was pretty talkative.
7. It was sure the most unique party.
8. I thought I'd literally pass out when I heard her mention you all.

SPELLING

NECESSITY FOR RULES

Misspelling is one of the most noticeable of written mistakes. Fortunately only about five hundred words present crucial spelling hurdles, and only a fraction of this number may be responsible for the errors which you make in your writing.

In spite of the apparent antagonism between spelling and logic, there are some basic rules that govern many of the most frequently misspelled words. Learning these rules is worth the effort. Then, too, mastery of a good basic list will tremendously improve anyone's spelling. Don't believe the adage that good spellers are born, not made.

Sp Learning How to Spell

You can improve your spelling rapidly if you really make the effort.

1. The first step is to want to improve. When you have finished your written work, go over it carefully to check your spelling.

2. Enunciate a word clearly to be sure that you have included all the syllables. Spelling is related to sound. Words are often misspelled because they are misspoken.

3. Is the word one that can be spelled by rule? A few simple rules cover the spelling of many of the most difficult words.

4. If still in doubt, use the dictionary. Even good spellers need dictionaries. No one needs to feel embarrassed about looking up words. In any formal writing every word must be spelled correctly, and it is simply good judgment not to take chances.

5. When you look up a word, impress it upon your mind. Merely to copy the correct spelling on your paper and then to dismiss it from your mind is not sufficient. Determine to spell the word without hesitation the next time.

6. Keep a list of the words you misspell in reports, themes, tests, and spelling exercises. Memorize the correct spelling.

7. Study the rules and special lists in this chapter. Do the exercises in order to fix the correct spelling in your mind. Consciously seek to recall and apply the rules in all your written work.

If you follow these seven suggestions, your spelling is bound to improve.

Sp 1   Pronunciation as an Aid to Spelling

Many words are misspelled because of incorrect pronunciation. If you say "canidate," you are likely to spell the word that way. You are headed for a similar mistake if you say "childern." When you look up a word in the dictionary, notice its pronunciation as well as its spelling.

See pages 140 to 147 for a detailed discussion of pronunciation.

Careless omission of syllables often leads to incorrect spelling. Study the following list to make sure that you are not guilty of the slovenly deletion of syllables. Practice the correct pronunciation until it becomes automatic.

WRONG	RIGHT	WRONG	RIGHT
accidently	accident*all*y	libary	lib*r*ary
boundry	bound*a*ry	literture	lit*e*rature
canidate	can*d*idate	occasionly	occasiona*ll*y
charactristic	charact*e*ristic	paticular	pa*r*ticular
choclate	choc*o*late	posponed	pos*t*poned
considable	consid*e*rable	probly	proba*bl*y
curosity	cur*i*osity	quanity	quan*t*ity
defnitely	def*i*nitely	reely	rea*ll*y
everbody	ever*y*body	reconize	recog*n*ize
Febuary	Feb*r*uary	representive	represen*tat*ive
genrally	gen*e*rally	sophmore	soph*o*more
goverment	gover*n*ment	suprise	su*r*prise
labratory	lab*o*ratory	temperture	temper*a*ture
lible	li*a*ble	unanmous	unan*i*mous

Adding extra syllables often leads to incorrect spelling. Pronounce these words correctly as you copy them:

WRONG	RIGHT	WRONG	RIGHT
atheletics	athletics	griev*i*ous	grievous
barbar*i*ous	barbarous	hinder*a*nce	hindrance
broadcast*ed*	broadcast	mischiev*i*ous	mischievous
drownd*ed*	drowned	rememb*er*ance	remembrance
elem	elm	suffer*a*ge	suffrage

Transposed letters also lead to incorrect spelling. The following words are frequently misspelled because of this pronunciation error. Practice the correct pronunciation.

WRONG	RIGHT	WRONG	RIGHT
childern	child*re*n	prespiration	pe*r*spiration
hunderd	hund*re*d	perscription	p*re*scription
preform	p*er*form	perserve	p*re*serve

191

EXERCISE 1. Pronounce each word in the preceding lists, noting and correcting any tendency you may have to make improper omissions, additions, or transpositions.

EXERCISE 2. Use the words in the preceding lists in correct oral sentences.

EXERCISE 3. Use twenty words from the preceding lists in correct written sentences.

EXERCISE 4. Practice pronouncing the following words aloud. Then write them from dictation. Make a list of the ones you missed; practice saying and writing them until you have achieved mastery.

accommodate	further	privilege
accurately	hurrying	probably
artistically	instinct	quantity
casualty	length	realize
commission	naturally	recommend
definite	necessary	reverence
description	occasionally	scenery
different	omission	separate
disappoint	opinion	specialty
eighth	opportunity	strictly
emphatically	optimist	superintendent
entirely	organize	temperance
everybody	partner	temperature
excellent	physiology	varieties
finally	primitive	ventilate

EXERCISE 5. Here are parts of a number of words which are frequently mispronounced and misspelled. Can you say and spell each word correctly?

cem...ry	iv..y	rec...ize
hei..t	lib...y	umb...la
hyg...ic	mem..y	veg...ble

Sp 2   Meaning of Words

Sometimes words are so similar in sound that it is essential to enunciate clearly and to listen carefully to determine which word is meant. In order to spell the following words correctly, you must know their separate meanings:

accept, except	emigrate, immigrate
affect, effect	eminent, imminent
all ready, already	farther, further
all together, altogether	formally, formerly
allusion, illusion	ingenious, ingenuous
baring, barring	lightening, lightning
censor, censure	loose, lose
choose, chose	mind, mine
continually, continuously	presence, presents
corps, corpse	quiet, quite
council, counsel	respectfully, respectively
decent, descent	sense, cents, since
defer, differ	statue, statute, stature
desert, dessert	than, then
device, devise	wail, whale

EXERCISE. Write sentences using correctly any ten sets of words from the preceding list.

Recognition of Homonyms

Some words sound alike but have different meanings and spellings. In speaking, an error in the use of a homonym is indistinguishable; but there is no such protection in writing. It is well to become familiar with the more common homonyms and their meanings.

Be sure you know which of the following homonyms is the word you want before you try to spell it. Look up the meanings of those unfamiliar to you.

air, heir	altar, alter
allowed, aloud	baring, bearing

berth, birth
board, bored
brake, break
canvas, canvass
ceiling, sealing
cite, sight, site
coarse, course
complement, compliment
dyeing, dying
fair, fare
hair, hare
heal, heel
hear, here
heard, herd
hole, whole
knew, new
lessen, lesson
pair, pear

passed, past
peace, piece
plain, plane
principal, principle
right, rite, write
road, rode
shone, shown
stake, steak
stationary, stationery
steal, steel
their, there, they're
threw, through
to, too, two
wait, weight
wave, waive
weak, week
whose, who's
yoke, yolk

EXERCISE 1. Write sentences using ten pairs of homonyms from the preceding list.

EXERCISE 2. See how many of the pairs of homonyms above you can use in a single, sensible sentence.

EXERCISE 3. Compile a list of twenty or more additional homonyms.

Sp 3   Some Helpful Rules

The following rules will make spelling easier:

Rule 1, Words ending in consonants

1. When words are accented on the last syllable and end in a single consonant preceded by a single vowel, double the consonant before a suffix beginning with a vowel.

admit-t-ance   begin-n-ing
compel-l-ing   equip-p-ed

2. When words of one syllable end in a single consonant preceded by a single vowel, double the consonant before a suffix beginning with a vowel.

drop-p-ed   plan-n-ed
sit-t-ing   man-n-ish

To apply these rules you must recognize the basic word. To decide whether *occurrence* has two *r*'s, you must think of the basic word, *occur*. There are three steps in the application of the rules.

a. The basic word must be either a one-syllable word or a word accented on the last syllable. *Sit* and *compel* meet this test; *open* does not.
b. The basic word must end in a single consonant. *Help* and *reform* do not qualify; *swim*, however, does.
c. The final consonant of the basic word must be preceded by a single vowel. The rule excludes *seed* and *look;* it applies to *scan* and *begin*.

The following rules also apply to words ending in consonants:

3. Words which end in double consonants usually retain both consonants when a suffix is added.

skillful   willful

4. With words ending in c, insert a k before a suffix that begins with e, i, or y so that the c will not sound like s.

picnic — picnicking   traffic — trafficked

EXERCISE 1. Write the past tense (*ed*) of the following words:

annul	expel	plan	rob
bar	omit	plug	slip
control	pin	regret	trip

EXERCISE 2. Write the present participle (*ing*) of these:

refer	fan	admit	begin
bet	hit	rid	occur
chat	pad	run	expel

EXERCISE 3. Write the following verbs in a column. Place a mark over the accented syllable of each word. Then, after each word, write first the present participle and then the past participle.

allot	consent	acquit	span
desert	drug	emit	tap
remit	infer	rebel	drop

EXERCISE 4. Add suffixes to the following: *colic, fill, ebb, dull, odd.*

Rule 2, Words ending in e

1. When a word ends in a silent e, the e is usually dropped before a suffix beginning with a vowel.

Exceptions to this rule occur in words like *noticeable, changeable, dyeing.*

admire — admiring	move — movable
advise — adviser	please — pleasant
double — doubling	use — usage

2. When a word ends in a silent e, the e is generally retained if a suffix beginning with a consonant is added.

Exceptions to this rule occur in *judgment* and *acknowledgment.* You will notice that even for these words, however, the dictionary gives *judgement* and *acknowledgement* as the second possible spellings.

bore — boredom	place — placement
complete — completely	safe — safety
excite — excitement	sincere — sincerely

3. After a soft c or g, the final e is retained before a suffix beginning with a or o. Drop the e before a suffix beginning with e or i.

advantage — advantageous
courage — courageous
notice — noticeable
outrage — outrageous
peace — peaceable

manage — managing
mortgage — mortgaged
notice — noticing
place — placed
wage — waged

4. When a word ends in double e, the two e's are generally retained when a suffix is added.

agree — agreeing   flee — fleeing

Rule 3, Words ending in oe

When a word ends in oe, both vowels are usually retained when a suffix is added.

canoe — canoeing   shoe — shoeing
hoe — hoeing   toe — toeing

EXERCISE 1. Write the present participle (*ing*) of the following words:

come	invite	save
grope	love	see
have	move	sense
hope	owe	serve
insure	please	shine

EXERCISE 2. Form adjectives by adding *ous* or *able* to the following words:

admire	desire	love
advantage	excuse	move
advise	fame	note
believe	forgive	receive
courage	grieve	trace
cure	imagine	value

197

EXERCISE 3. Form adverbs by adding the suffix *ly* to the following words:

complete	extreme	fortunate	game
leisure	rare	loose	scarce
separate	sincere	sure	true

Rule 4, Words ending in y

1. When a word ends in y preceded by a consonant, the y is usually changed to i before a suffix (except when the suffix begins with i).

beauty — beautiful   lively — livelihood
happy — happiness   study — studying

2. When a word ends in y preceded by a vowel, the y is usually retained.

pray — praying   obey — obeying
key — keying   joy — joyful

EXERCISE. Add the suffix *ful* to each of the following words:

bounty   duty   fancy

Add *ly* to these words:

crafty   gloomy   pretty

Add *ness* to these words:

deadly   ghastly   dastardly

Add *ing* to these words:

delay   prey   toy   annoy

Rule 5, Words ending in ie

When a word ends in ie, the e is generally dropped and the i is changed to y before a suffix is added.

tie — tying   die — dying

EXERCISE. Add a suffix to each of these words:

       lie   hie   belie   vie   untie

Rule 6, Words containing *ei* or *ie*

1. When the combination sounds like long e, *ei* follows *c;* *ie* follows other consonants.

Exceptions to this rule occur in such words as *leisure, weird, seize, neither.*

achieve	grieve	ceiling	perceive
chieftain	niece	conceive	receipt
field	relief	deceit	receive

> Write *i* before *e*
> Except after *c,*
> Or when sounded like *a,*
> As in *neighbor* and *weigh.*

2. When the combination sounds like long a, *ei* is correct.

eight	sleigh
reign	weight

3. When the combination sounds like long i, *ie* is usually correct.

Exceptions are found in words ending in *ght* like *height* and *sleight.*

tie	pie
hie	die

4. When the sound is short e or i, the combination is usually *ei.*

foreign	heifer
sovereign	their

5. When the letters are sounded separately, *ie* is the usual order.

diet	siesta
piety	fiesta

EXERCISE. Spell the *ei* or *ie* word that is pronounced
like each of the following:

air	peace	there
ate	rain	vain
lean	sealing	wait
nay	slay	way

Rule 7, Compound words

**Compound words made by joining two or more words
generally retain all the letters of the original words.**

stiff-necked   well-bred

Exceptions are found in words written as one word and
those to which *full* has been added: *cupful*. Other exceptions occur in compounds of *all* and *well*: *withal, welfare*.

Some Troublesome Words

Some words cause trouble because their spelling is different from their pronunciation. English is a particular of-
fender among languages in this respect because the pronunciation of some of our words has changed while the
spelling has remained static. You will need to memorize
the spelling of such words as the following:

colonel	lieutenant	rough
cough	pneumonia	sergeant
diphtheria	ptomaine	suite
khaki	rhythm	Wednesday

Review Exercises

EXERCISE 1. Which rule or rules apply to the spelling
of each of these words?

bountiful	hateful	remitting
colicky	manageable	staying
cowardliness	receiving	teeing
cure-all	refusing	vie
dieting	rein	vying

EXERCISE 2. Without first studying them, take the following words from dictation. Apply spelling rules whenever you are in doubt.

advantageous	lying	planned
believing	napping	repelled
canoeing	neighbor	skillful
deceive	niece	weighing
dutiful	omitting	well-bred
fiesta	paleness	witty
judgment	planed	worrying

Sp 4   Plurals of Words

1. Most nouns form the plural by adding s to the singular.

book — books	dog — dogs
boy — boys	house — houses

2. Nouns ending in s, sh, ch, x, and z form the plural by adding es.

church — churches	loss — losses
bush — bushes	tax — taxes

3. Nouns ending in o preceded by a vowel, and most musical terms, form the plural by adding s.

arpeggio — arpeggios	rodeo — rodeos
radio — radios	solo — solos

4. Some nouns ending in o preceded by a consonant form the plural by adding es.

echo — echoes	potato — potatoes
hero — heroes	tomato — tomatoes

5. Nouns ending in y preceded by a consonant change y to i and add es to form the plural.

city — cities	fly — flies
company — companies	party — parties

201

6. Nouns ending in y preceded by a vowel form their plurals by adding s.

alley — alleys   key — keys
journey — journeys   monkey — monkeys

7. Some nouns ending in f or fe form the plural by changing the f or fe to ves.

elf — elves   loaf — loaves
life — lives   shelf — shelves

Other nouns ending in f or fe form their plurals simply by adding s.

dwarf — dwarfs   oaf — oafs
fife — fifes   strife — strifes

8. A few nouns follow old declensions.

child — children   man — men
foot — feet   mouse — mice
goose — geese   ox — oxen
louse — lice   woman — women

9. Compound nouns usually form the plural by adding s or es to the principal word.

passer-by — passers-by
son-in-law — sons-in-law
board of education — boards of education

A compound noun made of two equal nouns generally makes both nouns plural.

manservant — menservants
woman friend — women friends

10. A few nouns are the same in both the singular and the plural.

sheep   deer
trout   salmon

11. Words taken directly from foreign languages usually retain the foreign plural.

alumna — alumnae   hypothesis — hypotheses
alumnus — alumni   parenthesis — parentheses
analysis — analyses   phenomenon — phenomena
basis — bases   radius — radii
datum — data   thesis — theses

12. Letters, signs, figures, and words used without regard to their meaning add 's to form their plurals.

Mind your *p's* and *q's.*
There are no *if's* in his vocabulary.
He earned three *A's* in school.

EXERCISE. Divide your paper into two columns and label one *singular* and one *plural.* Write each of the following words in the correct column; then supply the missing singular or plural for the other column.

alumna   daughter-in-law   halves
and   days   iceman
basis   deer   kitchen
bush   echo   quiz
cameo   editor in chief   salmon
cupful   glasses   x

Sp 5 Possessives

See page 36 for rules which govern the use of possessives.

EXERCISE 1. Write the possessive form of each of the italicized words in the following phrases:

the *girl* dress, the *reporter* beat, *Evelyn* and *Marjorie* home (same home), the *children* book, my *father-in-law* farm, the *dog* house, *James* coat, the *women* club, *boys* and *girls* glee club, the *cows* fodder

EXERCISE 2. Copy the following sentences, inserting apostrophes wherever necessary to show possession:

1. Coopers literary career began one evening in 1820.
2. At his wifes request he was reading aloud an English novel.
3. In Coopers opinion it was insipid, and he said so.
4. On his wifes challenge to write a better one, Coopers pride was aroused; and he wrote *Precaution*.
5. The book was thought to be an Englishwomans work.
6. Coopers desire for greater success was aroused.
7. Conscious of Americas literary inferiority, he sought an American setting for his next book.
8. He recalled that woodsmens tales had fired his imagination in his grandfathers home.
9. He had also experienced a sailors life, for he had been sent to sea for blowing up a students room at Yale.
10. Out of this background and not out of Scotts or anyone elses example came Coopers best novels.

Sp 6 Contractions

To make a contraction, place an apostrophe where one or more letters have been omitted. Exception: will not — won't

are not — aren't	does not — doesn't
cannot — can't	you would — you'd

The use of contractions in formal writing is inadvisable.

EXERCISE. Write the contraction for each of the following:

could not	I shall	there is
did not	is not	was not
do not	it is	we have
has not	of the clock	were not
have not	she is	would not
I am	should not	you are
I have	that is	you will

204

Sp 7   Hyphenated Words

A hyphen is used between words combined into a single term representing a new idea. We can be thankful that the hyphen is used less frequently today than formerly. The following rules cover the most necessary uses:

1. Use a hyphen between words which act as a single adjective modifier.

well-cared-for building   *forty-yard* line
worth-while trip   *poverty-stricken* family

Similar words used in the predicate to modify the subject are not hyphenated:

The building is *well cared for.*
His trip was *worth while.*

The hyphen should be omitted in compounds when the first word is an adverb ending in *ly.*

The neatly arranged papers were ready.
An entirely satisfactory plan was made.

2. Hyphenate numbers from *twenty-one* to *ninety-nine.*

3. Hyphenate two-word fractions only when the two parts form a single adjective.

a *one-third* share
a *one-eighth* solution

When the words are read separately as adjective and noun, do not use the hyphen.

He gave away *one third* of his fortune.
His share was *one fourth.*

4. Use a hyphen after a prefix that has been attached to a proper noun.

un-American   pre-Cambrian
pro-British   un-Christian

5. Place a hyphen after *self* when it is prefixed to a noun.

> self-control   self-defense

6. Hyphenate words in which there may be doubt as to meaning.

> They re-acted the entire ceremony.
> She reacted to the vaccination.
>
> He re-formed his plans.
> He reformed after New Year's Day.

7. Hyphenate words in which the joining of a prefix with the root causes an awkward combination of letters.

> co-operation   re-echo   re-enter

8. Consolidate a prefix and a root word unless the root word begins with the last letter of the prefix or with w.

> coeducational   re-enter
> nonessential   semi-invalid
> postgraduate   co-worker

Although there is a tendency in the English language to consolidate words, many expressions are still correctly written as separate words.

> all right   dining room   per cent
> ash can   en route   post card
> week end   high school   fish cakes

The following compounds are now properly written as single words:

> anywhere   somehow   outlaw
> somewhere   wherever   northeast
> anybody   whoever   thereupon
> nobody   myself   throughout
> anything   yourself   moreover
> something   overthrow   inasmuch
> anyhow   outdoors   heretofore

nonetheless	greenback	runabout
horsepower	typewritten	raincoat
horsepower	passkey	bookkeeper
newsboy	knockout	roommate

EXERCISE 1. Copy the following phrases, inserting hyphens wherever needed; consolidate words where necessary:

daughter in law	post graduate
fifteen yard line	president elect
who so ever	self made man
jumping off place	ten yards
one fifth share	thirty three

EXERCISE 2. See how many compounds of the following words you can find:

book   self   work   room   school

Spelling Lists

1. Crucial words for everyone

The following words are frequently misspelled. Because they are crucial words, it is important that you learn to spell them correctly.

accidentally	analyze	changeable
accommodate	anniversary	choose
accompanying	appreciative	colonel
achievement	appropriate	coming
acknowledgment	athletic	comparatively
across	beginning	compel
affects	behavior	conscientious
alleged	believing	consciousness
altogether	beneficial	consistent
amateur	benefited	conveniently
ammunition	bouquet	courteous
among	canceled	criticize

Spelling

dealt
definite
describe
description
despair
develop
dining
disappear
disappoint
discipline
dissatisfied
divide
dormitory
embarrass
equipped
existence
fascinating
February
fraternity
friend
government
guaranteed
gymnasium
hoping
hosiery
humorous
imitate
inadequate
incidentally
inconvenience
initiation
inquiries
installation
interruption
judgment
knowledge
laid

lead (metal)
led
lightning
lose
miniature
miscellaneous
ninety
noticeable
occasional
occurred
occurrence
omission
omitted
ordinarily
parallel
perceive
permanently
perspiration
physician
prairie
precede
preference
preferred
prejudiced
preparation
principal
principle
privilege
procedure
prove
psychology
pursuing
really
receive
recommend
reference
referred

regretting
religious
restaurant
ridiculous
roommate
sandwich
satisfactorily
scheduled
seize
separate
sincerely
solemn
sophomore
sorority
specifically
superintendent
supplementary
technical
they're
tournament
tragedy
transferred
truly
Tuesday
unanimous
unnecessary
until
using
usually
villain
voluntarily
Wednesday
whether
wholly
who's
yacht
you're

2. A list of words used frequently in college

abbreviate
accessible
accuracy
acquaintance
affectionately
anticipate
apparatus
auxiliary
bachelor
bureau
challenge
character
coherence
commemorate
concentrate
connoisseur
conqueror
criticism
curriculum
customary
debater
dictionary
disappointment
environment
equivalent

exaggerate
exhilaration
experiment
familiar
fascinate
illiterate
immediately
indispensable
ingenious
ingenuous
intelligible
irresistible
laboratory
legible
literature
maintenance
marriage
monotonous
opportunity
optimistic
pamphlet
pantomime
partial
pertinent
philosophy

pronunciation
propaganda
relinquish
remembrance
resemblance
rhythm
sacrilege
science
significant
similar
simultaneous
soliloquy
statue
stature
statute
subsequent
sufficiently
syllable
temperament
theater
tranquillity
valiant
variety
wretched
written

3. A list of business words

accessory
accommodation
accrued
accumulate
adjournment
advertisement
analysis
application

assistance
association
attorney
balance
beneficiary
bookkeeping
budget
bureaus

business
calendar
carriage
cashier
census
commercial
commissioners
competitors

209

confident	expired	misappropriate
congratulations	financial	necessary
controversy	franchise	personnel
convenience	granary	practice
cordially	illegal	prepaid
corporation	independence	proceed
current	inquiry	proprietor
cylinder	installment	questionnaire
decimal	intercede	receipt
defendants	inventory	recommendation
deferred	irrevocable	reconciliation
depreciation	justifiable	secretary
development	legacy	successor
economical	legitimate	thorough
enclosure	liabilities	trial
equipment	memorandum	truly
expenses	minimum	unusually

Review Exercises

EXERCISE 1. Artemus Ward misspelled words for humorous effect. Can you rewrite in correct orthography this excerpt from one of his essays?

I have no politics. Nary a one. I'm not in the bizniss. If I was I spose I should holler versiffrusly in the streets at nite and go home to Betsy Jane smellen of coal ile, in the mornin. I should go to the Poles arly. I should stay there all day. I should see to it that my nabers was thar. I should git carriages to take the kripples, the infirm, and the indignant thar. I should be on guard agin frauds and sich. I should be on the look out for the infamus lise of the enemy, got up jest be4 elecshun for perlitical effeck. When all was over and my candydate was elected, I should move heving & arth — so to speak — until I got orfice, which if I didn't git a orfice I should turn around and abooze the Administration with all my mite and maine. But I'm not in the bizniss.

EXERCISE 2. Copy the following friendly letter, correcting all the misspelling. There are twenty misspelled words.

Antioch Colledge
Yellow Springs, Ohio
October 30, 19—

Dear Dick,

I was suprised to know that you were planing to have an operation yester-day. I certenly hope that it was sucessful.

I now have a partime job in a bookstore. The bookstore was taken over this fall by a young newley maried couple who have big plans for promoshion. They are orderring about two hunderd dollars' worth of new stock and have good ideas for re-organising, maintainance, and generl improvments. It is extremily intresting work, and they are fine peopel to work for.

Sincerily yours,
Chuck

EXERCISE 3. Copy the following business letter, correcting all the misspelled words. There are twenty in all.

2407 Chestnut Street
Omaha 6, Nebraska
December 11, 19—

Miss Mary Sidwell
916 South 37 Street
Omaha 5, Nebraska

Dear Miss Sidwell:

Will you kindley renue my supscription to *The New Yorker* magasine for and other year. I am hopeing you will alow me the ninty-cent discont you menshioned when I spoke to you on the telaphone.

Will you also order a year's supscription to *Coronet* for Miss Ruth Jessen, 4907 Webster Street. If it is not to late, I should like to have this supscription begin with the Chrismas issew. However, this may not be possable. I know you will do you're best for me as you allways do.

Cordialy yours,
Richard Lane

Fun with Spelling

STUNT 1. Can you name an English word which has two *u*'s in succession? a word that has three double letters in succession? three words that end in *dous?*

STUNT 2. Can you think of a word that begins with *s* and ends with *s* with a *mile* between?

STUNT 3. Can you think of four words ending in *l*, such as *cupful?* Do not use again a word ending in *ful.*

STUNT 4. Can you think of ten words ending in *x?*

STUNT 5. If you have a friend who prides himself on his spelling, try him on these tricky words:

consensus	dissension	corroborate
sacrilegious	supersede	ecstasy
exhilarating	tranquillity	dissipate
questionnaire	assassinate	hypocrisy
millionaire	abscess	conspicuous
effervescent	penitentiary	chrysanthemum
picnicking	annihilate	inoculate

EFFECTIVE SENTENCES

SENTENCE FRAGMENTS

A fragment of anything is unsatisfactory. A fragment of cloth is insufficient for a dress, a fragment of a song is merely tantalizing, and a fragment of a conversation is highly annoying. Let's consider sentence fragments. Certainly if they can be eliminated from our speaking and writing, our communication will be clearer and more exact.

EF S   Definition

A fragment of a sentence is an incomplete expression of a thought.

EF S 1   Word, Phrase, Clause Omissions

If we know exactly how sentences are built, we have at least a fighting chance to avoid the fragment error. First of all, what is a sentence?

A __sentence__ is a group of words that expresses a complete thought. Every sentence has a subject and a predicate.

Let us start with a subject and a predicate. Then let us add words, phrases, and clauses. As a sentence grows, it becomes more complicated; and the possibilities for the sentence fragments are multiplied.

1. SUBJECT-PREDICATE: *Science has contributed.*
2. WORDS ADDED: Science has contributed *research, that precise study and investigation.*
3. PREPOSITIONAL PHRASE ADDED: Science has contributed *to the welfare of all.*
4. PARTICIPIAL PHRASE ADDED: Science has contributed countless men and women, *working tirelessly day and night.*
5. INFINITIVE PHRASE ADDED: Science has contributed *to save millions of lives.*
6. ADJECTIVE CLAUSE ADDED: Science has contributed information *that has made life easier.*
7. ADVERBIAL CLAUSE ADDED: Science has contributed *so that we may be healthier.*
8. NOUN CLAUSE ADDED: Science has contributed *what the world needs.*

The eight sentences point out the principal ways in which sentence fragments occur. Here are the eight thoughts as they are sometimes expressed. Contrast them with the first group, and you will find that only the first sentence remains unchanged.

1. Science has contributed.
2. Science has contributed research. That precise study and investigation.
3. Science has contributed. To the welfare of all.
4. Science has contributed countless men and women. Working tirelessly day and night.
5. Science has contributed. To save millions of lives.
6. Science has contributed information. That has made life easier.
7. Science has contributed. So that we may be healthier.
8. Science has contributed. What the world needs.

Word Fragments

1. Avoid using an appositive as a sentence.

WRONG: Everyone has heard of Leeuwenhoek. The Dutch janitor and shopkeeper.

RIGHT: Everyone has heard of Leeuwenhoek, the Dutch janitor and shopkeeper.

2. Avoid using a predicate without a subject.

WRONG: Received your interesting letter yesterday.

RIGHT: I received your interesting letter yesterday.

3. Avoid using part of a series as a sentence.

WRONG: I see you are taking French, English, and history. Also science and mathematics.

RIGHT: I see you are taking French, English, history, science, and mathematics.

4. Avoid using as sentences groups of words beginning with *for example, such as, especially.*

WRONG: I like stories about scientists. For example, the story about Leeuwenhoek.

RIGHT: I like stories about scientists; for example, the story about Leeuwenhoek.

EXERCISE 1. Rewrite these sentences, making the necessary corrections. You will find one that is correct.

1. Sometimes take the present status of science for granted. 2. Read yesterday about the Institute for Advanced Study at Princeton. 3. One of the faculty members is Albert Einstein. The great mathematician known for his theory of relativity. 4. Five million dollars was donated to establish the Institute. 5. A few hundred years ago scientists had a difficult time. Especially in any controversial field. 6. Certain facts were accepted as definitely true. Such as the flatness of the earth. 7. The skeptics imprisoned Galileo. The man who proved the movement of the earth around the sun. 8. They burned to death

Servetus. A man curious enough about human anatomy to do an autopsy.   9. Most early scientists received ridicule and scorn. Also hatred and persecution.   10. Intellectual curiosity was not always a virtue. Especially in some fields of thinking.

EXERCISE 2. Rewrite the following paragraph, making whatever corrections are needed:

Science in the early days was a mixture of honest curiosity and hoax. Let us consider Leeuwenhoek's period. The seventeenth century. See a number of evidences of a rising interest in science. In England was founded a scientific organization called The Invisible College. The forerunner of the Royal Society of England. Some of their experiments amuse us. Especially the one with the spider and the powdered unicorn's horn. Made a circle with the powder and put the spider in the middle. They believed the spider could not run out of the circle. Even such an experiment proves one thing. Namely, a growing interest in research.

Phrase Fragments

1. Avoid using a prepositional phrase as a sentence.

> WRONG: Leeuwenhoek lived as a humble janitor and shop-
> keeper. In the city of Delft, Holland.
> RIGHT: Leeuwenhoek lived as a humble janitor and shop-
> keeper in the city of Delft, Holland.

EXERCISE 1. Make the necessary corrections in this paragraph:

Leeuwenhoek found time to grind lenses. In addition to performing his duties as janitor of the city hall and as shopkeeper. With a kind of single-tracked mind. Leeuwenhoek kept grinding lens after lens. Through these lenses, he looked at all sorts of things. Like the stinger of a flea and the legs of a louse. He would spend hours peering through his lenses. For the sheer joy of it. Then with the soul of a true scientist. He looked at each specimen hundreds of times. Always under the same conditions. Then and then only would he draw his conclusions.

2. Avoid using a participial phrase as a sentence.

WRONG: At all hours, the neighbors could see Leeuwenhoek. Staring through his lenses.

RIGHT: At all hours, the neighbors could see Leeuwenhoek, staring through his lenses.

EXERCISE 2. In the following paragraph are a number of participial phrases used erroneously as sentences. Rewrite the paragraph, making the necessary corrections.

Looking at a small drop of rain water. Leeuwenhoek noticed many little creatures. Swimming around in it. Looking at them for hours. This Dutch scientist made sure of his finding. But he was puzzled. Where did they come from? Had they crawled in? Wiping a glass very clean. Leeuwenhoek put it under a rain spout. Again and again he was seen. Peering through his lenses. Looking at the same strange creatures. Determined to find the source of the "wretched beasties," as he called them. Leeuwenhoek caught water directly from the heavens. Once more he tried his experiment, and this time there were no "wretched beasties" in the water. They did not come from the sky, then, concluded Leeuwenhoek. Apparently satisfied with his findings.

3. Avoid using an infinitive phrase as a sentence.

WRONG: Of course Leeuwenhoek kept the water. To look at it again.

RIGHT: Of course Leeuwenhoek kept the water to look at it again.

EXERCISE 3. Rewrite the following, eliminating all infinitive phrases that are used as sentences:

It is fortunate that Leeuwenhoek thought it was important. To look at the water again. On the fourth day the little "wretched beasties" were seen. To be swimming about in the water. To have made this discovery. Leeuwenhoek must have been elated. His endless curiosity had led him. To make an important finding which would benefit all humanity.

It is fortunate, too, that the Dutch scientist continued in his slow, methodical way. To poke around in all sorts of experiments. In order to examine pepper. He decided. To soak it for a few weeks. Finally the time came for him. To examine the pepper through his lenses. He was utterly amazed. To see countless numbers of the "wretched beasties" on the pepper. Thus, a seventeenth-century Dutchman had learned how. To raise microbes. In the succeeding centuries, that discovery would be used. To produce such drugs as penicillin and streptomycin.

Clause Fragments

1. Avoid using an adjective clause as a sentence.

> WRONG: Everyone is familiar with the story of penicillin. Which has already saved countless lives.
>
> RIGHT: Everyone is familiar with the story of penicillin, which has already saved countless lives.

EXERCISE 1. Rewrite these sentences to avoid this error:

1. Penicillin was accidentally discovered by a scientist. Who was experimenting in his laboratory in London.
2. He had a glass culture plate. Which was alive with bacteria.
3. Suddenly his eye noticed something. That was unusual.
4. On the plate, there was a bit of green mold. Which seemed to be killing the bacteria around it.
5. Dr. Alexander Fleming was the kind of scientist. Who would catch the significance of such a sight.

EXERCISE 2. In the following paragraphs, there are several adjective clauses that have been used as sentences. Rewrite the paragraph, making the necessary corrections.

Leeuwenhoek's experiment three hundred years earlier had given a technique. Which eventually brought about the discovery of penicillin. Leeuwenhoek had raised his "wretched beasties" in a culture. Of which the base was pepper. In 1929, Dr. Fleming was raising bacteria. From which was to come one of the most valuable drugs in the world. There was a power in that little green mold. Which could kill other bacteria.

It is easy to recognize the possibilities for saving lives. That such bacteria could possess. Such bacteria injected into the human body could fight other bacteria. Which were destroying health. This was the premise followed by the scientists. Who set about in the production of penicillin.

2. Avoid using an adverbial clause as a sentence.

WRONG: After a small amount of penicillin had been extracted. A test was necessary.

RIGHT: After a small amount of penicillin had been extracted, a test was necessary.

WRONG: A number of mice were chosen for the experiment. As is the custom.

RIGHT: A number of mice were chosen for the experiment, as is the custom.

EXERCISE 3. Rewrite the following to eliminate the use of abverbial clauses as sentences:

1. After the fifty mice had been injected with a type of bacteria frequent in wound infections. The experiment was begun.
2. Twenty-five of them would also receive shots of penicillin. When the right time came.
3. If penicillin counteracted harmful bacteria. The twenty-five had a chance.
4. As you have probably read. The twenty-five not receiving penicillin were dead within seventeen hours.
5. Twenty-four of the twenty-five receiving the penicillin lived on. As though nothing had happened.

EXERCISE 4. Rewrite the following paragraphs, eliminating all adverbial clauses used as sentences:

As had been done by Leeuwenhoek three hundred years earlier in his experiments. The experiment with mice was repeated hundreds of times. Until the results of the experiment were positive. The

scientists would not allow penicillin to be used on human beings.
Finally, in 1941 a few human patients were chosen. Because all
other drugs had failed. Penicillin was a last chance. The results
were spectacular. As everyone knows.

Many scientific advances are made. When the horror of war
is present. Scientists knew that the lives of many young men
could be saved. If infection from war wounds could be curbed.
Penicillin could save thousands of lives. If only enough of it could
be produced. At first it could not be produced in large quantities.
As you know. The miracle of production was finally accomplished. After many organizations began to recognize the need.

3. Avoid using a noun clause as a sentence.

WRONG: Everyone knows. That penicillin was discovered in
England.
RIGHT: Everyone knows that penicillin was discovered in
England.

WRONG: How it was developed in both England and America.
Is also known.
RIGHT: How it was developed in both England and America
is also known.

EXERCISE 5. Rewrite the following to eliminate the use
of noun clauses as sentences:

1. Do you know? That streptomycin was discovered in the
United States.
2. What marvels it has accomplished. Is recognized everywhere.
3. Many persons do not know. Where the microbe was found.
4. A hundred years ago people believed. That cemeteries were
the cause of epidemics.
5. That the soil was contaminated. Was a common belief.

EXERCISE 6. Rewrite the following paragraphs, eliminating all noun clauses used as sentences:

All tests showed clearly. That the soil of cemeteries did not
contain disease bacteria. What scientists found. Was exceedingly

important. Apparently the soil had killed all disease bacteria. What scientists recognized then. Was the possibility of the soil's containing *good* bacteria. They knew beyond a doubt. That good bacteria will kill harmful bacteria.

Constant research finally paid dividends. Dr. René J. Dubos discovered a valuable soil microbe. We now know. That soil microbes can kill the bacteria resulting in pneumonia. Then Dr. Selman A. Waksman of New Jersey discovered in the course of his research. What scientists believe is one of the greatest contributions of our time. Dr. Waksman discovered streptomycin.

Review Exercises

EXERCISE 1. Find the sentence fragments among the following. Make whatever additions are necessary to produce complete sentences.

1. Dr. Waksman's research involved a staggering amount of work. 2. That a tiny amount of soil may contain eight million microbes. 3. To isolate the one right microbe from eight million. 4. Used a glass plate on which were living many disease microbes. 5. Then he streaked mud across the plate and waited. 6. If the disease microbes ceased to flourish on one part of the plate. 7. The next job, the discovery of which microbe had done the work. 8. The work seemed endless, but at last the right microbe was discovered. 9. Leeuwenhoek, peering at the "wretched beasties." 10. Skill and imagination and especially perseverance.

EXERCISE 2. Rewrite this paragraph so that it contains no sentence fragments:

Because scientists are working constantly for the betterment of mankind. Our lives are happier and healthier. Formerly many persons succumbed to diseases. Which now are easily curable. Millions of dollars are being spent in research. To help people like you and me.

UNITY IN SENTENCES

The quality of oneness is important in every sentence. Every part should contribute to a singleness of idea and a singleness of effect. If unity is lacking, the reader or listener is certain to feel like the gentleman who jumped on his horse and rode off in all directions.

EF S 2   Ways to Achieve Unity

1. Avoid linking unrelated independent clauses with *and* and *and so*. "Stringy" sentences lack singleness of thought.

> WRONG: It must take a tremendous amount of patience to be a research worker, and thousands of experiments must be done in the will-o'-the-wisp search.
>
> RIGHT: It must take a tremendous amount of patience to be a research worker. Thousands of experiments must be done in the will-o'-the-wisp search.

EXERCISE 1. Rewrite the following paragraph in whatever way you think best to achieve unity:

The production of such drugs as penicillin and streptomycin was at first discouragingly slow, and the microbes are raised in big tanks containing specially prepared broths. After the molds appear, scientists must extract the precious microbes; and so it took years of patient effort to get enough penicillin to save just a few lives, and very obviously the process was too slow to be of much help to humanity. Then the United States Department of Agriculture discovered a new broth which encouraged the growth of the mold, and in 1945 there was at last enough penicillin to treat seven million persons, and the rise in the production of streptomycin was proportionately high.

2. Avoid joining sentences with a comma or without any punctuation.

> WRONG: Penicillin is effective against eighty-nine diseases, certainly this substance is a boon to medicine.

RIGHT: Penicillin is effective against eighty-nine diseases.
        Certainly this substance is a boon to medicinee. (The
        clauses may also be linked with a semicolon.)

WRONG: Persons afflicted with tularemia used to suffer for
        months now with streptomycin they may be cured
        in a few days.

RIGHT: Persons afflicted with tularemia used to suffer for
        months. Now with streptomycin they may be cured
        in a few days. (A semicolon also may link clauses.)

EXERCISE 2. Rewrite the following sentences correctly:

1. The name of Louis Pasteur is known everywhere the pasteur-
ization of milk has done much to popularize his name.   2. The
vintners of Orléans appealed to him, their wine was spoiling.
3. He told them to heat the wine to 55° C in this way the wine
would not spoil.   4. The same process is used in the pasteuriza-
tion of milk its use has reduced infant death rates tremendously.
5. But let us go back to Leeuwenhoek, he, too, made a contribution in this field.   6. One day Leeuwenhoek through the use
of a mirror and his lenses examined the microbes in his own mouth
the sight of them horrified him.   7. Leeuwenhoek loved to drink
very hot coffee, he believed that it contained special curative
powers.   8. One morning he drank his steaming hot coffee by
chance he examined his mouth immediately afterward.   9. He
was more than amazed, there was not a single "wretched beastie"
in sight.   10. Leeuwenhoek had stumbled upon a way to kill
microbes, Pasteur's use of heat on the wine was simply a continuation of the idea.

**3. Avoid breaking into several choppy sentences an idea
which can be expressed in a single sentence.**

POOR: Next, the people of France appealed to Pasteur.
        They wanted him to save their silkworms. They
        were dying. They had some strange disease.

BETTER: Next, the people of France appealed to Pasteur
        to save their silkworms, which were dying of some
        strange disease.

EXERCISE 3. Rewrite the following groups of sentences, and notice the improvement in unity:

1. Pasteur studied the problem. It took five years. He found two diseases instead of one. They were killing the silkworms.
2. These were his findings. Specific diseases have their causes. They are caused by specific bacteria.
3. Inoculation is an important method. It provides immunization against disease.
4. The conquest of rabies was achieved. Pasteur accomplished this. It was in 1885. He did it through a process of immunization.
5. Pasteur made a broth. He used the spinal cord. It came from a rabbit that had died of rabies.
6. Pasteur inoculated fifty dogs. He used this broth. He wanted to immunize them against rabies.
7. Again he inoculated the dogs. This time he used the virus of rabies.
8. The immunization was successful. Not a single dog became affected by rabies.
9. One day a little boy and his mother appeared. They had gone to Pasteur's laboratory. They wanted help. The little boy's name was Joseph Meister.
10. The boy had been knocked down. He had also been bitten by a dog. The dog was undoubtedly mad.

Review Exercise

EXERCISE. The following paragraphs exemplify poor style for the three reasons you have just studied. Rewrite the paragraphs, working for sentence unity.

Fearfully Pasteur took the child as his patient without help the boy would surely die. His process of inoculation had been successful. It had saved every animal. Still it was a tremendous responsibility to take a human being, it would be tragic if the boy should die.

The boy was inoculated. Pasteur did it. He used a syringeful of broth. It had been made from the spinal cord of a rabbit.

The rabbit had died of rabies. On the following days fresh inoculations were made in all Joseph Meister received thirteen inoculations in ten days. Then Pasteur waited. He wanted to know the outcome of the experiment. It meant the success or failure of an idea.

Joseph Meister did not die he lived. Pasteur had given a life-saving idea to the world and can you name some of the many ways in which it is used?

4. Avoid loading sentences with unrelated ideas.

POOR: Joseph Lister, who was a Quaker, became interested in the killing of germs, those "wretched beasties" which Anthony Leeuwenhoek of Delft, Holland, had seen through his lenses.

BETTER: Joseph Lister became interested in the killing of germs.

EXERCISE 4. Rewrite each of these sentences, omitting all details which are unrelated to one idea. Notice how the sentences gain punch and definiteness when they are shorn of the unrelated parts.

1. Joseph Lister, the name is probably familiar to all of you, is known, and very justly so, as the founder of antiseptic surgery.
2. Modern military surgery, operations taking place in base hospitals often under gunfire, has an exceedingly low mortality rate.
3. During the Napoleonic Wars, which finally concluded with the Battle of Waterloo in 1815, the chief surgeon, by the name of Larrey, reported only two survivals in several thousand cases of amputation.   4. Fifty years later, the problem, a very serious one, bothered Dr. Joseph Lister, who at one time had been professor of surgery at Glasgow.   5. He heard that carbolic acid, a poisonous substance that comes from coal tar and other sources, was used to disinfect garbage.   6. Very shortly Lister, whose father was the father of modern microscopy, was using diluted carbolic acid on bandages and spraying the operating rooms, very crude affairs, with carbolic acid; and the results proved the wisdom of his idea.

5. Avoid the inclusion of too many details.

POOR: A historic search for the yellow-fever microbe took place in Cuba in 1900 at a time when thousands of American soldiers and even many of the staff officers in General Leonard Wood's office had died of the disease.

BETTER: A historic search for the yellow-fever microbe took place in Cuba in 1900.

EXERCISE 5. Find the unnecessary details in these sentences. Rewrite the sentences, and notice to what extent they have been strengthened by the omission of superfluous details.

1. People, including the natives and the Americans, had strange ideas about the cause of yellow fever, sometimes called "yellow jack." 2. When anyone died of yellow fever, his possessions, like clothing, bed linens, and draperies, were buried to eliminate any possible contamination to those who might touch his belongings; and frequently the house was burned in a frenzy to stamp out the horrible disease. 3. Nevertheless, in spite of all these rigid and sometimes too-drastic precautions taken by friends and relatives of the victims of yellow fever, people continued to die like flies. 4. One doctor, by the name of Carlos Finlay, whose name is now known in medical circles everywhere, asserted that yellow fever was caused by mosquitoes. 5. People simply marked him as a dreamer, one who sat around figuring up fantastic notions concerning the causes of yellow fever which no one could possibly believe, and went on burying the dead, of which there were tremendous numbers.

6. Avoid too-frequent use of parentheses and dashes.

POOR: Walter Reed (for whom the Walter Reed Hospital in Washington is named) was finally called in (June 25, 1900) for advice.

BETTER: Walter Reed was finally called in on June 25, 1900, for advice.

POOR: His fight against yellow fever — you probably read about it in the play *Yellow Jack* — is a monument to scientific curiosity — the kind Leeuwenhoek exemplified in his experiments.

BETTER: His fight against yellow fever is a monument to scientific curiosity.

The occasional use of parentheses and dashes is entirely permissible. However, some persons fill their writing with side remarks placed in parentheses or between dashes; and the writing, consequently, loses unity and strength. It is their *overuse* against which you are being warned.

EXERCISE 6. Rewrite the following sentences, making whatever corrections you think are necessary:

1. Dr. Carlos Finlay — he was an interesting kind of dreamer, all right — gave Walter Reed (Chairman of the Yellow Fever Commission) some mosquito eggs.

2. They hatched the eggs (the eggs were put in a warm place to do this) and made ready for their experiment — an experiment all the world would profit by.

3. This species of mosquito had silver markings on its back (there are between twenty and thirty kinds that carry diseases).

4. One of the men (Jesse Lazear, by name) took some mosquitoes (female) and allowed them to bite a number of men dying of yellow fever — they were then delirious.

5. The next step (how Pasteur would have applauded their care) was to allow those mosquitoes — absolutely steeped in the blood of yellow-fever victims — to bite persons who were entirely well (but probably wouldn't be so for long).

Review Exercise

EXERCISE. Rewrite the following sentences to give them unity:

1. James Carroll — a member of the Yellow Fever Commission with a wife and five children — allowed one of the fateful mosquitoes to sting him (August 27, 1900).

2. Three days later (August 30) Carroll came down with a violent case of yellow fever, the first symptoms of which are bloodshot eyes and a high fever.

3. Fortunately, Carroll pulled through (it was a tough fight, however) and continued the fight against yellow fever since more and more experiments had to be carried out to prove the truth (or untruth) of the mosquito theory, propounded by that old dreamer, Carlos Finlay.

4. On the thirteenth of September, Jesse Lazear was feeding his mosquitoes (he would put them in test tubes and then turn the tubes upside down on the arms of the sick so that the mosquitoes would drink their blood) when a mosquito — not one of his special ones — lighted on his arm and bit him.

5. Twelve days later Jesse Lazear died of yellow fever after having suffered high fever, rapid pulse, and all the other symptoms of that disease.

7. Avoid incomplete and illogical comparisons.

WRONG: The situation was so serious. (The word *so* generally requires a *that* clause to complete the meaning.)

RIGHT: The situation was so serious that more experiments had to be made.

WRONG: The situation was as serious, if not more serious, than it had ever been. (Take out the words *if not more serious;* does the sentence make sense?)

RIGHT: The situation was as serious as it had ever been, if not more serious.

WRONG: The bite of a female mosquito is more deadly than a male. (*Bite* is being compared with *male*.)

RIGHT: The bite of a female mosquito is more deadly than that of a male.

WRONG: Yellow fever is worse than any disease I ever heard of. (Since yellow fever is a disease, the sentence illogically says that yellow fever is worse than itself.)

RIGHT: Yellow fever is worse than any other disease I ever heard of.

WRONG: In fact, I think it is the worst of any other disease.
RIGHT: In fact, I think it is the worst of all diseases.

WRONG: I like these stories better than Patty.
RIGHT: I like these stories better than Patty does.

EXERCISE 7.   One of the sentences in the following group is correct, but all the others contain incomplete or illogical comparisons. Correct the sentences as you think best.

1. Mosquitoes are so annoying. 2. I think I dislike them more than Tom. 3. In the summertime, they are the worst of any other pests. 4. They annoy me more than any insect. 5. Did you know that a male mosquito is as gentle, if not more gentle, than a house cat? 6. Mrs. Mosquito causes much more damage than he. 7. The habits of Mrs. Mosquito are more objectionable than Mr. Mosquito. 8. The humming sound, caused by the flapping of her wings, is more irritating than any sound I know of. 9. The musical accomplishments of the female are definitely worse than the male. 10. Stories about research are so very interesting.

8. Avoid awkward sentences.

WRONG: Research is when a critical study or investigation is made.
RIGHT: Research is a critical study or investigation.

WRONG: The discovery of the cause of yellow fever was where science advanced.
RIGHT: The discovery of the cause of yellow fever was an advancement for science.

WRONG: Because men were willing to die for science caused others to live.
RIGHT: Because men were willing to die for science, others could live.
RIGHT: The fact that men were willing to die for science helped others to live.

EXERCISE 8. Rewrite the following sentences, eliminating any awkwardness which you may find:

1. Because the source of yellow fever was discovered caused the experimenters to redouble their efforts.   2. An experiment is where people test to prove or disprove something doubtful.   3. Trial and error is when the method is hit or miss.   4. Because people's lives depend on exactness causes scientists to reject the hit-or-miss method.   5. Truth is when all facts are exact.

Review Exercise

EXERCISE. All the following sentences lack unity for one of the eight reasons discussed in this section. Make the necessary corrections.

1. Every scientist recognizes the need to experiment again and again varying conditions can change results.
2. Leeuwenhoek peered at his "wretched beasties" repeatedly, and no wonder the neighbors thought him crazy.
3. Pasteur inoculated fifty dogs. He was working on rabies. He used the dogs in his experiments.
4. Joseph Lister (the English surgeon who had been influenced by Pasteur) used antiseptics (solutions of carbolic acid) many times before he came to any conclusions.
5. Certainly the Yellow Fever Commission was as careful, if not more careful, than these.
6. The Commission (made up of four persons — Reed, Carroll, Lazear, and a Cuban) carried on their experiments many, many times (in a scientific way).
7. The results of the experiments carried on by the Yellow Fever Commission in Cuba in 1900 showed the world the necessity in the extreme of finding ways to exterminate as quickly as possible the mosquito.
8. Extermination is where things are utterly destroyed.

COHERENCE IN SENTENCES

Coherence literally means "a sticking together." It involves a kind of teamwork among all the parts of the sentence; words, phrases, and clauses must all be arranged in a way that will make the idea crystal clear.

EF S 3   Ways to Achieve Coherence

1. Avoid misplacement of modifying (a) words, (b) phrases, and (c) clauses.

(a) Words:

> WRONG: We have only read about a few of the miracles of science.
>
> RIGHT: We have read about only a few of the miracles of science.

EXERCISE 1. Rewrite these sentences, placing the modifying words correctly:

1. We go through a week scarcely without hearing of some new discovery.   2. We only see surprising things.   3. Most diseases are nearly now conquered.   4. There only are a few which remain mysteries.   5. There hardly are any on which research is not being done.

(b) Phrases:

> WRONG: The new boy told us more about mosquitoes in history class.
>
> RIGHT: The new boy in history class told us more about mosquitoes.

EXERCISE 2. Rewrite these sentences, making sure that the phrases are placed near the words which they modify:

1. A mosquito carries malaria with its poisonous sting.   2. Doses were formerly given to people of quinine.   3. When the Japanese conquered the East Indies, the supply was cut off of quinine.

4. Mr. Smith suffers from malaria in the house next door. 5. A new medicine has given him relief by the name of atabrine.

(c) Clauses:

> WRONG: Atabrine was discovered by German scientists, which is a synthetic of quinine.
> RIGHT: Atabrine, which is a synthetic of quinine, was discovered by German scientists.

EXERCISE 3. Rewrite the following sentences, placing the adjective clauses near the words which they modify:

1. The Nazis realized the importance of a malaria counteragent who were planning the war. 2. Atabrine would give relief in five days, which was discovered in 1932. 3. The quinine treatment was long and painful that malaria sufferers had taken for years. 4. Fifteen little pills of atabrine would do the trick, which was the usual dosage. 5. Soldiers cannot win battles who are sick with malaria.

Review Exercise

EXERCISE. These sentences lack coherence because of a misplaced word, phrase, or clause. Correct them.

1. One ton of atabrine will almost cure 600,000 victims of malaria. 2. Thirty thousand persons could only be helped by a ton of quinine that suffer from malaria. 3. Doctors everywhere hailed the experiments with enthusiasm in their voices. 4. Persons were seen on the streets who a short time before had shaken with chills and fevers. 5. There only was praise for the new drug. 6. America almost was at a point of frustration without a substitute for the necessary quinine. 7. Part of the secret finally was uncovered which the Germans had guarded closely. 8. Dr. A. E. Sherndal unraveled the secret gradually of the Winthrop Chemical Company. 9. According to the German formula, several of the ingredients could not be procured in the United States that went into the making of the drug. 10. This hurdle only was an incentive which the Germans had set up.

232

2. **Avoid "squinting" modifiers.** A "squinting" modifier is one which because of its placement may refer either to the preceding or to the following word.

> WRONG: Drug companies were encouraged immediately to go into production. (As the sentence stands, we cannot tell whether the companies were immediately encouraged, or whether it was hoped that they would go immediately into production.)
>
> RIGHT: Drug companies immediately were encouraged to go into production.
>
> RIGHT: Drug companies were encouraged to go immediately into production.

EXERCISE 4. Can you point out the "squinting" modifiers in these sentences? How can the sentences be reworded to eliminate doubtful meaning?

1. The companies that co-operated willingly skyrocketed the production. 2. The shadows of war which were apparent increasingly frightened everyone. 3. Without atabrine, soldiers who contracted malaria suddenly might die. 4. During the war, atabrine was used successfully to save thousands of lives. 5. Moreover, millions of the pills which had been made fortunately were flown to our allies.

3. **Avoid unnecessary separation of parts of a sentence which belong naturally together.**

> WRONG: For a few cents a person is now able *to* entirely *cure* a case of malaria.
>
> RIGHT: For a few cents a person is now able entirely *to cure* a case of malaria.
>
> WRONG: The *Japanese*, even though they had conquered the East Indies, *were unable* to get quinine.
>
> RIGHT: Even though they had conquered the East Indies, the *Japanese were unable* to get quinine. (*Or*) The *Japanese were unable* to get quinine even though they had conquered the East Indies.

WRONG: The Dutch *had* before surrendering *scorched* their quinine trees.

RIGHT: The Dutch, before surrendering, *had scorched* their quinine trees. (*Or*) Before surrendering, the Dutch *had scorched* their quinine trees.

EXERCISE 5. These sentences lack coherence because parts which naturally belong together are separated. Rewrite the sentences, correcting them as you think best.

1. It is interesting to because of atabrine visualize the relief that will be brought to millions. 2. Experiments, as you already know, have been tried in several states where malaria because of swamp conditions is prevalent. 3. The experiments have in every case on record been successful. 4. People no longer have to, as was formerly the case, die of the dreaded disease. 5. Over three million persons, according to prewar records, die yearly as a result of malaria. 6. Atabrine can, without any doubt, save millions. 7. Moreover, governments everywhere are to the best of their abilities stamping out the breeding places of mosquitoes. 8. Swamps wherever it is possible are being drained. 9. Oil has, as you know, been spread on water to by smothering kill the young mosquitoes as they hatch. 10. Moreover, insecticides have to a certain extent proved to be valuable.

4. Avoid connecting parts of a sentence illogically.

In connecting an adverbial clause with an independent clause, it is exceedingly important that the proper subordinate conjunction be chosen. Since subordinate conjunctions carry different meanings, it is impossible to use them interchangeably.

WRONG: Although we read the stories of modern research workers, we can see the influence of Leeuwenhoek.

RIGHT: When we read the stories of modern research workers, we can see the influence of Leeuwenhoek.

WRONG: I read where Texas fever was once a scourge.

RIGHT: I read that Texas fever was once a scourge.

Sometimes a co-ordinate conjunction is used where the meaning demands a subordinate conjunction.

WRONG: Texas fever was a dread disease among cattle, and science conquered it.

RIGHT: Since Texas fever was a dread disease among cattle, science determined to conquer it.

EXERCISE 6. Rewrite these sentences, making sure that the clauses are connected logically:

1. Since cattlemen in the South bought Northern cattle and put them in their fields, the trouble began. 2. If a short time had passed, the Northern cattle sickened and died. 3. No one would listen to them, and the cattlemen insisted that ticks were killing the cattle. 4. The cattlemen made these wild statements, and people simply shook their heads and thought they were a little crazy. 5. Perhaps you have read where those cattlemen were right. 6. Theobald Smith was put in charge of the search, but he was the right man for the job. 7. While he was born in the city, he liked the country. 8. As he was chosen, he went to the scene of the trouble. 9. The cattlemen talked to him about ticks, but he listened. 10. He recognized where they had reason for their beliefs.

5. Avoid elliptical clauses.

In an elliptical clause there is an omission of a word or words which are clearly implied. Unless care is exercised in the use of elliptical clauses, they may dangle; and the result is usually not only confusing but also humorous.

WRONG: While experimenting, all evidence pointed toward the ticks.

RIGHT: While experimenting (*or* While he was experimenting), Smith realized that all evidence pointed toward the ticks.

WRONG: Do not kill a tick until full of blood.

RIGHT: Do not kill a tick until it is full of blood.

EXERCISE 7. Make the necessary corrections in the following sentences:

1. When working, time was forgotten. 2. After putting infected cattle and noninfected cattle in the same field, every development was watched. 3. After dragging out his microscope, countless examinations were made. 4. No conclusions were drawn until finished. 5. While picking ticks off the animals, the sun beat down unmercifully. 6. Although living only about twenty days, plenty of damage is done by a tick in that time. 7. After laying approximately two thousand eggs, death comes. 8. When examining the blood of an animal dead of Texas fever, strange little microbes were found. 9. After repeating the examination many, many times, the same results were always found. 10. While experimenting with some baby ticks which never had been on cattle, the solution came.

6. Avoid dangling verbals: (a) participles, (b) gerunds, and (c) infinitives.

(a) Dangling participial phrases:

> WRONG: *Finding* that the baby tick was the bearer of disease, the *problem* was solved. (Can the problem find anything?)
>
> RIGHT: *Finding* that the baby tick was the bearer of disease, *Smith* solved the problem. (Notice that in this sentence it is Smith who does the finding.)
>
> WRONG: *Having solved* that problem, another *one* awaited him.
>
> RIGHT: *Having solved* that problem, *Smith* found another one awaiting him. (*Having solved* modifies *Smith*.)

EXERCISE 8. In the following sentences, there are a number of dangling participles. Find them, and then rewrite the sentences to eliminate dangling modifiers.

1. Buying Northern cattle, these were the cattle found by the cattlemen to be dying. 2. Putting on his thinking cap, the

problem was tackled by Smith.   3. Not showing a sign of Texas fever, Smith saw the Southern cattle continue to graze unconcernedly.   4. Attaching themselves to Northern cattle, damage was wrought by the death-dealing ticks.   5. Watching some Northern calves, the idea occurred to Smith.   6. Having been bitten by ticks, a mild case of Texas fever would take place. 7. Occurring in calfhood, the effects of the disease were milder. 8. Having recovered, the disease did not bother the calves again. 9. Seeing this happen to Southern calves, too, the solution was evident to Smith.   10. Having all the clues, the solution is probably apparent to you also.

(b) Dangling gerund phrases:

WRONG: After seeing the clues, the solution was evident. (Did the solution see the clues?)
RIGHT: When Smith saw the clues, the solution was evident.

WRONG: In reading articles about the experiment, the facts are clear.
RIGHT: When we read articles about the experiment, the facts are clear.

EXERCISE 9. In nine of the following ten sentences, there is a dangling gerund phrase. Find the phrases, and reword the sentences so that one can tell exactly to whom or what the gerund refers.

1. By getting immunity in calfhood, Texas fever could not harm Southern cattle.   2. In shipping nonimmunized Northern cattle into tick-infested areas, trouble was inevitable.   3. In getting the fever when fully grown, the chances for recovery were slight. 4. After reading of Pasteur's work in immunity, we recognize his influence on Theobald Smith.   5. By using a vaccine made of the spinal cord of a rabbit dead from rabies, the principle of immunity was discovered by Pasteur.   6. After inoculating a person who had been bitten by a mad dog, an immunity to rabies was set up by Pasteur.   7. By watching the effect of ticks on calves, the same principle of immunity was recognized by Smith.   8. After

having mild cases when young, there was no danger later.
9. By having vaccinations and inoculations against various
diseases, immunity is given to us.   10. By taking an ounce of
prevention, epidemics may be avoided.

(c) Dangling infinitive phrases:

> WRONG: To find the ending of the experiment, there are
> stories in your library.
> RIGHT: To find the ending of the experiment, look in your
> library.

> WRONG: To get the facts, several sources should be read.
> RIGHT: To get the facts, you should read several sources.

EXERCISE 10.   Eight of the following sentences contain
dangling infinitive phrases. Make the necessary corrections.

1. To get the right books and magazines, the librarian should
be consulted.   2. To find the solution to the problem of the ticks,
Smith's recommendations are interesting.   3. To understand the
suggestions, they should be studied.   4. To learn about present
tick control, ask some farmers.   5. To get their ideas, your questions should be in order.   6. To find out about the value of cattle from India, you should ask a Texan.   7. To know of their use
in Texas as a method to combat ticks, a Texan can tell you.
8. To see pictures of Brahma cattle, *The National Geographic
Magazine* has some.   9. To know about these sacred cows, your
history teacher will tell you.   10. To understand their importance, a native of India should be questioned.

Another dangling phrase construction to avoid is the
one that begins with *due to*. The words *due to* are an adjective expression and therefore must modify a noun or a
pronoun. When *due to* introduces a phrase at the beginning
of a sentence, it usually dangles. There are two solutions
to the problem: (1) use *due to* as a predicate adjective after
a linking verb or (2) substitute the phrasal preposition
because of or *on account of*.

WRONG: Due to research, we are healthy. (*Or*) We are healthy due to research. (The phrase *due to research* modifies *healthy*, which is an adjective. Adverbs, not adjectives, modify adjectives; and it will be remembered that *due to* is an adjective expression.)

RIGHT: Our good health is due to research. (*Or*) We are healthy because of research.

Another dangling phrase, similar to *due to*, is one introduced by *caused by*, also an adjective expression.

WRONG: Our living conditions improved, caused by tireless research.

RIGHT: The improvement in our living conditions was caused by tireless research.

Review Exercise

EXERCISE. All but one of the following sentences lack coherence for one reason or another. Rewrite the poor sentences, making certain that all parts fit neatly together like those of a jigsaw puzzle.

1. Rubbing his magic lamp, fame and fortune came to Aladdin. 2. After apparently rubbing another kind of lamp, scientific miracles occur today. 3. Did you ever read where the insect world might destroy us? 4. The human race would be destroyed due to overwhelming numbers of insects. 5. We know that scientists have been at work constantly to keep insect life in check. 6. The discovery of DDT has done much to solve the problem. 7. The flies can be destroyed which carry malaria. 8. Afflicted communities will use it, and many of the 4000 persons who die each year of malaria in this country will be saved. 9. DDT was, as you know, used in the war in the South Pacific. 10. When used, many species of insect life were held in check. 11. There only was praise for it. 12. To know more about it, many stories are available. 13. Sprayed from planes, many insects were killed by it. 14. By doing this, disease was held in check. 15. The magic lamp saved lives that produced DDT.

239

CLARITY

Actually, if sentences are entirely coherent, they are also clear. The two qualities, coherence and clarity, are closely related.

EF S 4   Ways to Achieve Clarity

1. Avoid using indefinite subjects.

The words *they*, *you*, and *it* are the chief offenders. These three words should usually have definite antecedents; we generally know who *they* and *you* and *it* are. However, when we are forced to *guess*, their use is not good.

> WRONG: They say that blood plasma is one of the miracles of science.
> RIGHT: Blood plasma is one of the miracles of science. (*Or*) Doctors say that blood plasma is one of the miracles of science.

> WRONG: When a person is in an accident, you are often given plasma.
> RIGHT: When a person is in an accident, he is often given plasma.

In informal conversation or writing, *you* is frequently used. In more formal communication, the pronoun *one* is substituted.

> INFORMAL: You then may escape shock.
> FORMAL: One then may escape shock.

The word *it* may be used as an expletive and be entirely correct. The word *it* may be used as a pronoun and refer so definitely to an antecedent that there is no doubt about the meaning. However, when *it* is not an expletive or does not have a definite antecedent, its use should be avoided.

> EXPLETIVE: *It* is good to hear that.

> PRONOUN WITH DEFINITE ANTECEDENT: *Plasma* has saved
> thousands of lives; *it* is a godsend.
>
> PRONOUN WITHOUT DEFINITE ANTECEDENT: *It* says in the
> paper that blood banks must be enlarged.
>
> SENTENCE RECAST: According to an article in the paper,
> blood banks must be enlarged.

EXERCISE 1. Rewrite these sentences, eliminating all
indefinite subjects. Obviously, not every *they*, *you*, or *it* in
the sentences is indefinite.

1. They often sell plasma to persons who need it. 2. Because
they often have more blood than they need, they sell it to
hospitals. 3. If a hospital accepts a donor, you are paid for it.
4. It says in the paper that the blood is refrigerated. 5. Then
they examine it very carefully in a laboratory. 6. Your blood
is examined for harmful microbes. 7. It says in the article that
they take no chances. 8. You can feel entirely safe when they
give you plasma. 9. It would be too bad if anyone should have
to die just because they haven't enough plasma. 10. They say
that some communities are making certain that it will not
happen.

2. Avoid unnecessary shifting of (a) the subject of the sentence, (b) the voice of the verbs, (c) the tense of the verbs,
and (d) person.

(a) Subject of the sentence:

> WRONG: Surgery has advanced tremendously, and millions of
> lives have been saved.
>
> RIGHT: *Surgery* has advanced tremendously and (*it*) has
> saved millions of lives.

(b) Voice of the verbs:

> WRONG: Often surgeons take doomed persons, and they are
> restored to health.
>
> RIGHT: Often surgeons *take* doomed persons and *restore*
> them to health.

241

(c) Tense of the verbs:

See page 26 for a discussion of the *sequence of tenses.*

WRONG: Often in the old days a person became ill and dies.
RIGHT: Often in the old days a person *became* ill and *died.*

WRONG: My grandfather says to me last night, "There weren't any anesthetics."
RIGHT: My grandfather *said* to me last night, "There *weren't* any anesthetics."

(d) Person:

Shifting from first person to third or from second to first is very confusing. If you start with *you*, do not shift to *one* or *we* or some other pronoun.

WRONG: In surgery under gunfire, you were given a cannon ball; and one could bite on it during the operation.
RIGHT: In surgery under gunfire, *you* were given a cannon ball; and *you* could bite on it during the operation.

WRONG: When we consider surgery today and when we think of the marvelous anesthetics discovered to relieve our suffering, everyone is sincerely grateful.
RIGHT: When *we* consider surgery today and when *we* think of the marvelous anesthetics discovered to relieve our suffering, *we* are sincerely grateful.

EXERCISE 2. Rewrite each of these sentences to eliminate unnecessary shifting of the subject of the sentence, of the voice and tense of verbs, or of person:

1. Refrigeration is a new kind of anesthetic, and is said by patients to be painless.   2. If one must have an amputation, you may be given refrigeration anesthesia.   3. Cold numbs; and, consequently, no pain is felt by the patient.   4. It was used in a trial amputation in 1943 and proves its value.   5. An eighty-three-year-old man has stubbed his foot and was going to lose his foot and ankle.   6. His foot was packed in crushed ice, and

then the surgeon waited an hour.   7. At the end of that time, the surgeon was satisfied that the ice has numbed the foot and ankle; and the operation was performed.   8. We read that the operation was completely successful, and thus one is once again awed by the miracles of science.   9. The use of ice is effective because it slowed down the processes of the body.   10. When the body is chilled, less poison is produced; and, consequently, there are not so many chances for shock.

3. Avoid using pronouns which do not refer definitely to particular antecedents.

WRONG: Bob went with his friend Al to the library so that he could find a book about refrigeration anesthesia.

RIGHT: Bob went with his friend Al to the library so that Al could find a book about refrigeration anesthesia.

WRONG: Finding his pet dog on the library steps, he put his book in his hip pocket and chased the dog home.

RIGHT: Finding his pet dog on the library steps, Al chased him home. (Because of the humorous implications, it is better to omit the doubtful phrase.)

WRONG: Running down the street, he chased Huxley with a bone in his mouth.

RIGHT: Running down the street, Al chased Huxley, who had a bone in his mouth.

WRONG: Escaping into his own yard, he (Huxley) buried his bone.

RIGHT: Escaping into his own yard, Huxley buried his bone.

WRONG: Al's father is a doctor, the study of which interests him tremendously.

RIGHT: Al's father is a doctor. Medicine is a subject which interests Al tremendously.

EXERCISE 3. Correct these sentences:

1. After going through the card catalogue with his friend, he found some books on medicine.   2. That evening Al saw Huxley

with his book on medicine between his paws.   3. He apparently liked his book.   4. Al's father had named him for the English biologist, Thomas Huxley.   5. He was born in 1825.   6. Seeing the book on medicine, he commended him on his choice.   7. Al's father is a very good doctor, the importance of which should not be minimized.   8. He told Al more about refrigeration anesthesia, in which he was very much interested.   9. Shaking his head and rolling his big brown eyes wisely, he was listened to by Huxley. 10. Al was glad that he could answer his questions.

4. Avoid using the expletive *it* and the pronoun *it* in the same sentence.

> WRONG: It is true that it is a very simple method.
> RIGHT: It is true that refrigeration anesthesia is a very simple method.

EXERCISE 4.   Rewrite these sentences to avoid possible confusion:

1. It is known that it was used in Napoleon's retreat from Moscow.   2. It is true that it was a dreadful military disaster. 3. During the whole of it, it was extremely cold.   4. It was necessary to perform many amputations, and it was anesthesia that was used.   5. It is said that it was much less painful when the men were numbed by the cold.

5. Avoid mixing figures of speech.

> WRONG: Those who experiment for science have no bed of roses; but, despite all, they are willing to wade through it. (Does one *wade* through a *bed* of roses?)
> RIGHT: Those who experiment for science have no bed of roses; but, nevertheless, they are willing to endure the hardships.

> WRONG: They have climbed the ladder of success to the very heart of the problem.
> RIGHT: They have gone successfully to the very heart of the problem.

EXERCISE 5. Rewrite these sentences, eliminating all mixed figures of speech:

1. Science has gained a foothold on the page of time. 2. Experimenting in tubs of ice is a rough road. 3. Allowing oneself to be covered with ice for days would be the last straw on that rocky road. 4. Faith in the eventual outcome was the mainspring which took these scientists to the pinnacle of success. 5. Whether refrigeration anesthesia will stand the acid test of the shifting grains of sand is yet to be proved.

Review Exercise

EXERCISE. Find among the following the sentences which are not clear. Rewrite them in whatever way you think best.

1. They say that in an injury poisonous toxins are released in the blood. 2. These toxins circulate in the blood stream, and shock is produced. 3. Obviously, it is very serious if it happens. 4. The cold treatment reduces the toxins, and the spread of bacteria is delayed. 5. Many uninjured persons died in the blitz, and the cause is shock. 6. Many scientists are considering the use of ice in such cases. 7. Last night the doctor told my father that he had "immersion foot." 8. My father is a plumber and has a tough row to hoe to make one coin to rub against another. 9. He stood in icy water for hours, and "immersion foot" was developed as a result. 10. Putting ice bags on his numb feet, they say they always recover.

SUBORDINATION

To subordinate means simply "to make or consider of less value or importance." If parts of a sentence are of equal importance, *co-ordination* results. If the parts are unequal in value, they should be so arranged that one or more parts will receive the major emphasis. Thus, *subordination* results.

CO-ORDINATION: <u>All branches of science are exact,</u> but <u>surgery is one of the most exact.</u>

Less Important

SUBORDINATION: <u>Because an operation is a delicate proce-</u>

More Important

<u>dure, a surgeon must be extremely skillful.</u>

EF S 5   Ways to Effect Proper Subordination

1. Avoid making compound sentences of clauses of unequal importance.

WRONG: Dr. Harvey Cushing was a surgeon, and he specialized in brain surgery.

RIGHT: Dr. Harvey Cushing was a surgeon who specialized in brain surgery.

WRONG: In 1895, Dr. Cushing was a young intern; and one out of ten survived brain surgery.

RIGHT: When Dr. Cushing was a young intern in 1895, only one out of ten survived brain surgery.

WRONG: The reason for so many failures was lack of complete information, and everyone knew it.

RIGHT: Everyone knew that the reason for so many failures was lack of complete information.

EXERCISE 1. Rewrite the sentences in which the meaning is obscured by improper subordination:

1. Twenty-five years had passed, and the odds were reversed.
2. In his lifetime, Cushing operated on two thousand persons;

and they had brain tumors.   3. He dared to explore the unknown, and thousands are now living, and they would have died otherwise.   4. He was in Harvard Medical School, and something happened, and he almost gave up medicine.   5. He was administering ether during an operation, and the patient died.   6. Cushing felt so bad about the loss of the patient, and he helped to devise a chart, and it indicates the patient's pulse and respiration.   7. That chart is the one that is still being used.   8. Cushing studied in Europe for a year under a famous surgeon, and that surgeon inspired Cushing to study the brain. 9. In his experiments, he put a transparent "window" in an animal's skull, and he could make observations.   10. Cushing made the observations, and the animal was under an anesthetic.

2. Avoid putting the principal statement of a sentence in a subordinate clause.

WRONG: He recognized the effect of blood pressure on his problem when he made an important discovery.

RIGHT: When he recognized the effect of blood pressure on his problem, he made an important discovery.

WRONG: There was no instrument to measure blood pressure because Cushing began a search.

RIGHT: Because there was no instrument to measure blood pressure, Cushing began a search.

WRONG: He was in Italy while he found a device to measure blood pressure.

RIGHT: While he was in Italy, he found a device to measure blood pressure.

EXERCISE 2.   Rewrite the sentences in which you find poor subordination.   Be sure that each independent clause carries the important idea.

1. You have ever had a complete physical examination if you have had your blood pressure taken.   2. The doctor put a little armlet around your arm when you had Dr. Harvey Cushing to thank.   3. Dr. Cushing, having discovered the device in Italy,

brought it to America, which he did immediately. 4. It was necessary to know the location of brain tumors because Dr. Cushing traced all the nerves of the body. 5. Now a doctor sees the part of the body affected when he knows the location of the tumor. 6. Because this is possible, Dr. Cushing did the minute research. 7. As he devised new instruments, he continued in the work. 8. He needed something special whenever he invented it. 9. Each new discovery that he made meant the saving of more lives. 10. He kept working and studying as the mortality rate of his operations kept dropping.

3. Avoid excessive subordination.

Notice that too many dependent clauses may obscure the meaning of the sentence.

POOR: Although some surgeons who operated on brains which had growths insisted that an operation if it was to be successful should be done with as much speed as was possible, the operations which Dr. Cushing conducted often took three or four hours, which very obviously was a long time.

BETTER: Although some surgeons specializing in brain tumors insisted that an operation should be done speedily, Dr. Cushing's operations often took three or four hours.

EXERCISE 3. The meaning of each of these sentences is weakened because of excessive subordination. Rewrite the sentences, making the necessary corrections.

1. An operation which Dr. Cushing performed when he was in France while World War I was in progress is proof of what his hands, which were very skillful, could do when necessity arose, as it often did. 2. While he was in France, he was asked to operate on a French soldier in whose head was a piece of shrapnel which no one had been able to extricate because it was so deeply embedded in his brain. 3. Dr. Cushing, who invented the instruments which he needed whenever he needed them, took a six-

inch nail which he made blunt and which he attached to a magnet.
4. When Dr. Cushing operated on the soldier, who had been in great pain, he used the nail, which was magnetized, as a searching tool which he hoped would pull out the piece of shrapnel which was embedded in his brain.   5. Although Dr. Cushing hoped that the nail, which was magnetized, would pull out the shrapnel the first time that it was inserted into the wound, which was several inches deep, he was not discouraged when it did not come the first time or the second or the third time that he tried but tried again, which was the fourth time.   6. Suddenly the little piece of shrapnel that was embedded in the brain of the French soldier who lay on the operating table was caught by the miraculous little device which Dr. Cushing had invented because it was the sort of thing that he needed for that particular operation. 7. With the many casualties which are caused by any war that takes place, Dr. Cushing, who was anxious to help in any way that he could, frequently operated seven or eight times a day. 8. Moreover, as was his custom whether he was at home or whether he was in a front-line hospital, he kept minute records of each operation which he performed because each one gave him added information in the medical field to which he had given his life.   9. While he was in France, during which time the war was continuing, he was stricken with polyneuritis, which is an infection of the nervous system and which is very rare.   10. The infection which he had brought on a numbness which spread over his body so that he could move only with great difficulty.

4. Avoid using the *and which* or *but which* construction except to join two adjective clauses.

WRONG: The numbness reached his hands and which had given life to hundreds.

RIGHT: The numbness reached his hands, which had given life to hundreds.

WRONG: This was a personal calamity for Dr. Cushing and which the world shared.

RIGHT: This was a personal calamity for Dr. Cushing and one which the world shared.

WRONG: Fortunately the numbness gradually left his hands but which did not ever leave his legs.

RIGHT: Fortunately the numbness gradually left his hands, but it did not ever leave his legs.

If *two or more* adjective clauses are being joined, the *and which* and *but which* constructions are correct.

RIGHT: Still Dr. Cushing overcame the calamity which had struck him and which never left him.

RIGHT: In him was a will which could be handicapped but which could not be downed.

EXERCISE 4. Rewrite the sentences that are incorrect.

1. Dr. Cushing received another blow and which was a crushing one. 2. One day he was about to enter the operating room and which was in readiness. 3. On the operating table lay a woman who was suffering from a brain tumor and who had been blinded by it. 4. He was handed a message which told of the death of a son. 5. It had been an automobile accident and which had taken his son's life. 6. Dr. Cushing's response to that emergency showed a greatness of spirit and which we all admire. 7. He was a man of great spiritual strength and whom we respect. 8. He performed the operation and which had been planned. 9. His grief, and which was a personal matter, had to be submerged in work, and which was duty. 10. There was a man and who was a great American.

5. Avoid weakening subordination by inserting *and* or *but* before phrases.

WRONG: Dr. Cushing continued research and to the end of his life.

RIGHT: Dr. Cushing continued research to the end of his life.

WRONG: He devised electrical "knives," and making them of fine wires.

RIGHT: He devised electrical "knives," making them of fine wires.

EXERCISE 5. Correct each of these sentences:

1. The electrical "knives" could be used and with greater safety than the ordinary surgical knives. 2. Dr. Cushing in many ways advanced science, and giving new techniques and new devices. 3. Moreover, he helped the poor and in many ways. 4. Thus, he made life richer, and giving health and happiness to many. 5. He is a shining example and among the great scientists of the world.

Review Exercise

EXERCISE. Find among the following the sentences weakened by improper subordination. Rewrite them, making the necessary corrections.

1. We consider the great scientists, and we recognize certain qualities in common.
2. Each has possessed patience, and which is a necessary quality.
3. Leeuwenhoek who peered through his lenses which he painstakingly ground himself so that he might see his "wretched beasties," as he called them, never wrote down a conclusion which he had reached until he had seen exactly the same thing hundreds of times.
4. Pasteur tried to find a safeguard against rabies, and inoculating fifty dogs before daring to come to a conclusion.
5. Walter Reed fought against yellow fever, which was killing people like flies and which defied treatment.
6. We read of Reed's many experiments when we are awed.
7. Theobald Smith worked tirelessly, and he wanted to find the cause of Texas fever.
8. Cushing believed there were better ways to perform an operation when he experimented until he found them.
9. Their determination to find the right answer and only the right answer can be seen and in many ways.
10. Doing things the easy way is not the method and which scientists seem to follow.

251

EMPHASIS

The person who says, "Now let me emphasize . . ." may be able to achieve the desired emphasis through certain tricks of sentence arrangement.

EF S 6   Ways to Achieve Emphasis

1. Place an attention-seizing word at the beginning of the sentence.

> WEAK: The doctor suddenly fainted.
> EMPHATIC: Suddenly the doctor fainted.

Obviously, in no piece of writing or speaking would you begin every sentence with an attention-seizing word. Too much emphasis can be as bad as too little. The following exercise merely shows the possibilities of this kind of emphasis.

EXERCISE 1. Rearrange each of these sentences to give it a startling beginning:

1. You must surely have heard of the Mayo brothers. 2. They are known universally for their contributions to medicine. 3. These men, kind, generous, and skillful, deserved their fame. 4. The Mayo Clinic has undoubtedly saved thousands of lives. 5. Dr. Will and Dr. Charlie worked conscientiously and consistently to alleviate pain.

2. Place the key words of the sentence near the end.

> WEAK: The boys learned much from their father, who was a doctor.
> EMPHATIC: From their father, who was a doctor, the boys learned much.
> WEAK: There were practically no hospitals in those early days.
> EMPHATIC: In those early days, there were practically no hospitals.

EXERCISE 2. Rewrite these sentences, placing the key word or words at the end:

1. The elder Dr. Mayo used neighbors' spare bedrooms for his operating rooms. 2. Dr. Mayo had devised many of his instruments like Dr. Cushing. 3. By the local blacksmith some of them had been forged. 4. Dr. Mayo performed many successful operations with the aid of his two sons and under such crude conditions. 5. The boys were learning about surgery from their earliest years, therefore.

3. Repeat key words to give emphasis.

WEAK: From their father, the Mayo brothers learned many skills. They used these in later years.

EMPHATIC: From their father, the Mayo brothers learned many skills. These skills they used in later years.

EXERCISE 3. How could these groups of sentences be improved through the repetition of key words?

1. An amazing story is told of one operation. Surely it succeeded despite all odds.
2. The boys were there to give assistance. Their help included sterilizing instruments, holding the instruments, and doing odd jobs.
3. To a young doctor was given the responsibility of administering the ether. That was a very serious job.
4. In the middle of the operation, he toppled to the floor in a faint. That period of unconsciousness certainly came at the worst possible time.
5. There was no time to revive him. To bring him to, might mean the difference between life and death to the woman on the operating table.

Repetition is sometimes very annoying. It should be used only to give occasional punch to sentences. Notice in the following how offensive repetition can be when it is not a planned and purposeful repetition:

POOR: Dr. Mayo *told* Charlie to administer ether. Charlie heard what his father *told* him to do, but he was *only* nine and *only* a little boy for his age. Nevertheless, the *only* thing for him *to do* was what his father *told* him *to do*.

BETTER: Dr. Mayo *told* Charlie to administer ether. Charlie heard what his father *said*, but he was *only* nine and *not* very tall for his age. Nevertheless, he *did* as his father *directed*.

Sometimes the use of pronouns can eliminate unpleasant repetition of nouns. However, each pronoun must have a definite antecedent.

POOR: *Charlie* was too short to reach the patient's face. Quickly *Charlie* looked around the room and spied a cracker box. In a second, *Charlie* was on the cracker box and doing as *Charlie's* father had directed.

BETTER: *Charlie* was too short to reach the patient's face. Quickly *he* looked around the room and spied a cracker box. In a second, *he* was on the cracker box and doing as *his* father had directed.

EXERCISE 4. Rewrite this paragraph, making whatever corrections you think are necessary:

In 1871, the elder Dr. Mayo went to New York for a year of study. While Dr. Mayo was in New York during the year, Dr. Mayo became absorbed in the work of Pasteur and Lister. Pasteur and Lister in their work with microbes and antiseptics had revolutionized the work in medicine. The elder Dr. Mayo absorbed from the teachings of Pasteur and Lister all that he could. Dr. Mayo was determined to carry back to Minnesota the benefit of what he had learned.

4. Arrange the parts of a series in a logical or an ascending order of importance.

WEAK: Dr. Mayo mortgaged his home, scrimped, and saved to buy a microscope.

EMPHATIC: Dr. Mayo scrimped, saved, and mortgaged his home to buy a microscope.

EXERCISE 5. Rewrite each of these sentences, placing the details of the series in an ascending order:

1. The six-hundred-dollar microscope was very precious and new and shiny. 2. The boys liked to make discoveries, to jot down their findings, and to look at specimens through it. 3. In their father's office there was a skeleton that was battered and ugly and old. 4. They learned from it their lessons in anatomy, called it old Chief Broken-Nose, laughed at it. 5. Their father, the microscope, and Chief Broken-Nose were their early inspirations for learning.

5. For the most part, use the active voice since it creates a livelier style than the passive voice.

POOR: In 1883, a tornado whipped through Rochester, Minnesota. Buildings *were destroyed*, twenty persons *were killed*, and three hundred *were injured* by it.

BETTER: In 1883, a tornado whipped through Rochester, Minnesota, *destroyed* buildings, *killed* twenty persons, and *injured* three hundred.

EXERCISE 6. How might these sentences be rewritten to give them a livelier tone?

1. No hospital was had by Rochester at that time. 2. His patients were being taken care of by Dr. Mayo in four spare bedrooms in different private homes. 3. Quickly temporary quarters were furnished by the town officials. 4. The need for a hospital was indicated by this dreadful emergency. 5. Very often progress is hastened by some unexpected event.

6. Give the most important idea of the sentence the proper proportion of space.

POOR: After the passing of the emergency that had struck Rochester with such terrific force and with such serious results, plans for a hospital were made.

BETTER: After the emergency had passed, plans for a hospital were made.

EXERCISE 7.   In each of the following sentences, determine the part that should be emphasized.   If another part
of the sentence has been given a disproportionate amount
of space, make the necessary changes.

1. Because of his age and perhaps the weariness that comes with
long years of service, for such is the way of life, the elder Mayo
gave his sons the responsibility of managing the new hospital.
2. At that time, for we must remember it was 1889 and people
had not yet been educated to the idea of hospitals, people dis-
trusted hospitals.   3. However, because of their skill, which was
tremendous as all will testify who were ever treated by them, Dr.
Will and Dr. Charlie proved the success of the plan.   4. The fond-
ness that the two brothers felt for each other and the easy way
in which they carried on their affairs can be seen in a story which
is true which is told of their dividing their practice geographically.
5. Later in their clinic, which came as a natural result of the success
which they experienced in their hospital, each took different parts
of the human body for his field of specialization.

**7. Do not let wordiness obscure the parts of the sentence
that should be emphasized.**

> WEAK: By the year 1910, Rochester, situated in rural Min-
> nesota, was referred to by doctors and laymen from all
> over the country as "the medical crossroads of the world."
> EMPHATIC: By 1910, Rochester was generally referred to as
> "the medical crossroads of the world."

EXERCISE 8.   Reduce the wordiness in these sentences,
and notice the improvement in emphasis:

1. The Mayo brothers decided with their usual breadth of
vision that their clinic should be a center of training for doctors
who wished to learn more about the new and better methods of
surgery.   2. One of the many visitors who attended the clinic
tells of an operation — a very complicated one — which he and a
large group of other surgeons saw Dr. Will Mayo perform with
great skill and ease.   3. As he worked and with the large group

watching each movement that he made, Dr. Will described in soft, easy tones each of the steps that he was making, how each was made and the purpose of each, so that everyone would understand fully all that he was doing. 4. One crisis after another occurred, each of which was exceedingly serious and to practically any other surgeon would have meant defeat; but each one Dr. Will took care of, as one might expect, in his way, which was always quiet and efficient. 5. The doctors who watched, many of them with years of experience and accustomed to practically any kind of emergency, finally having seen almost more than they could bear, began to slip out quietly from the room in which the operation was taking place.

8. Use periodic sentences occasionally to give emphasis.

A *periodic sentence* is one that reaches "grammatical completeness only at the end." It may begin with phrases and dependent clauses, but its meaning is not clear until the subject and predicate are reached at the end of the sentence. The periodic sentence is in contrast with the *loose sentence*, which is "grammatically complete at one or more points before the end."

PERIODIC SENTENCE: Because they were interested in research which would lead to prevention as well as cure, *the brothers established the Mayo Foundation.*

LOOSE SENTENCE: *The brothers established the Mayo Foundation* because they were interested in research which would lead to prevention as well as cure.

The *occasional* use of the periodic sentence gives emphasis since the reader or listener is forced to *wait* to find out the meaning.

EXERCISE 9. For practice, change each of these loose sentences into a periodic sentence:

1. A medical college was set up with the million and a half dollars which they gave to the University of Minnesota for the

work of the Mayo Foundation.   2. The college was set up at the clinic because it possessed all the necessary facilities for observation and practice.   3. A student was not permitted to watch even a simple operation until he had spent a year learning how to diagnose.   4. The Mayos discouraged unnecessary surgery with their strong emphasis on correct diagnosis.   5. Dr. Charlie began the research on the use of iodine to prevent goiter although he himself was famous everywhere for his goiter surgery.

9. Use balanced sentences occasionally for emphasis.

The word *balance* indicates the structure. A *balanced* sentence is one made up of two or more co-ordinate clauses in which the phrases are similar in structure.

> BALANCED SENTENCE: Cure is surely important, but prevention is even more important.
>
> BALANCED SENTENCE: A general practitioner must know much about many diseases; a specialist in a clinic must know much about one disease.

EXERCISE 10. For each of the following, supply a second part that balances the first:

1. At a clinic one doctor may specialize in the heart, –?–.
2. The heart specialist examines your heart, –?–.
3. A person who goes through a clinic has the advice of many doctors, –?–.
4. The Mayo Clinic has given help to the great and the rich, –?–.
5. The rich are charged according to their wealth, –?–.

EXERCISE 11. Make up balanced sentences, using these key words:

1. football — baseball	6. work — play
2. night — day	7. duty — pleasure
3. friend — enemy	8. sickness — health
4. truth — falsehood	9. present — past
5. age — youth	10. fact — fiction

10. Use parallel structure occasionally for emphasis.

The word *parallel* also indicates the kind of structure that will result. In using parallel structure, try always to be consistent. For example, a series may be made up of words, of phrases, or of clauses. A series of words should not contain a clause; a series of clauses should not contain a phrase.

WRONG: The influence of Leeuwenhoek, Pasteur, and what Lister accomplished in the field of antiseptics goes on and on.

RIGHT: The influence of *Leeuwenhoek*, *Pasteur*, and *Lister* goes on and on. (three nouns)

WRONG: By developing a microscope, by discovering the value of inoculation, and in the use of antiseptics, these three scientists greatly advanced the cause of science.

RIGHT: *By developing a microscope, by discovering the value of inoculation,* and *by finding the power of antiseptics,* these three scientists greatly advanced the cause of science. (three phrases beginning with *by*)

WRONG: Throughout the ages, true men of science have been those who know, that never cease in their search for knowledge, and from whom the world has received benefit.

RIGHT: Throughout the ages, true men of science have been those *who know, who never cease in their search for knowledge,* and *who use their knowledge for the benefit of others.* (three parallel adjective clauses)

EXERCISE 12. Rewrite these sentences, making the parts parallel:

1. A few years ago the king of Siam, suffering from an eye ailment and who wanted to have it remedied and having known the reputation of the distinguished eye surgeon, Dr. John M. Wheeler, came to this country.

2. Dr. Wheeler called in Mr. Edgar B. Burchell, a man who is a self-taught bacteriologist, that is an authority on the skull, and because of whose skill surgery has been made safer.

3. The king of Siam recognized Burchell's extraordinary ability, becoming curious, and later he questioned Dr. Wheeler about him.

4. He learned that Burchell was born on New York's West Side, how he was one of nine children, and the way he was affected by the misery of sickness all around him.

5. He was unhappy, terribly disappointed, and feeling bitter when, because of poverty, he was forced to leave school.

11. Separate the parts of a sentence when one part obviously requires emphasis.

> WEAK: Burchell did not forget his ambition to be a doctor, decided to get some kind of job near doctors, and landed a job as janitor in the New York Eye and Ear Infirmary.
>
> EMPHATIC: Burchell did not forget his ambition to be a doctor and decided to get some kind of job near doctors. He landed a job as janitor in the New York Eye and Ear Infirmary.

EXERCISE 13. How might these sentences be made more emphatic through a separation of parts?

1. The young man scrubbed on his hands and knees twelve hours a day, didn't mind it a bit, and had his evenings free for secret "experiments" in the laboratory.

2. The surgeons' frogs and guinea pigs began to disappear, no one could understand why, and one surgeon asked Burchell to keep an eye on them.

3. Burchell went to lectures, listened to scholarly discussions, and learned.

4. The interns didn't like some of their jobs and taught Burchell how to do them, and soon he was a laboratory assistant.

5. As a boy, he had listened to stories about Horatio Alger and had loved them, but his own story equaled any Horatio Alger story.

12. Place ideas of lesser value in a subordinate position.

WRONG: Because Burchell allowed no obstacle to stand in his way, he was determined to succeed.

RIGHT: Because Burchell was determined to succeed, he allowed no obstacle to stand in his way.

For a full discussion of this topic, see pages 246 to 251.

Review Exercise

EXERCISE. Rewrite each of these sentences to give it proper emphasis:

1. At the infirmary, all his jobs were done well by Burchell.
2. The officials decided to send him to Vienna for study because he showed such remarkable ability.
3. He was in Vienna while Dr. Neumann showed him his collection of skulls.
4. Burchell made up his mind immediately to make better ones.
5. He bought some bones; then he bleached, hinged them together, sawed, and bored to produce a collection far superior to Neumann's.
6. Burchell's knowledge of the skull, where the nerves and arteries are, of variations in formation is universally recognized.
7. He has a famous eye collection in addition to a collection of skulls.
8. Burchell helped to devise a way to remove particles of metal from the eye. These little specks had been dangerous, difficult, and sometimes an impossible job to remove.
9. Burchell has been given an honorary Doctor of Science degree in recognition of his long years of service.
10. The roll of honor includes names like Leeuwenhoek, Pasteur, Lister, Reed, Cushing, the Mayos; and Burchell's name belongs there, too.

VARIETY

Variety is the final touch that gives color and interest and the proverbial spice to sentence structure. Sentences all built according to the same blueprint are dull and monotonous.

EF S 7   Ways to Achieve Variety

1. Use compound parts to relieve sentence monotony.

Compound subjects, compound verbs, compound direct objects, compound predicate nouns, compound objects of prepositions are some of the possibilities.

> POOR: The Bible was one book that influenced Edgar B. Burchell. Gray's *Anatomy* was another.
>
> BETTER: The Bible and Gray's *Anatomy* were two books that influenced Edgar B. Burchell.

2. Use different kinds of sentences as they are classified according to structure.

Too many simple sentences result in a choppy, uninteresting style. A mixture of simple, compound, complex, and compound-complex sentences gives the desired variety.

See the discussion of sentences beginning on page 2.

3. Use both loose and periodic sentences.

A *loose sentence*, you remember, is one which is "grammatically complete at one or more points before the end." A *periodic sentence* is one that reaches "grammatical completeness only at the end."

> LOOSE SENTENCE: *We remember another great scientist* who was influenced by the Bible.
>
> PERIODIC SENTENCE: When the name of George Washington Carver is mentioned, *we remember his reliance upon God.*

4. Use different kinds of sentences as they are classified according to meaning.

Most persons use declarative sentences more than any other kind. The occasional use of an interrogative, an exclamatory, or an imperative sentence will add variety.

EXERCISE 1. Rewrite the following sentences according to the directions in parentheses:

1. Faith made Dr. Carver the great man that he was. Intelligence was there, too. His unflagging perseverance was another quality. (Combine, using a compound subject.)
2. He wondered this. Why had the Creator made the peanut? (Combine, making a complex sentence.)
3. He separated the elements of the peanut. He studied them carefully. He made combinations of the elements. He found three hundred commercial products based on the peanut. (Combine, using a compound predicate.)
4. He did all this laborious research for a reason. (Change to an interrogative sentence.)
5. He gave his life to science because he possessed a great love for humanity. (Change to a periodic sentence.)

5. Use a variety of sentence length.

Too many short sentences make a choppy style; too many long sentences make a slow, heavy style. A little of one and a little of the other can give variety.

6. Use an occasional series of words, phrases, or clauses.

SERIES OF WORDS: Dr. Carver separated *the oils, the gums,* and *the resins.*

SERIES OF PHRASES: His searching mind produced new uses *for peanuts, for sweet potatoes,* and *for cotton.*

SERIES OF CLAUSES: *When we consider his background, when we remember his struggle for education,* and *when we realize his contribution to humanity,* we are humbled.

7. Use the inverted order occasionally.

In the inverted order, the predicate comes first.

              Subj.   Verb
REGULAR ORDER: *Carver was born* of slave parents.

                 Verb   Subj.
INVERTED ORDER: There *were* dreadful *tragedies* in his youth.

                                     Verb
INVERTED ORDER: From these beginnings *came* a great
   Subj.
scientist.

8. Use verbals occasionally.

PARTICIPLE: *Determined* to succeed, Carver drove on.

GERUND: *Overcoming* obstacles was not easy.

INFINITIVE: The boy was hungry *to learn.*

EXERCISE 2. Rewrite these sentences according to the directions in parentheses:

1. Carver's education for the first ten years came from Webster's blue-back speller. (Use inverted order.)
2. He thirsted for knowledge. He mastered the speller before he started to school.   (Combine, using a participial phrase.)
3. Carver's early education came from the woods. It was supplemented by Webster's spelling book. He went to a one-room school in Missouri for a year. (Combine, using a series.)
4. He spent three years at Simpson College in Iowa. Then he went to Iowa State College. He won many friends. He also won his Bachelor of Science degree in 1894. (Combine to eliminate the choppy style.)
5. He was very good in chemistry. The college offered him a position in the laboratory. He was glad to accept. (Reword to eliminate the short, choppy sentences.)

9. Use appositives occasionally.

ADJECTIVE CLAUSE: Booker T. Washington, who was head of Tuskegee Institute, asked Carver to join his staff.

APPOSITIVE: Booker T. Washington, head of Tuskegee Institute, asked Carver to join his staff.

10. Use direct discourse to break monotony.

INDIRECT DISCOURSE: Booker T. Washington said that he would be proud if Carver would come to Tuskegee and cast down his bucket.

DIRECT DISCOURSE: Booker T. Washington said, "I'd be proud if you would come here and cast down your bucket."

11. Use words which blend together harmoniously.

POOR: Carver happily took Tuskegee's token.

BETTER: Carver happily accepted Tuskegee's offer.

EXERCISE 3. Rewrite these sentences according to the directions in parentheses:

1. Carver saw that cotton, which was the chief crop of the South, was failing. (Rewrite, using an appositive.)
2. It seemed as though Carver was asking himself what he could do to help. (Change to direct discourse.)
3. The planters were appalled by the paltry crops which were produced. (Eliminate inharmonious words.)
4. The planters said to Carver that he must help them or they would be ruined. (Change to direct discourse.)

12. Use a variety of sentence beginnings.

By beginning sentences in various ways, much interest can be added. Here are some of the ways:

(1) Begin some sentences with prepositional phrases.

PHRASE AT END: Dr. Carver set to work with his usual zeal.

PHRASE AT BEGINNING: With his usual zeal, Dr. Carver set to work.

(2) Begin some sentences with adverbial clauses.

CLAUSE AT END: He suggested the planting of sweet potatoes and peanuts after he had studied the problem.

CLAUSE AT BEGINNING: After he had studied the problem, he suggested the planting of sweet potatoes and peanuts.

(3) Begin some sentences with an adverb.

> ADVERB AT END: The planters followed his advice slowly.
>
> ADVERB AT BEGINNING: Slowly the planters followed his advice.

(4) Begin some sentences with an adjective.

> ADJECTIVES WITHIN SENTENCE: The planters, hesitant and doubtful, were waiting.
>
> ADJECTIVES AT BEGINNING: Hesitant and doubtful, the planters were waiting.

(5) Begin some sentences with a participial phrase.

> PHRASE WITHIN SENTENCE: Dr. Carver, planting a field of his own, proved the value of rotation of crops.
>
> PHRASE AT BEGINNING: Planting a field of his own, Dr. Carver proved the value of rotation of crops.

(6) Begin some sentences with an infinitive phrase.

> PHRASE AT END OF SENTENCE: It was necessary to enrich the land.
>
> PHRASE AT BEGINNING: To enrich the land was necessary.

(7) Begin some sentences with a nominative absolute.

> CLAUSE AT BEGINNING: After Dr. Carver had proved his point, sweet potatoes and peanuts were planted in abundance.
>
> NOMINATIVE ABSOLUTE AT BEGINNING: Dr. Carver having proved his point, sweet potatoes and peanuts were planted in abundance.

(8) Avoid beginning too often with the same word.

> POOR: I like the conclusion of the story. I had wondered what Dr. Carver would do if there were too many sweet potatoes and peanuts. I think humanity owes him a debt.
>
> BETTER: I like the conclusion of the story. His solution of the problem of an overproduction of sweet potatoes and peanuts was clever. Certainly humanity owes him a debt.

EXERCISE 4. Rewrite each of these sentences, giving it a new beginning:

1. Dr. Carver discovered in the peanut vitamins A and B.
2. More peanuts were used after he discovered how to use them in salad dressing.   3. The products using peanuts gradually increased.   4. Dr. Carver, slow, thorough, and patient, was determined to find a solution to the problem.   5. He saved the market for peanuts by finding three hundred products based on them. 6. Dr. Carver turned his attention to the sweet potato after the peanut problem was solved.   7. It was a great achievement to find over a hundred products based on the humble sweet potato. 8. There were many products which he made from sweet potatoes. There was flour. There was a "tapioca." There was a product which could be used as coffee.   9. Dr. Carver was giving his life to humanity, forgetting the tragedies of his boyhood. 10. The world has been made better and happier through him.

Review Exercises

EXERCISE 1. Rewrite each of the following, making whatever corrections you think are necessary:

1. In all ways, George Washington Carver an exceedingly modest man.
2. The peanut planters were grateful to Dr. Carver for his help to show their gratitude they sent him a sizable check.
3. Dr. Carver, although he was grateful to them for their thoughtfulness, returned the check.
4. He writes to them that God didn't charge anything for his work and that he wouldn't either.
5. During his lifetime he accumulated money and which he neither needed nor wanted.
6. In a bank crash in 1933 (as you will remember there were many such incidents in the early 1930's which left many persons destitute), Dr. Carver lost most of his money.
7. It didn't bother him. He said that he wasn't using it himself.
8. When he gave all the rest of his money away for the purpose of founding the Carver Creative Research Laboratories.

9. Everything that he did — and very obviously his contributions go on and on in many different fields — was for the good of humanity.

10. He was only interested in improving life for others.

EXERCISE 2. Eight of the following sentences should be rewritten:

1. Anyone mentions Dr. Carver, and he always speaks of his simplicity.
2. Enjoying life as he found it, an automobile was unnecessary.
3. He chose his clothes carelessly, and they were put on for covering rather than for beauty.
4. They say that his appearance before the Ways and Means Committee of Congress was a memorable occasion.
5. He was given fifteen minutes to plead the cause of the Southern peanut planters.
6. The members of the committee were tired, it came his turn to speak.
7. When he started to speak, no one was in the mood to listen.
8. Dressed in coat and trousers and that didn't match, his speech began.
9. In simple, sincere language he told his story that tale was so extraordinary that the committee listened in spite of themselves.
10. He finished, and they begged that he tell them more.

EXERCISE 3. Rewrite these sentences, according to the directions in parentheses:

1. The members of the committee voted for his recommendation, listened, and applauded. (Arrange verbs in series in ascending order of importance.)
2. He had been allotted only fifteen minutes, but he spoke for two hours. (Subordinate one clause.)
3. A bronze plaque was dedicated to him at Tuskegee in 1931 because of his great service to science. (Change to a periodic sentence.)

4. Because no plaque was really necessary, the memory of him is enshrined in the hearts of all Americans. (Give proper subordination.)

5. The name of George Washington Carver, born of slave parents and forced to work his way through college, belongs with those of Leeuwenhoek, Pasteur, Lister, Reed, Cushing, and the Mayos. (Eliminate wordiness.)

EXERCISE 4. Rewrite the following friendly letter, making the necessary corrections in sentence structure:

> 798 Cherry Lane
> Grand Rapids 5, Michigan
> November 22, 19—

Dear Ted,

Have been wanting to write to you for some time but have been spending all my time doing some extra reading. As I told you in my last letter. Mr. Reagan gave me a book. It was *The Mayos — Pioneers in Medicine.* The author was Regli. I started reading it, and I didn't think it would interest me. Before I had gone far in it. I couldn't lay it down.

I keep thinking this. I'd like to be a doctor. I'd like to do something and which would help others. Although my grades (or should we talk about grades at this time of the year?) show that I'm no brain trust. Nevertheless, I think I'd make a good doctor. So, I'm reading books like *The Horse and Buggy Doctor, Magic in a Bottle.* I'm also reading *Behind the Sulfa Drugs.*

You'll probably remind me. At various times I've wanted to be a policeman, a streetcar conductor, and pull people's teeth. You must admit, however, that though my fancy in the past has flitted hither and yon like a butterfly, lately it has been sticking like glue to science.

I only have talked about myself in this letter. Maybe I'm already a "buggy" doctor.

> Sincerely,
> *Bob*

EXERCISE 5. Rewrite the following business letter, improving all sentences which seem weak:

798 Cherry Lane
Grand Rapids 5, Michigan
December 1, 19—

Holland Book Shop
1223 Ohio Street
Chicago 17, Illinois

Gentlemen:

I am looking for a book about Walter Reed. I believe there is a play and which is about him and which is called *Yellow Jack*. I think the authors are Howard and De Kruif.

If you have this book in stock. Will appreciate your sending it to me. I do not know the price, and will you send it to me C.O.D.?

Thanking you.

Yours very sincerely,
Robert Channing

EXERCISE 6. Rewrite the following letter:

Holland Book Shop
1223 Ohio Street
Chicago 17, Illinois

Mr. Robert Channing
798 Cherry Lane
Grand Rapids 5, Michigan

Dear Mr. Channing:

Having received your order, the book is now on its way to you. We can be of any service to you in the future, and we hope you will let us know.

Yours truly,
J. T. Holland

THE PARAGRAPH

UNITY OF THE PARAGRAPH

The old saying "United we stand; divided we fall" is applicable in the building of paragraphs. Unity, or oneness, is the first essential quality.

Par Definition

A paragraph is a sentence or a group of sentences developing a single idea.

Usually a paragraph consists of a group of sentences. In the case of direct quotations, however, paragraphs are frequently made up of single sentences.

> "What comes after seventy-five?" asked the six-year-old boy of his father.
> "Seventy-six," came the answer.
> "That's the spirit!" said the boy, delighted with his own joke.

EXERCISE 1. Each of the following paragraphs fails because it does not keep to a single idea. Find in each the

271

sentence or sentences which detract from the unity of thought.

1. Dry ice has been used to create rain and snow. With the right kind of clouds and the right temperature, dry ice can make the moisture in the clouds turn to rain or snow. Vincent J. Schaefer of the General Electric laboratories developed the method. With the proper conditions, a dollar's worth of dry ice can produce a sizable snowstorm. This control of weather will be of help in the development of winter resorts. Fifteen dollars' worth will result in a deluge of rain.

2. Vilhjalmur Stefansson has exploded many of the myths concerning the arctic. According to Stefansson, the temperature in the summer often goes to 90°. Flowering plants, including poppies, bluebells, and even the common dandelion, are in great abundance. Stefansson is a famous explorer who has spent many years of his life in the arctic regions. Moreover, the buzzing of flies and mosquitoes is no uncommon sound. Usually Northern mosquitoes are not disease carriers. The abundance of plant, animal, bird, and insect life in the arctic has been well established; and, thus, the myth of the barren North is exploded.

3. Daniel Boone learned to walk in the forest without leaving a trail. He followed the beds of streams to disguise his path. He jumped over chasms by clinging to wild grapevines. That is the sort of stunt one sees adventurers do in the movies. He made friends with the right Indians. Thus, Daniel Boone learned the intricate ways of successful trail blazing.

4. Superman has had a healthful influence on the youth of America. At least three million persons follow his adventures avidly. His adventures are syndicated in more than two hundred newspapers. Superman is a kind of modern Robin Hood, fighting injustice, intolerance, and all sorts of evils. In some ways, Jesse James was the same sort of person. In some of the comic strips, he has urged his young readers to go to the dentist and to work hard at school. During the war, he was constantly lending his support to various important drives. Buck Rogers is another popular cartoon figure.

5. Some romantic figures in fiction are so highly exaggerated that they become caricatures. Caricaturing depends upon distortion to produce a particular result. Cartoons are caricatures. Superman is not a caricature. Cartoonists always picture Mr. Roosevelt with a toothy smile; they emphasize Mr. Truman's glasses and Mr. Hoover's high, stiff collar. Dickens was a master at caricaturing. He made Uriah Heep an unforgettable type of false humility; he made Bill Sykes the exemplification of criminality. Because one characteristic is emphasized to the exclusion of all others, such characters are caricatures rather than representations of real people.

EXERCISE 2. Study some of your own paragraphs, and decide whether they have unity. If changes are necessary, make them; and then notice the improvement.

Par 1   The Topic Sentence

The sentence which states the main idea of the paragraph is called the topic sentence.

The topic sentence is an important guidepost to both the writer and the reader. Certainly the formulation of a topic sentence helps the writer to stay on a single track: he knows he must make every sentence in the paragraph help to explain and amplify the meaning of the topic sentence. For the reader, a topic sentence is important since it provides the gist of the idea of the paragraph. It tells him exactly where he is headed.

In paragraphs of exposition and argumentation, the topic sentence usually appears first. However, it may appear within the paragraph, at the end, at both the beginning and the end; and sometimes it is implied rather than stated. (Paragraphs of narration and of description usually do not have topic sentences since the meaning is made clear in other ways.)

The paragraphs that follow show the various positions of the topic sentence. The first one appeared originally in *The New Yorker*.

1. Topic sentence at the beginning

At last there appears to be a means of dealing with historical novels. A new machine called Ultrafax, combining radio, photography, and television, recently sent the entire text of *Gone with the Wind* three miles through the air at the speed of light. There is your solution for historical novels: Point the thing straight up, put on a novel, and let it go. Why has nobody thought of this splendid machine before?

E. B. WHITE [1]

2. Topic sentence within the paragraph

Many autobiographers, among them Lincoln Steffens and Gertrude Atherton, describe earthquakes their families have been in. *I am unable to do this because my family was never in an earthquake, but we went through a number of things in Columbus that were a great deal like earthquakes.* I remember in particular some of the repercussions of an old Reo we had that wouldn't go unless you pushed it for quite a way and suddenly let your clutch out. Once, we had been able to start the engine easily by cranking it; but we had had the car for so many years that finally it wouldn't go unless you pushed it and let your clutch out. Of course, it took more than one person to do this; it took sometimes as many as five or six, depending on the grade of the roadway and conditions underfoot. The car was unusual in that the clutch and brake were on the same pedal, making it quite easy to stall the engine after it got started, so that the car would have to be pushed again.

JAMES THURBER

3. Topic sentence at the end

The psychology of the clam has no doubt been exhaustively studied, but possibly the observations of an independent investi-

[1] Copyright 1948, *The New Yorker Magazine, Inc.*

gator (who has dug for clams twice or thrice ere now) may not be altogether without value. The world has a low opinion of the clam's mentality. In common parlance, clam is synonymous with fool; and indeed he is the Nabal of bivalves; folly remaineth with him. Why else should he reveal his presence to his human enemy by spouting thin jets of water through his proboscis? A truly wise beast like the oyster or the mussel remains passive and undemonstrative at the approach of danger. The clam would seem to be of a nervous, excitable temperament. The approach of the spade compressing his muddy home apparently angers or frightens him, and he spouts in a sort of hysterical fury. Can it be that he thinks he is defending himself by putting out the rash beholder's eye? Or insulting him by spitting in his face? *The popular advice not to be a clam is justified by the observed facts.*

ARCHIBALD MacMECHAN

4. Topic sentence at both the beginning and the end

The coon is probably the most courageous creature among our familiar wild animals. Who ever saw a coon show the white feather? He will face any odds with perfect composure. I have seen a coon upon the ground, beset by four men and two dogs, and never for a moment losing his presence of mind, or showing a sign of fear. *The raccoon is clear grit.*

JOHN BURROUGHS

5. Topic sentence implied: *Authors should not be expected to be as clever in real life as they are in their books.*

After all, is it not expecting too much to expect a novelist to talk as cleverly as the clever characters in his novels? Must a dramatist necessarily go about armed to the teeth with crisp dialogue? May not a poet be allowed to lay aside his singing robes and put on a conventional dress suit when he dines out? Why is it not permissible for him to be as prosaic and tiresome as the rest of the company? He usually is.

THOMAS BAILEY ALDRICH

EXERCISE 1. In each of the following paragraphs, find the topic sentence. Then study each of the other sentences to determine whether it helps to explain the idea given in the topic sentence.

1. The ghost that got into our house on the night of November 17, 1915, raised such a hullabaloo of misunderstandings that I am sorry I didn't just let it keep on walking, and go to bed. Its advent caused my mother to throw a shoe through a window of the house next door and ended up with my grandfather shooting a policeman. I am sorry, therefore, as I have said, that I ever paid any attention to the footsteps.

JAMES THURBER

2. Travelers, I will admit, differ temperamentally, differ in their wants and needs; but for me the Pullman Company will never improve on its classic design of upper and lower berth. In my eyes it is a perfect thing, perfect in conception and execution, this small green hole in the dark moving night, this soft warren in a hard world. In it I have always found the peace of spirit which accompanies grotesque bodily situations, peace and a wonderful sense of participation in cosmic rhythms and designs. I have experienced these even on cold nights when I all but died from exposure, under blankets of virgin gossamer.

E. B. WHITE

3. I cannot answer this question. The reasons go back too far for me; but the fact remains that it has been decided that when not tragic, and even sometimes when tragic, aunts are comic. Not so comic as mothers-in-law, of course; not invariably and irremediably comic; but provocative of mirth and irreverence. Again I say, why? For taken one by one, aunts are sensible, affectionate creatures; and our own experience of them is usually serious enough; they are often very like their sisters our mothers, or their brothers our fathers, and often, too, they are mothers themselves. Yet the status of aunt is always fair game to the humorist; and especially so when she is the aunt of somebody else.

E. V. LUCAS

4. Delightful as literature is, however, it has more lasting values than as a source of pleasure, amusement, and relaxation. It is, especially for the young reader, the most important source of ideas and ideals. Literature is the record of what men have thought and felt about life, and from that record the modern reader can enrich his own meager experience with the thoughts and emotions of the past. Especially important in this respect is contemporary literature, for as our modern life becomes more complex and diverse no single person can hope himself to experience all life. Yet every man wants to know more of life than lies within his grasp. The eternal spirit of youth is eagerness for experience, a great curiosity about life in the past and in the present. For this eagerness for knowledge, this "divine discontent" of youth, there is no better satisfaction than the quest for an understanding of the ideas and ideals expressed in literature of the past and of the present.

BOAS AND SMITH

5. Even today the spirit and rites of ancient Christmas are kept up, more or less in their full rigor and spendor, by a race of beings that is scattered over the whole earth. This race, mysterious, masterful, conservative, imaginative, passionately sincere, has its way in spite of us. I mean the children. By virtue of the children's faith, the reindeer are still tramping the sky, and Christmas Day is still something above and beyond a day of the week; it is a day out of the week. We have to sit and pretend; and with disillusion in our souls we do pretend. At Christmas, it is not the children who make believe; it is ourselves.

ARNOLD BENNETT

EXERCISE 2. Pick out the topic sentences of some paragraphs in your literature book. Then check them for unity.

EXERCISE 3. For each of the following paragraphs, supply a topic sentence that would be suitable:

1. –?–. When she [Tallulah Bankhead] was a child in a Washington suburb, a kindly gentleman named Cordell Hull let her

ride his ponies. She has swapped cabled pleasantries with her friend Winston Churchill. An admirer, Lord Beaverbrook, once gave her a party attended by such eager guests as the Aga Khan and Rudolph Valentino. Jock Whitney, the Prince of Wales, the Duke of Kent, Ronald Coleman — they have all flitted through the spotlight that trails Tallulah wherever she goes.

Time[1]

2. A newspaper account recently told the story of a boy who had been struck by the broken end of a live wire, which touched one side of his face, burning and paralyzing it. In court the boy's lawyer asked the little fellow to turn toward the jury and smile. He tried. One side of his face smiled, but the injured side just puckered up in a pitiful contortion. The jury took just twelve minutes to award the boy $20,000. –?–.

Coronet

3. What is the primary instinct which leads men to literature? –?–. From primitive man crouching about a fire in a cave listening with delight to the story of the killing of the hairy mammoth with stone-tipped arrows to the boy curled in an armchair by the fireplace reading with delight the story of Custer's last stand as the Redskins circled ever nearer and nearer — from that day to this a good story has been able "to hold children from play and old men from the chimney corner."

BOAS AND SMITH (*Adapted*)

4. –?–. If the illness or loss is a relatively minor one, the letter may be written in a light and bantering vein. But when a person is gravely ill or has suffered a really serious loss, any attempt to be facetious is in very bad taste and should be avoided. Even though your bright and witty letter may be written with the best intentions in the world, to cheer the invalid or unhappy victim of misfortune, you can be sure it will be resented. –?–.

LILLIAN EICHLER WATSON[2]

[1] Courtesy of *Time*, Copyright Time Inc., 1948.

[2] Reprinted by permission of Prentice-Hall, Inc., from *Standard Book of Letter Writing* by L. E. Watson. Copyright 1948 by L. E. Watson.

5. –?–. No matter what the combination of guests, young or old or very young, it is always the same, a perfect party, the best ever! Each guest seems as responsible as the hostess; it is the thing Charleston does best of all — give a party. Nowhere else do gaiety and dignity blend with such perfect harmony. Differences are left at the door; they can be settled somewhere else; the party is the thing. No cliques, no men gathered in one corner and women in another; the throng is mobile, it moves easily; all seem glad to be here, all go away refreshed. We never hire entertainers nor plan amusements; just meeting each other seems pleasure enough to most of us.

ELIZABETH O'NEILL VERNER

EXERCISE 4. For each of the following theme topics, write the topic sentence of the opening paragraph. Why will you try not to repeat the title in your topic sentence?

1. The Most Unforgettable Character
2. Little White Lies
3. What I Dislike about Radio
4. Football, a Builder of Character
5. The Meaning of Tolerance
6. A Place I Remember
7. My Favorite Kind of Reading
8. Chief Cause of Failure
9. A Great American
10. The Hidden Springs of Poetry

Par 2   Arrangement of Details

A good paragraph should have coherence as well as unity. One sentence should flow into the next in an orderly, logical manner. The butterfly method of flitting from hither to yon and then back to hither is confusing.

The following is a very poor adaptation of a paragraph taken from *Inside U.S.A.* by John Gunther. As you will see, there is *no* orderly arrangement of details.

POOR: Maine's chief distinction is, however, not size but character. One element in this is intrepidity. Another factor is the complete simplicity and financial integrity of almost all old Maine citizens. Another element is humor. The state is largely marked by fingers of land poking out into the sea; in the most literal sense its lobstermen and other fishermen make their living by combat with the elements. This is not as wry and bitter as is humor in Vermont, say; it has a glow; it has been softened by the Atlantic fogs. Money doesn't count for everything in their scale of values; people will spend their last cent on a coat of pale yellow paint for their houses; drop a pocketbook in the streets of Augusta, and a dozen passers-by will return it. Still the humor can be sharp. For instance Bert Sinnett, an old retired lobsterman and a member of one of the ancient families of Maine, was once called as a witness in a lawsuit.

Q. Your name is Bert Sinnett?
A. Yes.
Q. You live in Bayley Island?
A. Yes.
Q. Lived there all your life?
A. Not yet.

In the paragraph, as Mr. Gunther arranged it, notice that the topic sentence is proved by three points: (1) One element is intrepidity. (2) Another factor is the complete simplicity and financial integrity. (3) Another element is humor. All the details are arranged under those three points.

GOOD: Maine's chief distinction is, however, not size but character. One element in this is intrepidity. The state is largely marked by fingers of land poking out into the sea; in the most literal sense its lobstermen and other fishermen make their living by combat with the elements. Another factor is the complete simplicity and financial integrity of almost all old Maine citizens; money doesn't count for everything in their scale of values; people will spend their last cent on a coat of pale yellow paint for their houses; drop a pocketbook in the streets of Augusta, and a dozen passers-by will return it. Another element is humor. This is not as wry and bitter as is humor in Vermont, say; it has a glow; it has been softened by the Atlantic fogs. Still, it can be sharp. For instance Bert Sinnett, an old retired lobsterman and a member of one of the ancient families of Maine, was once called as a witness in a lawsuit.

Q. Your name is Bert Sinnett?
A. Yes.
Q. You live in Bayley Island?
A. Yes.
Q. Lived there all your life?
A. Not yet.

JOHN GUNTHER

EXERCISE 1. Here are four topic sentences which Mr. Gunther used for four paragraphs in his book *Inside U.S.A.* Beneath each topic sentence are a number of details. Can you organize the details of each paragraph in the proper order?

1. But easily South Dakota's greatest distinction is in the realm of — pheasants!

    a. 40,000 out-of-state licenses issued annually
    b. 50,000,000 pheasants in the state
    c. Open season approximately two months
    d. Fee for residents $1.00, fee for outsiders $20.00
    e. According to one man, "We have more pheasants than Republicans — and you can't even count the Republicans!"
    f. Limit of five birds a day
    g. Sioux Falls known as "pheasant capital of the world"

2. On its eight- to twelve-foot-thick rug of soil Nebraska lives quite well — provided the weather smiles.

    a. Average size of farms 191 acres (more than twice the size of average American farm)

    b. Thirty-second state in population

    c. Third dairying state (after Wisconsin and New York)

    d. More than a billion dollars invested in 121,000 farms

    e. Sixth in production of foodstuffs

    f. Exports corn, wild hay, wheat, alfalfa, feeder cattle, feeder hogs, butter, eggs

    g. Farms 61% more mechanized than those of national average

3. Whenever I go to Philadelphia, which is as often as I can, because I like it, I stroll down Chestnut Street and look at Independence Hall.

    a. Plaque in central lobby, "Frame of Government" of William Penn

    b. At Independence Hall on September 17, 1787, Constitution signed

    c. Here on June 10, 1775, George Washington made commander in chief of Revolutionary forces

    d. Wording on plaque: "Government is free to the people . . . and more than this is tyranny oligarchy and confusion."

    e. Here on November 3, 1781, twenty-four British standards captured at Yorktown presented to Congress

    f. Here on July 4, 1776, Declaration of Independence adopted

4. Consider now, in purely physical terms, what TVA has done in the fourteen years since its foundation, at a total cost of about 750 million dollars.

    a. Amount of TVA construction since 1935 equal to that of entire railway development in U. S. for a hundred years

    b. Ten times more material used in TVA dams than in Grand Coulee

    c. Twenty-six dams in TVA system

    d. Materials used in dams sufficient to fill hole ten feet in diameter straight through to China

    e. Thirty-five times more material used in TVA dams than in Boulder Dam

    f. Two and a half times more concrete used than in Panama Canal

EXERCISE 2. Each of the following contains ingredients for a good paragraph. After you have arranged the sentences in the order which you think is best, turn to pages 139 and 794 of *Inside U.S.A.* by John Gunther; and check your work with the original of these paragraphs.

1. The only authentic crop from a tree is the cone. As a matter of fact they are not. The timber tycoons had a slogan once — "trees are a crop." But the lumber industry was based for a couple of generations on the philosophy of harvesting a "crop" that was not renewed. So, in a sense, these trees do make a crop — every 80 to 180 years. It takes a minimum of 80 years for a Douglas fir to reach saw-log size, from 140 to 180 for a ponderosa pine.

2. Another is the use of dyes injected into the root of the cotton plant; cotton so dyed keeps color better than that dyed in the mills, and the process is much cheaper. This development was originally worked out by Russian agronomists in the Soviet Union. The scientists work almost as hard on cotton as they do on wheat. The bewildered visitor may soon see cotton fields blooming in orange, purple, green, magenta, and baby pink! One recent development has been the creation of a new fiber, naturally grown, called "Ramie," which has a tensile strength greater than that of cotton and makes clothes that wear much longer.

EXERCISE 3. Benjamin Franklin made an interesting recommendation to those who want to learn how to write. Take notes on a piece of writing that is well done. Then put the notes away, and do not look at them until the wording of the original has been forgotten. After some time has elapsed, take out the notes and write on the same subject, using the same ideas. Finally, check with the original.

This recommendation can be followed in part with the four paragraph outlines in Exercise 1. For checking, the originals of these paragraphs will be found on pages 248, 251, 600, and 736 of *Inside U.S.A.* by John Gunther.

Par 3   Transitional Devices

As you have seen, the orderly arrangement of sentences in a paragraph helps to produce coherence. Sentences can also be blended into a coherent pattern (1) through the use of transitional words and phrases, (2) through the use of pronouns to refer to antecedents in preceding sentences, and (3) through the repetition of key words.

1. Use transitional words and phrases.

Because these connecting words and phrases carry different meanings, they cannot be used interchangeably. It is important, consequently, to know their varying purposes.

> TO ADD IDEAS: *furthermore, likewise, similarly, in like manner, again, too, moreover, besides, also*
>
> TO ILLUSTRATE: *by way of illustration, for instance, for example, in the case of*
>
> TO COMPARE: *similarly, likewise, in the same way*
>
> TO CONTRAST: *on the other hand, nevertheless, yet, still, however, notwithstanding, on the contrary, in contrast to this, otherwise*
>
> TO SHOW PURPOSE: *for this reason, with this object in mind*
>
> TO CONCLUDE: *therefore, accordingly, consequently, as a result*
>
> TO SHOW ORDER IN TIME OR SPACE: *first, in the second place, next, then, to begin with, finally, here, there, beyond*

Notice the use of transitional words and phrases in the following excerpts. Notice, too, how their use knits the sentences closely together.

We washed the body, and wrapped it, still in its oilskins and sea boots, in a sheet. *Then* we placed it reverently in a canvas bag that had been made, with a place at the foot for pieces of iron and heavy weights to bear it down.

ALAN VILLIERS

The propeller does throw a blast of air backward, but the engineers would be only too happy to keep that air from hitting any part of the airplane. It is a nuisance. *Moreover*, the wings don't need a blast of air.

WOLFGANG LANGEWIESCHE-BRANDT

But I would remind you, *first*, that the music of poetry is not something which exists apart from the meaning. *Otherwise*, we could have poetry of great musical beauty which made no sense, and I have never come across such poetry.

T. S. ELIOT

He [Boswell] had no pride, no shame, and no dignity. The result was that a multitude of inhibitions passed him by. *Nevertheless*, he was by no means detached.

LYTTON STRACHEY

He [Goldsmith] left that celebrated university, the third university at which he had resided, in his twenty-seventh year, without a degree, with the merest smattering of medical knowledge, and with no property but his clothes and his flute. His flute, *however*, proved a useful friend.

THOMAS BABINGTON MACAULAY

EXERCISE 1. Copy each of these sentences and follow it by a second sentence which you compose. Link the two sentences with a transitional word or phrase. Try to use as many different transitional words and phrases as you possibly can.

1. Football is a good bodybuilder.
2. Assuredly a letter of condolence is hard to write.
3. Picnics always involve such undesirables as ants, flies, potato salad, and deviled eggs.
4. Autumn is one of the most beautiful times of the year.
5. American slang would surely mystify a visitor from Mars.

Transitional devices are helpful in denoting passage of time or in indicating position. In the following passage, transitional devices are used to show the order of events:

For a while I sawed and hacked at it [a shark] by myself, but its skin was much too tough for one man to handle. *At length* Tony was forced to hold the tail and Gene the head, while I slit open the stomach. *First* we cut out the liver, divided it into three large pieces, and ate that. But *still* we were hungry. *Next* we further explored the stomach, finding to our surprise two six-inch sardines, one of which had been bitten entirely in two when the shark had swallowed it. Never in my life have I tasted better meat than that shark liver, which even when raw resembled chicken liver, or the sardines, which tasted to our ravenous appetites like the tastiest kind of herring. *Finally* we devoured the rest of the shark's innards. *By now*, we had thoroughly lost what prejudices we may have had against eating raw fish.

HAROLD F. DIXON [1]

EXERCISE 2. List the transitional words and phrases that you would use in writing a paragraph on these topics:

1. Preparation for a Picnic
2. A Strange Noise at Night
3. First Swimming Lesson
4. Christmas Morning
5. Frying an Egg
6. A Room at Home
7. A Classroom
8. Interior of a Church
9. A Park
10. A Favorite Spot

[1] Courtesy of *Life*, April 6, 1942, issue.

2. Use pronouns to refer to antecedents in preceding sentences.

Notice in these excerpts how definitely the pronouns in italics refer to words in preceding sentences:

Rashes "come out" in writing as they do upon the face. *They* are a symptom of youthful disorders and often spring from mental indigestion.

HENRY SEIDEL CANBY

Doctor Meredith removed to Hannibal, by and by, and was our family physician there, and saved my life several times. Still, *he* was a good man and meant well.

MARK TWAIN

In the days when the undergraduate literary societies turned over their private collections to the college library, certain volumes of juvenile fiction, esteemed too frivolous for general circulation, were sequestered in a remote corner of that gallery. Very likely *some* of *them* are still there . . .

CHRISTOPHER MORLEY

Some of my misery was loneliness and some of it fear of old William Pollexfen, my grandfather. *He* was never unkind, and I cannot remember that *he* ever spoke harshly to me, but it was the custom to fear and admire *him*.

WILLIAM BUTLER YEATS

EXERCISE 3. Copy each of these sentences, and write a suitable sentence to follow it. In each sentence which you make up, use a pronoun that will refer definitely to an antecedent in the first sentence.

1. Johnny Appleseed did more than plant apples.
2. The development of atomic energy is more serious than we like to contemplate.
3. Helen Keller is an example of what determination can do.
4. Children are a great worry and an uncertain comfort.
5. My name is John Doe.

3. Repeat key words.

Notice how the sentences in these excerpts are tied together through the repetition of key words.

Until recently Americans have traveled in Europe to see architecture and traveled in their own country to view natural scenery. Today we are beginning to discover the *architecture* of the United States.

PHILIP N. YOUTZ

A book is great when it speaks to the best minds. It is popular when it speaks to the most *minds*.

CARL VAN DOREN

Yet once and for all the truth is best. The *truth* does not ultimately harm. The *truth* is healing when accepted, deep down, and the *truth* is that the world was not made to be an easy place to live in.

FELIX ADLER

Probably the fear of ghosts, as well as the belief in them, had its beginning in dreams. It is a peculiar *fear*. No other *fear* is so intense; yet none is so vague.

LAFCADIO HEARN

EXERCISE 4. Copy these sentences. Follow each with a sentence of your own, this time using the repetition of a key word as the linking device.

1. Women's hats are usually objects of merriment.
2. An unpedigreed hound dog is the kind for me.
3. Then came a moment of horrible, heartbreaking anxiety.
4. A liar is worse than a thief.
5. A lovely face appeared at the train window.

Transitions between Paragraphs

If you will examine the paragraphs in some of your books, you will find that frequently a transitional word, phrase, or sentence is used at the beginning of a paragraph for the purpose of linking it with the one immediately preceding. You may find expressions like the following:

1. In regard to this last point . . .
2. Finally, we know . . .
3. After that . . .
4. Still the situation . . .
5. So matters stood.
6. However, . . .

Notice the linking that takes place between the paragraphs in these two selections:

1. . . . At last it [a snake] vanished, and turning I fled from the ground, thinking that never again would I venture into or near that frightfully dangerous spot in spite of its fascination.

Nevertheless, I did venture. . . .

W. H. HUDSON

2. . . . The shock was not caused by any suspicion that he [my father] was not telling the truth, as it appeared to him, but by the awful proof that he was not, as I had supposed, omniscient.

This experience was followed by another. . . .

EDMUND GOSSE

EXERCISE 5. Here are the last sentences of five paragraphs. For each of these, write the first sentence for a paragraph that would follow. Write it so that it forms a link with the preceding sentence.

1. Very obviously the plot of a play is exceedingly important.
2. That night I drove my car into the garage, determined to forget my troubles.
3. Education, therefore, is one steppingstone to success.
4. The experience, I thought, had taught me a lesson.
5. Consequently, I decided that silence meant peace.

EXERCISE 6. To find examples of the use of transitional words, phrases, and sentences, analyze the paragraphs in some of your books.

Par 4   Methods of Development

Paragraphs may be developed in a number of different ways. Different kinds of subject matter demand different sorts of treatment, and sometimes even a combination of methods may be used. The following are the methods most commonly used:

1. Paragraphs may be developed by <u>details.</u>

But sooner or later we always get back to the recurrent theme of size, the concept of the grandiose. Texas is the place where you need a mousetrap to catch mosquitoes, where a man is so hardboiled that he sleeps on sandpaper sheets, where the grapefruit are so enormous that nine make a dozen, where Davy Crockett fanned himself with a hurricane, where a flock of sheep can get lost in the threads of a pipeline, where canaries sing bass, where if you spill some nails you will harvest a crop of crowbars, where houseflies carry dog tags for identification, where if you shoot at a javelina (peccary) it will spit your first bullet back, then race it toward you, and where that legendary creature Pecos Bill, the Texas equivalent of Paul Bunyan, could rope a streak of lightning.

JOHN GUNTHER

2. Paragraphs may be developed by <u>example.</u>

Children are precocious in their attitude toward stories. They know what they like and why they like it, and they are perfectly willing to express their opinions with brutal frankness. Once a storyteller gathered a group of six-year-olds around her and began in the accustomed fashion: "Once upon a time . . ." To this, one of the moppets remarked quickly, "I've already heard that one!"

MARY JACKSON

3. Paragraphs may be developed by <u>comparison, contrast, and analogy.</u>

I admire wit, but I have no real liking for it. It has been too often employed against me, whereas humor is always an ally. It never points an impertinent finger into my defects. Humorous persons do not sit like explosives on a fuse. They are safe and easy comrades. But a wit's tongue is as sharp as a donkey driver's stick. I may gallop the faster for its prodding, yet the touch behind is too persuasive for any comfort.

CHARLES S. BROOKS

4. Paragraphs may be developed by <u>definition and explanation</u>.

Clamming may be defined as the art or science of extricating the clam from his native mud. The process sounds extremely simple. There is the mud in which the clam lies embedded a few inches below the surface. Here is the hunter armed with a narrow shovel or a five-pronged stable fork. The clam must passively abide your onset. He cannot run away; he cannot fly in the air. You assail him with your digging implement. Insert it at the right place, turn over the mud, and there is the clam ready to hand over to Mrs. Cook for the chowder or the stew.

ARCHIBALD MacMECHAN

5. Paragraphs may be developed by <u>reasons and results</u>.

Miggle's memory was stupendous. Not only was she up on everyone's life history, but she enumerated so many appalling anecdotes concerning myself that I began to wonder what under heaven had prompted her to look me up. She recalled my unfortunate phase of trying to look like Theda Bara with ten-cent store earrings and my hair pulled out at the sides like horse blinkers. She brought up the old ugly scandal of the time I put wet blotters in my shoes before an unprepared-for German quiz, because someone had told me it would make me faint, and it didn't. She twitted me with once receiving the mark of 3 in an algebra exam when 60 was passing. (The 3 was for being present.) And she made me feel I was definitely a borderline case when to my horror she remembered the time I had had a crush on the captain of the

291

hockey team — a memory that so alarmed me I blushed a deep scarlet. She referred to the time I had sent ten cents for a sample of henna rinse that had turned my hair green, and she laughed happily over the thought of the youth I had imported for the May prom. He had worn spectacles and belonged to the Elizabethan Club, and I had considered him a rare spirit; but to Miggle who had commandeered a half-back from Penn State (the jade!) he was still a riot. She even knew how old I was — a fact she stated with triumph, adding "You're a year older than I, but then I graduated the year before you." I was beginning to dislike Miggle intensely.

CORNELIA OTIS SKINNER

6. Paragraphs may be developed by a <u>combination of methods.</u>

In the following paragraph, notice the use of contrast and of example:

A building's wall and roof used to be considered mere barriers. They might be decorated on the outside, but their main purpose was to keep the weather out. Modern architects think of a wall as a filter between the outside and inside environments. For example, the wall of a factory in a hot climate should reflect outside heat and absorb inside heat, passing as much of it as possible to the outside. In a cold climate, the wall should gather all possible heat from sunlight, while keeping inside heat from moving out. Modern materials, such as sheet metal, mineral wool, and glass brick, allow the architects to design efficient "filter walls."

Time [1]

EXERCISE 1. By what method or combination of methods does it seem to you that each of the following paragraphs has been developed?

1. A curious exemplification of the power of a single book for good or harm is shown in the effects wrought by *Don Quixote*

---

[1] Courtesy of *Time*, Copyright Time Inc., 1948.

and those wrought by *Ivanhoe*. The first swept the world's admiration for the medieval chivalry silliness out of existence; and the other restored it. As far as our South is concerned, the good work done by Cervantes is pretty nearly a dead letter, so effectually has Scott's pernicious work undermined it.

MARK TWAIN

2. Whoever has made a voyage up the Hudson must remember the Kaatskill Mountains. They are a dismembered branch of the great Appalachian family, and are seen away to the west of the river, swelling up to a noble height, and lording it over the surrounding country. Every change of season, every change of weather, indeed every hour of the day, produces some change in the magical hues and shapes of these mountains, and they are regarded by all the good wives, far and near, as perfect barometers. When the weather is fair and settled, they are clothed in blue and purple, and print their bold outlines on the clear evening sky; but sometimes when the rest of the landscape is cloudless, they will gather a hood of gray vapors about their summits, which, in the last rays of the setting sun, will glow and light up like a crown of glory.

WASHINGTON IRVING

3. A second common device for securing tone color is *alliteration*. Alliteration is the repetition usually of the initial sound or sounds of a word. It is thus similar to rhyme though different in position. Sometimes, as in "The Scythe Song," it is highly appropriate to the sense of the poem, but often it is of value merely as beautiful sound in itself.

BOAS AND SMITH

4. A few months before Muggs [a dog] died, he got to "seeing things." He would rise slowly from the floor, growling low, and stalk stiff-legged and menacing toward nothing at all. Sometimes the Thing would be just a little to the right or left of a visitor. Once a Fuller Brush salesman got hysterics. Muggs came wandering into the room like Hamlet following his father's ghost. His eyes were fixed on a spot just to the left of the Fuller Brush

man, who stood it until Muggs was about three slow, creeping paces from him. Then he shouted. Muggs wavered on past him into the hallway grumbling to himself, but the Fuller man went on shouting. I think Mother had to throw a pan of cold water on him before he stopped. That was the way she used to stop us boys when we got into fights.

JAMES THURBER

5. In the heart of the rabbit fear constantly abides. How her eyes protrude! She can see back and front and on all sides as well as a bird. The fox is after her, the owls are after her, the gunners are after her, and she has no defense but her speed. She always keeps well to cover. The northern hare keeps in the thickest brush. If the hare or rabbit crosses a broad open exposure it does so hurriedly, like a mouse when it crosses the road. The mouse is in danger of being pounced upon by a hawk, and the hare or rabbit by the snowy owl, or else the great horned owl.

JOHN BURROUGHS

6. Another phase of life here which has lost something through refinement is the game of croquet. We used to have an old croquet set whose wooden balls, having been chewed by the dogs, were no rounder than eggs. Paint had faded, wickets were askew. The course had been laid out haphazardly and eagerly by a child, and we all used to go out there on summer nights and play good-naturedly, with the dogs romping on the lawn in the beautiful light, and the mosquitoes sniping at us, and everyone in good spirits, racing after balls and making split shots for the sheer love of battle. Last spring we decided the croquet set was beyond use, and invested in a rather fancy new one with hoops set in small wooden sockets, and mallets with rubber faces. The course is now exactly 72 feet long and we lined the wickets up with a string; but the little boy is less fond of it now, for we make him keep still while we are shooting. A dog isn't even allowed to cast his shadow across the line of play. There are frequent quarrels of a

minor nature, and it seems to me we return from the field of honor tense and out of sorts.

E. B. WHITE

7. Rickets in children comes from undernourishment, and so does rickets in writing. The author with rickets does not know enough, has not read enough, is not sufficiently experienced, to write. An editor would say of his manuscripts, "Written well, but nothing in them." If your writing suffers from rickets, what you need is medicine for your intellect and imagination. Tonic your brain and let writing wait for convalescence.

HENRY SEIDEL CANBY

8. What has brought the poor reader to his sorry state? How account for the effortless skill of the efficient reader? Much of the answer to these questions can be given in the phrase, "*eye movements.*" The poor reader does not use his eyes properly. He has built up and thoroughly refined a set of incorrect eye habits, and by continuous practice and repetition has developed these habits to the point where they are almost ineradicable. The eyes of a skillful reader function so well that there is no realization of their functioning.

NORMAN LEWIS

9. Fast planes of the future will probably look like the Navy's new jet fighter, the Chance Vought XF7U-1, which completed its initial flight tests last week. The new fighter has short, broad wings "swept back" at an angle of 45° or better. There is no tail; two stabilizers with rudders are attached to the trailing edges of the wings. Two Westinghouse turbojet engines drive the plane at better than 600 m.p.h.

Time [1]

10. A *symbol* is much like an image except that it is not necessarily a picture. It is any concrete object used to stand for an abstract idea. The cross, for instance, is a symbol for Christianity, the crescent for Mohammedanism, the stars and stripes for the

[1] Courtesy of *Time,* Copyright Time Inc., 1948.

United States. The use of symbols is natural. Certain objects are almost universally used to stand for certain ideas. The Rock of Gibraltar serves as a symbol for anything firm and unshakable. Mountains have always stood in men's minds for the eternal strength and patience of God.

BOAS AND SMITH

EXERCISE 2. What method of development would you use in writing a paragraph based on each of the following topic sentences?

1. My grandmother hoarded things like a magpie.
2. An outstanding student is one who possesses a number of special qualities.
3. Fair-weather friends are good only in fair weather.
4. The comics have gained their present popularity for a number of reasons.
5. Astrology and astronomy have the stars in common.
6. What constitutes good sportsmanship?
7. The study of English has certain practical benefits.
8. Only the present is important.
9. Psychology and psychiatry should not be confused.
10. Each of us remembers certain fears of childhood.
11. We must first determine what *tolerance* means.
12. Eat pickles and ice cream at midnight — if you want to.
13. In every respect, the house was falling apart.
14. Little brothers are both a blessing and a nuisance.
15. He was the old-fashioned kind of druggist.

EXERCISE 3. Using topic sentences suggested in EXER-CISE 2, write a paragraph developed by each of these methods:

1. Details
2. Example
3. Comparison, contrast, and analogy
4. Definition and explanation
5. Reasons and results
6. Combination of methods

Par 5   Length of Paragraphs

Paragraphs may be ineffective because they are either too short or too long. On the other hand, it would be incorrect to say that paragraphs should be like "the bear's soup" — just in between. Sometimes a short paragraph may be necessary to give emphasis, and a long paragraph may be necessary to develop the topic sentence adequately.

In determining the proper length of a paragraph, one should consider the following:

1. Avoid paragraphs which are short because of a lack of development.

POOR: Daniel Boone represents the eternal spirit of adventure. He fought the Indians a large part of his long life.

BETTER: Daniel Boone represents the eternal spirit of adventure. He fought the Indians a large part of his long life. Tired of his dull and debt-ridden life, he hewed his way through the wilderness to Caintuck, as it was known by the Indians. He built the Wilderness Trail so that others could follow him, and founded the first town in the new country. Finally, in his old age, with the love of adventure still burning, he pushed westward for more elbowroom. It is small wonder that Daniel Boone's name has come to be synonymous with adventure.

2. Avoid breaking into short paragraphs a thought that should be developed in one.

POOR: The trail to Caintuck represented many dangers and hardships. Indians lurked in the thick underbrush, waiting to attack and kill.

The underbrush itself was almost impassable. The trees were dense, and vines and undergrowth made traveling slow as well as dangerous.

BETTER: The trail to Caintuck represented many dangers and hardships. Indians lurked in the thick underbrush, waiting to attack and kill. The underbrush itself was

297

almost impassable. The trees were dense, and vines and undergrowth made traveling slow as well as dangerous.

3. Avoid joining ideas which should be developed in separate paragraphs.

EXERCISE 1. Into how many paragraphs should the following be divided?

Daniel Boone's first journey to Caintuck ended in financial failure. When he returned home after an absence of two years, he had to report that the Indians had stolen from him his horses and his pelts. He had nothing but a dream in his heart and a memory of the rich black soil in the new land and of the wealth that could be made through trapping and hunting. Daniel Boone's second attempt ended no more happily than the first. In fact, the second attempt was completely disastrous. In 1773, six families of Carolina decided to follow Daniel to the new country. Taking his own family, too, Daniel Boone headed north. On the way, they were beset by a band of Cherokees who killed a number of the men and who kidnaped Daniel's sixteen-year-old son to torture and kill him as a warning that the white men were not to try again to cross into the domain of the redskins.

EXERCISE 2. Rewrite the following, making whatever changes you think are necessary:

Daniel Boone's trail to Kentucky was the one used by the Indians. It is no wonder they tried to stop the white men from using it.

The famous Wilderness Trail was finally made in 1775. It was in that year that a bargain was effected with the Cherokees, giving them goods in return for a large part of Caintuck.

Daniel Boone was the one selected to hew the trail. As soon as the bargain had been completed, he and a band of men began hacking down the trees and underbrush to make a way for the many who would follow.

The Indians, despite the treaty, were a constant threat. The trail blazers were attacked once, and four of them were killed. Even after the settlement at Boonesborough was established, Indian uprisings were frequent and serious. Kentucky proved to thousands to be the promised land. Those who were harassed by debt flocked there. Those who were finding it increasingly hard to make a living saw in Kentucky an answer to their problems. And, finally, there were thousands who, like Daniel Boone himself, had adventure in their hearts. So from all the neighboring territories, people came flocking to Kentucky; and, thus, a new state had its beginnings.

EXERCISE 3. Study for size the model paragraphs given in this chapter. Do any seem too long or too short? Do any seem to lack proper development?

EXERCISE 4. Look at the paragraphs in some of your other books. Find examples of very short but effective paragraphs. Find also a number of paragraphs which are long but which you believe should not be changed.

EXERCISE 5. Study a number of paragraphs which you have written, and criticize them for length.

Par 6   Kinds of Paragraphs

Four special kinds of paragraphs are used frequently.

1. Introductory paragraph

Some writers do not believe in the use of introductory paragraphs, preferring instead to plunge immediately into the middle of things. Others believe that an introductory paragraph is valuable since it tells the reader what he is to expect. It also puts him in the proper mood.

An introductory paragraph does not need to be long, and it certainly should not be made up of aimless chitchat to fill up space. If an introductory paragraph does not catch the reader's interest, he probably will not bother to read on. Consequently, the first paragraph demands that the writer "put his best foot forward."

Here is the introductory paragraph of an essay called "Breaking the Ice." Notice how it serves to arouse interest.

The woman I envy is she whose gift of gab never fails her: the woman who gossips easily with the individual who washes her hair, who exchanges warm little jokes with waiters, and who can think of something to tell the elevator man that isn't the weather report. . . . I never know how to begin, and so I don't. The result is awkward.

CORNELIA OTIS SKINNER

2. Concluding paragraph

The last impression that a reader receives is almost as important as the first. The concluding paragraph, therefore, should be a pulling together of all the threads, a rounding out, thus impressing upon the reader the fact that that which was begun in the introductory paragraph has been accomplished.

Below is the concluding paragraph of the same essay. Notice how gracefully it takes leave of the subject.

I don't know if others experience similar difficulties with opening remarks. Probably not. Such speculations make me feel hopelessly inadequate and I wonder whether to consult Freud or Emily Post concerning it. Perhaps an astrologer might reassure me that the stars ordained me to be that way and that my constellation is the Goat. Perhaps the best course is to remain silent and pass as an eccentric.

CORNELIA OTIS SKINNER

3. Transitional paragraph

Like transitional words and phrases, a transitional paragraph serves to bridge. It is usually brief, and its only function is to lead the reader gently from one paragraph to the next. The following example is preceded by a paragraph which discusses the first way by which a poet creates feeling and is followed by a discussion of the second way:

> The first way, then, by which a poet creates feeling is through pictures, sometimes painted in detail and sometimes suggested in just a few words.
>
> BOAS AND SMITH

4. Division, or topic, paragraph

This kind of paragraph has a function similar to that of a topic sentence. A topic sentence gives the main idea of a paragraph. Sometimes several paragraphs are needed to develop a single point. When this is the case, a division, or topic, paragraph is frequently used to indicate to the reader that certain aspects of a problem are going to be developed in the following paragraphs. This example is followed by paragraphs which deal with the four points it mentions:

> Four typical causes of minor friction are questions of *tempo*, the brotherly reform measure, supervised telephone conversations, and tenure of parental control. These are standard group-irritants that sometimes vex the sweetest natures.
>
> FRANCES AND GERTRUDE WARNER

EXERCISE 1. Write an introductory and a concluding paragraph on one of the following subjects:

Mosquitoes	Hero Worship	Handshakes
Voices	Loafing	Silent Talkers
My Shoes	Parasites	"They Say — "

EXERCISE 2. Study some of the essays and articles in your literature book for the use of introductory and concluding paragraphs. Study some of the chapters in a history or science text for examples of the use of transitional and division paragraphs.

EXERCISE. Each of the following paragraphs is weak. Rewrite the paragraphs to show examples of good form.

1. Daniel Boone wanted to fight in the War of 1812 and was thoroughly annoyed to be turned down. The reason he was rejected was the fact he was then seventy-eight years old. One of the most colorful figures to fight in the War of 1812 was Andrew Jackson. Jackson was put in charge of the militia of the State of Tennessee to quell the Creek Indians. They had been stirred up by the British. Andrew Jackson's conduct of that campaign won for him his famous nickname. He refused to take any special privileges for himself; he was the leader. He ate the same kind of food. He slept on the same hard ground. When the crucial battle of Tallapoosa took place, he was violently ill. He fought fearlessly. The Creeks were beaten. They called him "Old Hickory."

2. I want to tell about Jackson at the battle at New Orleans. The British were completely defeated. The British had ten thousand trained troops. Many of the inhabitants of New Orleans sneered at Jackson and his rough ways. Jackson's army was made up of volunteers and some of Lafitte's pirates. Jackson disregarded the people and set himself to the defense of the city. The coming battle was no small matter. Again his fearlessness and dogged determination to win led to a great victory.

3. Andy, aged thirteen, was sent to a British prison camp during the Revolution. He contracted smallpox there. He and his brother were both sent to prison. This is the reason Andy was sent there. He refused to clean the boots of a British officer. The officer struck him with his saber. Then he was marched off to prison. Almost every history book tells this story as being illustrative of Andrew Jackson's rugged independence and his fighting heart. For many years, Andrew Jackson was considered by some to be the lowest sort of rowdy. Uncouth, they called him. He would rather fight than conciliate. His rugged independence was much too rugged for them. The wrong sort of people liked him and voted for him. He was the essence of the common man.

LETTER WRITING

INDIVIDUALITY AND CORRECTNESS

Letters used to be copied from handbooks of forms suitable for all occasions. Today, however, a premium is placed upon both individuality of expression and correctness of form.

Let 1   The Business Letter

Your letter of application may win for you the job you want most. Certainly the mastery of good business-letter writing will help make the wheels of everyday living run more smoothly and efficiently.

1. Form of the Business Letter

If a business letter gives a poor first impression, the reader may unconsciously form an adverse opinion. He may even be reluctant to read beyond the first few sentences. Consequently, appearance is important.

As you see from the sample letter on the following page, a business letter has six parts. Notice the placement of each one as well as the use of margins, of capital letters, and of punctuation marks.

1.
722 East Market Street
Dayton 7, Ohio
April 29, 19—

2.
Personnel Manager
Sike's Department Store
1003 Third Street
Dayton 10, Ohio

3.
My dear Sir:

In the <u>Herald</u> I saw your advertisement for a stenographer, a position for which I should like to apply. I very much enjoy stenographic work, and I hope my qualifications will meet your requirements.

I am eighteen years old, and in June I shall be graduated from Central High School. I type 60 words a minute neatly and accurately and take 120 words a minute in dictation. All my grades are above average.

4.
For the past two summers I was employed by Field's Book Shop and am working there now on Saturdays.

The following have given me permission to use their names as references:

Mr. Lawrence K. Carter, Principal of Central High School
Miss Lois Mallon, Dean of Girls, Central High School
Dr. M. C. Field, Field's Book Shop

I should be glad to come for an interview. My telephone number is Waverly 1883W.

5.
Very sincerely yours,

Alice McGee

6.

1. HEADING

The heading of a letter contains the writer's address and the date. The form may be either block or indented.

Route 4, Box 10
Richmond 4, Virginia
May 10, 19—

Route 4, Box 10
Richmond 4, Virginia
May 10, 19—

2. INSIDE ADDRESS

The inside address indicates the name and the address of the recipient of the letter. It is placed flush with the left margin and follows the same form as the heading — block or indented.

Alston's Garage
116 Fairview Road
Waterville, Maine

Alston's Garage
116 Fairview Road
Waterville, Maine

3. SALUTATION

The salutation is the greeting of the letter. It is always placed flush with the left margin and is followed by a colon. Here are some frequently used salutations:

Dear Mr. Smith:
My dear Mr. Smith:
Dear Sir:
My dear Sir:

Gentlemen:
Dear Mrs. Jones:
My dear Dr. Brown:
Dear Miss Wilson:

The *My dear Mr. X:* salutation is considered more formal than the *Dear Mr. X:* form.

The only abbreviations which one should use are *Mr.*, *Mrs.*, and *Dr.* " Prof." and " Rev." should never be used.

4. BODY

Obviously, the body of the letter, the part that carries the message, is the most important part. A good business letter should be correct, clear, concise, and courteous. Businessmen must be able to read a letter quickly and easily. As a consequence, the writer of a business letter should know exactly and precisely the point or points he wants to make; and he should arrange them in an orderly sequence.

The following are suggestions worth remembering:

1. Make the first sentence indicate the reason for the letter.
2. Make the closing sentence clinch the point of the letter.
3. Concentrate on the facts, and be certain that all facts are correct.
4. Avoid any mention of irrelevant personal matters.
5. Avoid wordiness.
6. Put each new idea in a new paragraph.
7. Make the tone of the letter friendly, sincere, and lively.

5. COMPLIMENTARY CLOSE

The choice of both the salutation and the complimentary close depends upon the relationship of the writer to the receiver of the letter. The following are a number that can be used:

Yours sincerely,	Respectfully yours,
Yours very sincerely,	Yours respectfully,
Very sincerely yours,	Cordially yours,
Yours truly,	Very cordially yours,
Truly yours,	Yours very cordially,

In the model letter on page 304, notice that the complimentary close is aligned with the heading.

6. SIGNATURE

Always sign your name in ink, giving both your first and last names. If your letter is typewritten, you may type your name under your signature so that the recipient of the letter will not be puzzled over the spelling of your name.

The following show correct ways of signing letters:

1. A man signs:

   Bruce Adams   (No title before the name)

2. An unmarried woman signs:

   Ellen Bryant   or   *(Miss) Ellen Bryant*

3. In business correspondence, a married woman signs:

   Ann Mowry
   (Mrs. S. J. Mowry)

4. If the woman is a widow, she signs:

   (Mrs.) Louise Dale

The Use of Margins

You have probably been told that a letter should be placed on a sheet of paper much as a picture is placed in a frame. Obviously, this necessitates a wise use of margins. How long is your letter going to be? A short letter placed at the top of a page leaves too much white space at the bottom. A long letter begun too low on the page forces crowding at the end. Before beginning your letter, determine its approximate length.

Occasionally a letter must run over to the second page. Where the runover constitutes only a line or two, rewrite the letter, confining it to one page. However, do not make reductions at the expense of your margins.

As one authority has said, "You are known by your margins." Be generous in your use of white space. Make your margins set off your letter, thus enhancing its appearance.

EXERCISE. Examine some letters for their use of margins.

Spacing of the Parts

The placement of the parts of a letter on a page is highly important. The following skeleton letter indicates the spacing required by many business firms. It gives the formula for a letter typed in single space.

Single space →	Heading
Two to four spaces →	
Single space →	Inside address
Two spaces →	
Two spaces →	Salutation
Single space →	First paragraph
Two spaces →	
Single space →	Second paragraph
Two spaces →	
	Complimentary close
	Signature

In business letters that are typed single space, it is permissible to omit an indentation of paragraphs; paragraphs are indicated by the double spacing that separates them.

In a handwritten letter, space should be left between the heading and the inside address, between the inside address and the salutation, and between the last line of the letter and the complimentary close. There should, however, be no spacing between the salutation and the first line of the body of the letter.

Folding the Letter

Look at the sketches below. Numbers 1 to 4 inclusive show how to fold a letter to fit a long envelope, while numbers 5 to 8 show how to fold the same sized letter to fit a short envelope.

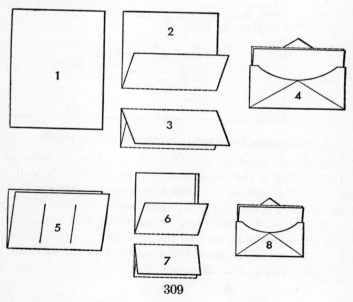

The following is an explanation of the numbering of the sketches shown on page 309:

1. Business stationery $8\frac{1}{2}'' \times 11''$
2. Turn up bottom third of sheet and crease.
3. Turn down top third to within $\frac{1}{8}''$ of bottom.
4. Place letter in envelope, keeping open edge at top.
5. Fold bottom half up to within $\frac{1}{4}''$ of top edge.
6. Turn on side and fold bottom third up.
7. Fold top third down to within $\frac{1}{8}''$ of bottom.
8. Place letter in envelope, keeping open edge at top.

Addressing the Envelope

Every envelope should carry two addresses, as this sketch shows:

Return address
```
Alice McGee
722 East Market Street
Dayton 7, Ohio
```

Address
```
              Personnel Manager
              Sike's Department Store
              1003 Third Street
              Dayton 10
              Ohio
```

In addressing an envelope, remember these points:

1. Every envelope should carry a return address as well as that of the person to whom the letter is directed.

2. In the address, the name of the town or city and that of the state should be on separate lines.

3. The same form (block or indented) that is used in the letter should be used on the envelope.

4. Abbreviations should be avoided, with the exception of such titles as *Mr.*, *Mrs.*, and *Dr.*

2. Kinds of Business Letters

There are as many different kinds of business letters as there are needs for them. The following, however, are the kinds most frequently used:

(a) Letter of application

The purpose of a letter of application is to sell yourself. There are certain tricks in the art of selling. The following will be helpful:

a. Type the letter, if possible.

b. Make the letter interesting, as well as exact and complete.

c. State the position for which you are making application.

d. Give information concerning age, education, training, experience, and references.

e. Indicate willingness for an interview.

f. Do *not* mention your personal troubles.

g. Do *not* refer to your lack of advantages.

h. Do *not* enlarge upon your accomplishments; state facts and let the employer judge.

i. Do *not* criticize a former employer.

j. Do *not* waste words.

On page 304 is an example of a letter of application. Notice the statements in the first and last paragraphs. Notice, too, both the arrangement of information in paragraphs and the spacing of the parts.

EXERCISE 1. Look in the "Help Wanted" section in your newspaper, and choose a position that interests you. Write a make-believe letter of application for it. Be sure that the form is correct and that you have supplied all the necessary information.

EXERCISE 2. Arrange the following letter of application in correct form, and address a make-believe envelope for it:

route 6 box 11 winona mississippi november 22 19—
collinss hardware store 149 main street jackson 2 mississippi gentlemen your advertisement in sundays gazette for a clerk during the christmas holidays interests me and i should like to make application for the position the last four summers i have clerked in smiths hardware store here in winona and have become familiar with hardware stock i am nineteen years of age and will be graduated from high school in may if you are interested in my application the following persons can tell you something about my record and qualifications mr john k long principal lee high school winona mississippi miss jane logan lee high school winona mississippi mr carl smith smiths hardware store winona mississippi i shall be glad to come to jackson for an interview at any time that is convenient for you yours very sincerely robert cox.

EXERCISE 3. For practice, write a letter of application for one of the following positions. Use your own address for the heading, and make up an address for the firm. When you have finished, address an "envelope."

> receptionist at a radio station
> waitress at a summer hotel
> soda-fountain clerk
> mechanic at a garage
> clerk in a store
> helper on a farm

EXERCISE 4. Exchange with a classmate your letter written in EXERCISE 3. Study his letter for content, for organization of ideas, and for form. Decide whether the letter reveals something of his personality or whether it sounds merely like a form letter. Discuss with him your opinion of the letter.

(b) Order letter

299 London Drive
Madison 3, Wisconsin
December 13, 19—

Shane and Shorley
1059 Michigan Avenue
Chicago 5, Illinois

Gentlemen:

I should like to order the following, which were advertised in yesterday's *Times*:

1 album of Bing Crosby's Christmas records	$3.94
1 Reflex camera	9.98
2 white handkerchiefs for men @ .75	1.50
	$15.42

My check is enclosed.

Yours very sincerely,
James Montgomery

313

EXERCISE 1. Write a letter to Mills Book Shop, 448 South Ludlow Street, Indianapolis 3, Indiana, ordering two copies of *Ivanhoe* by Scott, one copy of Blackmore's *Lorna Doone,* and one copy of Robert Louis Stevenson's *Treasure Island.* All the books are priced at one dollar. Address an "envelope."

EXERCISE 2. Write to Crile's Department Store, 14 Riverview Boulevard, San Francisco 6, California, ordering four articles of clothing which presumably you have seen advertised. Address an "envelope."

EXERCISE 3. Choose one article which you have seen advertised in your newspaper. Write a letter that you would send to order it. Obviously, when only one article is ordered, it is not necessary to set it off in block form as in the model letter on page 313.

(c) Letter asking for an adjustment

299 London Drive
Madison 3, Wisconsin
December 23, 19—

Shane and Shorley
1059 Michigan Avenue
Chicago 5, Illinois

Gentlemen:

The articles which I ordered from you arrived yesterday, and unfortunately an error has been made. I ordered one album of Bing Crosby's Christmas records, and I received the *Brigadoon* album instead.

Will you be kind enough to make the exchange? I have already mailed the *Brigadoon* album to you.

Very truly yours,

James Montgomery

EXERCISE 1. In EXERCISE 1 on the preceding page, you ordered three books. Let us say that by error you were sent Stevenson's *Kidnapped* instead of *Treasure Island*. Write a letter asking for a correction.

EXERCISE 2. In EXERCISE 2 on the preceding page you ordered certain articles of clothing. Let us say that one of the articles was badly soiled or damaged. Write the kind of letter that should be sent.

EXERCISE 3. You have received a bill from a local department store. The items are listed correctly, but the total amount due is wrong. Write a letter asking for an adjustment.

EXERCISE 4. Through the Nason Book Store, 987 Darby Road, Harrisburg, Pennsylvania, you have ordered a subscription to *Coronet*. You are receiving *The Reader's Digest* instead. Write a letter asking for a correction of the error.

(d) Letter of inquiry

Route 3, Box 11
Xenia, Ohio
November 17, 19—

American Book Company
88 Lexington Avenue
New York 16, New York

Gentlemen:

Do you have a book on typewriting which I can use to teach myself how to type? If you have such a book, will you be kind enough to send me the name of it and the price.

Sincerely yours,
Bettina Hunter

EXERCISE 1. Write a letter to Pogue's Department Store, 19 Elgin Avenue, Grand Rapids 2, Michigan, asking about a particular kind of sweater which you like but which was not included in an advertisement you recently saw. Address the "envelope."

EXERCISE 2. Write a letter to Tall Pine Camps, Lake George, New York, asking whether you might there earn part of the expenses of your summer's vacation. Address an "envelope."

EXERCISE 3. Write to the state librarian at your capital city to inquire about certain books that deal with a subject on which you are planning a term report. Add that you would like to borrow the books if they are available. Address an "envelope."

EXERCISE 4. In a letter of inquiry or of request, it is usually customary to enclose a self-addressed, stamped envelope. Make one example of this kind of envelope.

3. Diction of Business Letters

Good business English is no different from any other kind of English. In ordinary conversation, one would never think of saying, "We beg to advise," "Attached you will find," or "We beg to remain." Why, then, do we find such expressions in many business letters? The best advice is *write as you would talk*. Avoid stereotyped expressions, as you avoid them in all other kinds of written work.

DO NOT SAY	SAY
We shall advise you	We shall let you know
At any early date	Soon
We shall request that you	Please
Enclosed you will find	I am enclosing
We take great pleasure	We are very glad
Yours of the 10th inst. received	Your letter has been received

EXERCISE 1. Put each of these stereotyped phrases into plain, understandable English:

1. awaiting your reply
2. due to the fact that
3. in the course of
4. trusting you will send
5. we extend our thanks
6. take this opportunity
7. under separate cover
8. referring to your letter
9. the writer has checked
10. until such time as

11. along these lines
12. owing to the fact that
13. as per instructions
14. even date
15. at the earliest moment
16. thanking you in advance
17. in re the matter of
18. your letter is at hand
19. in view of the fact
20. permit me to say

EXERCISE 2. Study a number of business letters. Make a list of the stereotyped expressions that you find.

4. Spelling in Business Letters

Taking dictation necessitates an understanding of words, including differences in meaning and in spelling.

EXERCISE. Your teacher will dictate the following sentences for you to write. If you misspell any of the words in italics, use your dictionary to check their meanings.

1. Everyone will *accept except* the president.
2. We do not have *access* to the figures on *excess* profits.
3. The *effect* of the work *affected* the morale of the group.
4. Someone will *canvass* the territory to determine customers' preferences in *canvas*.
5. Everyone is *conscious* of the *conscientious* attempt.
6. It is necessary to *elicit* from the client the basis of his *illicit* business.
7. The arrival of the *eminent* statesman is *imminent*.
8. At the end of the *fiscal* year, the *physical* plant had expanded greatly.
9. In the *past* month, three bills have been *passed*.
10. The *principal* of the school stands for certain *principles*.

Let 2 The Friendly Letter

As William James has said, "As long as there are post-men, life will have zest." That zest increases every time we receive a friendly letter that is rich and happy and warm.

1. Form of the Friendly Letter

The form of a friendly letter follows that of a business letter, with two exceptions. A friendly letter does not have an inside address; and a comma, instead of a colon, follows the salutation. A friendly letter may be either typed or hand written.

1.
> 518 Wells Street
> Sistersville, Virginia
> November 14, 19—

2. Dear Brad,

3.
> Yesterday I baked some cookies for you. You'll pretend horror at the thought of me as a cook; but before you express your opinion, let me tell you what happened. In the midst of my labors, the house across the street caught on fire. Then, perhaps in sympathy, our furnace backfired and filled the house with smoke as thick as pea soup. Finally, as I was removing the cookies from the oven, the gang arrived; you can imagine what happened. Now you know all; let your conscience be your guide.

> We all send our love. Judging by your letters, you are having a marvelous time.

4.
> Your kid sister,

5.
> *Jill*

318

EXERCISE. Identify the five parts of the friendly letter on page 318.

2. Qualities of a Good Friendly Letter

There are a number of qualities which help to make a good friendly letter, but the following are the most important:

(a) Keep the "you" attitude.

EXERCISE. Each of the following sentences has only the "I" or "we" attitude. What changes can be made to show an interest in "you," too?

1. Everyone here is very well. 2. Our basketball season has just started. 3. We had a wonderful Thanksgiving. 4. I hope to make better marks this term. 5. Dad gave me a new album of Benny Goodman records.

(b) Be courteous.

EXERCISE. Each of the following sentences is an example of unintentional rudeness. Rewrite the sentences to express your thoughts more courteously. With some, an entirely new sentence is necessary.

1. Since I haven't anything else to do, I thought I'd write you a note.
2. I've been meaning to write to you for a long time, but I've been terribly busy.
3. I'm writing to you now because I know you'll be hurt if I don't.
4. When you left, I told you I'd write to you; so here goes.
5. This is such a dull day that I thought I'd write to you.
6. I must close now; I have some work to do.
7. That's all for now. I'm off to the movies.
8. Well, I've told you everything; so I'll close.
9. This is a stupid letter, but I've been in a rush.
10. Hastily yours,

(c) Make your first and last sentences interesting.

Here are the first sentences of three famous letters. Notice how they catch interest immediately.

> You are the first friend to whom I write this morning.
>> JOHN RUSKIN

> Truth is such a rare thing, it is delightful to tell it.
>> EMILY DICKINSON

> Have I displeased you? I hoped the opposite.
>> NAPOLEON

The following last sentences illustrate pleasing ways to conclude letters:

> Think of me, sometimes, when the Alps and ocean divide us — but they never will, unless you wish it.
>> LORD BYRON

> I shall be here for a few days still. Be my good angel to the extent of throwing me a scrap of your beloved writing.
>> GEORGE BERNARD SHAW

EXERCISE. Find a collection of letters, and study the first and last sentences of a number of them.

(d) Use easy, familiar words.

If in your conversation with your friends you are accustomed to using long words, you should continue to do so in your letters. Otherwise, use the short, familiar words you ordinarily employ. In that way you will make your letters sound just as though you are talking.

EXERCISE. What words do you ordinarily use instead of the following?

for the purpose of	correspond	approximately
purchased	peruse	retain
at the present time	with regard to	endeavor

3. Kinds of Friendly Letters

The chatty news letter is probably the kind most frequently written. In addition to this kind are the following:

(a) Letter of request

Some letters of request obviously are business letters. Others, however, are properly friendly.

302 East Market Street
Council Bluffs, Iowa
February 2, 19—

Dear Miss Allen,

Will you give me permission to use your name as a reference? I am applying for a part-time position as stenographer at the First National Bank and must give the name of someone who is familiar with my abilities — or lack of them.

May I use your name, please?

Sincerely yours,

Katherine McCoy

(b) Letter of appreciation for favor granted

302 East Market Street
Council Bluffs, Iowa
February 10, 19—

Dear Miss Allen,

I can't begin to thank you for your kindness in allowing me to use your name as a reference. Whatever you said about me must have been all right, for I now have the position. I'll do my best to make you proud of me.

Thank you again for your help.

Yours truly,

Katherine McCoy

EXERCISE 1. If there is a real occasion for your having to write to someone to ask permission to use his name as a reference, write the letter now. Otherwise, write a make-believe letter of request. Address an "envelope."

EXERCISE 2. Write a letter of appreciation for permission to use a friend's name as a reference.

(c) Thank-you letter

> Route 5, Box 2
> Chattanooga 3, Tennessee
> December 28, 19—

Dear Grandmother,

What a Christmas I had this year! Everything was just right—and I mean just right. The sweater that you sent me is the best-looking one I ever had, and it fits me to a T. The fact that you knit it for me makes it all the better.

You're a sweetheart, Grandmother. I love you, and I thank you.

> Yours very gratefully,
> Jim

EXERCISE 1. If there is a thank-you letter which you should write, write it now.

EXERCISE 2. Sometimes we receive gifts which we do not like. Nevertheless, courteous, friendly thank-you notes must be written. Write a thank-you note for one of the following:

a pincushion   a crocheted doily
a book of fairy stories   an apron
a sea shell with a picture on it

EXERCISE 3. The following is an excerpt of a letter in the book *Dere Mable — Love Letters of a Rookie* by Edward Streeter. Write the paragraph as you think the rookie should have written it.

Thanks for the red sweter, Mable. We aint allowed to use them. But you dont want to feel bad about that cause I got lots of others and didnt need it anyway. An tell your mother thanks for the preserves an cake. I think thats what they was. They must have packed them between a steam roller and a donkey engin from the looks. Joe Loomis picked out most of the glass and tried some. Hed eat anything, that fellow, Mable. He said it must have been pretty good when it started. Tell that to your mother. I know it will please her.

(d) Letter of condolence

A letter of condolence is one of the hardest we have to write. However, if it is the right kind, it can bring more comfort than all the flowers and printed cards in the world. Here are a few *don't's* to remember:

Don't be gay or flippant.

Don't dwell on details that will heighten the grief of the reader.

Don't quote passages of poetry or of the Bible.

Don't use flowery language.

Ann, dear,

I didn't hear until this morning that you had lost your mother. This is a dreadful shock to you and her many friends, who loved her. You and your mother have had so many happy years together that I know the memory of them must be helping you even now.

I am coming to see you in the next few days. In the meantime, you have my love and deepest sympathy.

Your friend,

Carol

473 Elm Street
Boone, North Carolina
April 5, 19—

EXERCISE 1. If there is a letter of condolence which you should write, do it now.

EXERCISE 2. Write a letter of condolence to someone who has experienced one of the following:

(a) a severe injury suffered in an accident
(b) the death of a grandmother
(c) the loss of home and possessions through fire

(e) Letter of invitation

Broad Acres
Villa Nova, Pennsylvania
May 7, 19—

Dear Chuck,

Can you come for dinner on Saturday evening, May 15, at six-thirty?

My cousin, Jock Williams, is going to be here for the week end; and I should like you to meet him.

I do hope that you can come.

Sincerely,

Alice

(f) Letter of acceptance

714 Rutgers Avenue
Swarthmore, Pennyslvania
May 9, 19—

Dear Alice,

Thank you for inviting me to your house for dinner on Saturday evening, May 15, at six-thirty. I shall be there.

You have talked so many times about Jock that I'm looking forward to meeting him.

See you Saturday!

Your friend,
Chuck

(g) Letter of regret

714 Rutgers Avenue
Swarthmore, Pennsylvania
May 9, 19—

Dear Alice,

I'm sure that I'm the unluckiest fellow in the world. I have a new job that requires my "presence" on Saturday evenings. This sad fact means that I cannot accept your invitation.

I'll telephone sometime Friday to find out when it will be convenient for me to run over to meet Jock. I do want to meet that cousin of yours.

Thank you for inviting me; I'm sorry that I can't be with you.

Sincerely yours,
Chuck

EXERCISE 1. Write to invite a friend to one of the following:

a week end at your home	a New Year's party
a camping trip	a Sunday-evening supper

EXERCISE 2. Write an acceptance and a regret to one of the invitations suggested in EXERCISE 1.

(h) Formal invitations and replies

A formal invitation is generally printed; the acceptance or regret is handwritten.

Invitation

Mr. and Mrs. Jonathan Parnell

request the pleasure of your company

at an informal dance

Thursday, the second of February

at nine o'clock

Essex House

R.S.V.P.

Acceptance

Miss Shirley Wayne
accepts with pleasure
Mr. and Mrs. Jonathan Parnell's
invitation for dancing
on Thursday, the second of February
at nine o'clock
at the Essex House

Regret

Miss Shirley Wayne
regrets that she is unable to accept
Mr. and Mrs. Jonathan Parnell's
kind invitation for dancing
on Thursday, the second of February
at nine o'clock
because of a previous invitation

Review Exercises

EXERCISE 1. Draft a letter of application for a job that you would like to have. Address the "envelope."

EXERCISE 2. Write to B. Altman and Company, Fifth Avenue, New York, ordering one flannel lounging robe for men, navy blue, large size, price $11.95; one pair of leisure slippers, navy blue, size 10, price $6.95; two pairs of men's pajamas, white, size C, price $4.50 each. Pay for the order by check. Address an "envelope."

EXERCISE 3. One of the articles ordered in EXERCISE 2 was not received. Write a letter inquiring about it.

EXERCISE 4. Write a chatty news letter to one of your friends living in another community. This letter is really to be sent.

EXERCISE 5. Write a letter to a teacher or to a parent, asking him or her to be a chaperon at one of your school functions. Address an "envelope."

EXERCISE 6. Write a letter to someone who has done a favor for you. Mail the letter.

EXERCISE 7. Write a letter to a firm or to a college requesting a catalogue.

EXERCISE 8. Write a formal invitation to a school party. Then write a formal note of acceptance and one of regret.

EXERCISE 9. Letters of condolence are written also to persons suffering from minor ailments. In such letters, a lighter tone is permissible. Write to a friend who is indisposed because of:

mumps	pinkeye	loss of voice
hives	stiff neck	toothache

EXERCISE 10. Rewrite correctly each of the following:

1. I remain, Yours very sincerely, John Doe
2. Please be advised we are out of stock.
3. Having nothing better to do, I take my pen in hand.
4. You will never get over the death of your mother.
5. I cannot tell you the affect your letter had on me.

EXERCISE 11. Lord Chesterfield wrote to his son, "In short, let me see more of you in your letters." What is the importance of this statement in both business and friendly letters?

LIBRARY TECHNIQUES

VALUE OF THE LIBRARY

A library is a useful tool, and it is well worth your while to learn how to use it effectively. A knowledge of the resources of your school or public library and an understanding of the way in which they are organized are necessary if you are to utilize them efficiently in research, either now or later.

Lib 1   Arrangement of Books

The plan most commonly used in school and public libraries in the United States is the Dewey Decimal System. Under this plan, the books are divided according to their subject matter into main divisions, such as history, science, religion. Each group is given a number between 0 and 1000. This number is written on the back of every book of that group. The books are then placed on the shelves in the order of their numbers, from left to right in each section of shelves. By means of this classification, books can be found quickly and easily.

Here are the numbers as they are assigned to the different classes of books:

000–099	General works	500–599	Science
100–199	Philosophy	600–699	Useful arts
200–299	Religion	700–799	Fine arts
300–399	Sociology	800–899	Literature
400–499	Language	900–999	History and travel

Looking at this outline, what number would you expect to find on a biology book? on a music book? on a book of fiction?

Logically, fiction would be placed with literature in the 800 class. However, because fiction is generally used more often than other kinds of books, most libraries place it on a special shelf, usually the most accessible one. Books of fiction carry the initial of the family name of the author, rather than a class number. The books are then arranged alphabetically according to the letters on the backs. In a library which has a large collection of fiction, each author is assigned a number, which is written on the backs of all his books, preceded by his initial, like this:

AUTHOR'S NAME	NUMBER
Abbot	A126
Adams	A211
Allee	A422

In this way, the books of each author are kept together.

Large libraries, including some high-school libraries, use similar author numbers on their nonfiction books, placing them on the backs of the books under the class numbers.

Biography is generally removed from the history shelves where it might normally appear. It is usually shelved next to the fiction. A book covering the life of one person is an individual biography. It is marked 92 (*not* 092) or B, depending upon the library. Beneath the 92 or the B is placed the initial of the person whom the book is about. These books are then arranged on the shelves alphabetically by initials. What number and letter would you expect to find on a life of George Washington? A book which contains accounts of the lives of two or more persons is a collective biography. It is marked 920, is usually placed immediately before or after the individual biographies, and is arranged alphabetically by author.

EXERCISE 1. Go to your library and see how efficiently you can carry out the following directions:

Find the shelves lined with books numbered from 000 to 099. Select one book in this class and jot down the author, title, and number. Walk around the library from left to right. Find one book in each of the classes listed on page 330 and write the name of the author, the title, and the number. Notice that books with the same number are arranged alphabetically by author. Does your library use author numbers? Where is the fiction located? Select one book of fiction and write the name of the author, the title, and the letter (or letter and author number). Find an individual biography and a collective biography and do the same for each. Which, of all the classes, contains the largest number of books?

As you can see from the outline on page 330, each of these divisions is general. In the average school library, there will be several hundred books in each division; and in a large library, there may be thousands. Each will include a number of different kinds of books, all on the same general subject. For instance, history will include ancient, medieval, modern, and the histories of individual countries. It would be awkward for the reader if he were obliged to search through so many books in order to find one on a specific era or country. For this reason, the main classes are further divided, each one into ten subclasses;

and each of these, in turn, into ten smaller classes. Let us take science as an example:

   500   Science
        510   Mathematics
                511   Arithmetic
                512   Algebra
                513   Geometry
                        513.1   **Plane geometry**
        520   Astronomy
        530   Physics
        540   Chemistry
        550   Geology
        560   Paleontology
        570   Biology
        580   Botany
        590   Zoology

The other sciences are divided just as mathematics is in the example. For instance, chemistry is divided into analytical chemistry, organic chemistry, and others. This process of division continues as the subject narrows. Notice how the use of decimals makes it possible to expand the system indefinitely.

The shelves which you investigated in your first exercise hold the books which you are permitted to borrow from the library. There is also a collection which may not be taken from the library because the books are in constant use. These are the reference books. They are shelved apart from the others but arranged in the same way. Each number, however, is preceded by the letter R.

In school libraries, the books are arranged on open shelves; and you are permitted to go to them to find your own books. In large public and college libraries, only a part of the collection is open to the reader. The other books are kept on closed shelves, called *stacks*, which are not accessible to the visitor. In such cases, he must ask a librarian for his books. To secure them, he fills out a slip of paper giving the authors, titles, and numbers of the books that he wants. For this reason, the number on the back of a book is referred to as the *call number*. It includes the class number and the author letter.

Where are the reference books kept in your library?

EXERCISE 2. Find one book on each of the following subjects, and write the name of the author, the title, and the call number:

chemistry, physics, geology, painting, music, party games, poems, plays, history of the Crusades, history of England, history of the United States, English grammar, Spanish grammar, Latin grammar, life of Abraham Lincoln, novel by Charles Dickens, manners, United States Government

Many college libraries use the Library of Congress Classification. As you will see, it differs somewhat from the Dewey Decimal System. However, if you understand the general principles of classification, you will have no difficulty in using either system. It is necessary for you only to understand, not to memorize, a system of classification, because you will always be able to find the call number of a book by consulting the card catalogue.

LIBRARY OF CONGRESS CLASSIFICATION

A	General works	M	Music
B	Philosophy, religion	N	Fine arts
C	History	P	Language and literature
D	Foreign history	Q	Science
E,F	American history	R	Medicine
G	Geography, anthropology	S	Agriculture
H	Social sciences	T	Technology
J	Political science	U	Military science
K	Law	V	Naval science
L	Education	Z	Library science, bibliography

Lib 2   The Card Catalogue

The card catalogue is the index to the library. It lists by author, title, and subject the books owned by the library and locates each one by giving its call number. It gives also the name of the publisher, the date of publication, the number of pages, and sometimes a list of contents; and it tells whether or not the book is illustrated.

The catalogue is made of cards arranged alphabetically and kept in drawers, which are labeled. There are usually three cards for a book, one with the name of the author, one with the title, and one with the subject at the top. Below are samples of the cards used. Only the tops of the cards are given. You need not be concerned with the printing at the bottom of a card. It is there only for the convenience of the librarian.

1.
```
92      Goss, Madeleine (Binkley) 1892–
B          Deep-flowing brook, the story of
        Johann Sebastian Bach.  N.Y. Holt,
        1938.
           239 p. illus.
```

This card means that there is in the library a book by Madeleine Goss (her maiden name was Binkley, and she was born in 1892) titled *Deep-flowing Brook*. This book was published in New York by Henry Holt and Company in 1938. It has 239 pages and is illustrated. Its call number is 92 B. This is an author card, and it is filed under the author's name. You will find all the cards for books by this author in the same place in the catalogue, arranged alphabetically by the first word of each title, unless this word is an article. In that case, its placement is governed by the second word.

If you want to find the book *Deep-flowing Brook*, turn to the D's and you will find this card:

2.
```
92          Deep-flowing brook.            1938.
B          Goss, M.B.
```

This card tells you that the book was written by M. B. Goss and published in 1938; and its call number is 92 B. If you want further information about it, you will have to turn to the author card.

Suppose that you wish to find a book about Johann Sebastian Bach: turn to the B's and look up *Bach*. You will find this card:

3.
```
92          BACH, JOHANN SEBASTIAN
B          Goss, M.B.
              Deep-flowing brook, the story of
          Johann Sebastian Bach.  N.Y. Holt,
          1938.
              239 p. illus.
```

Bach is the subject of this book, and *Goss* is its author. Notice that the subject is in capital letters and is indented. The subject is usually written in capital letters or in red. It is always indented so that it is even with the beginning of the title, while the author's name is never indented. With this arrangement, you can always distinguish the author's name from the subject of the book.

In addition to this card, you will find others which list books about Bach, arranged in alphabetical order by the names of the authors. Thus, by looking for any subject in its alphabetical place, you will find all the books that your library has on that subject, each on a separate card, arranged alphabetically by author.

When a subject is a large one, with separate books written on different phases of it, it is divided into subtopics. These subtopics are arranged under the main subject, in alphabetical order. For example, all the books on the Second World War are arranged under "World War, 1939–45." Since many books have been written on the war in its different phases, it is necessary to divide them according to specific subjects, such as "Aerial Operations," "Causes," "Diplomatic History." All the subtopics are arranged alphabetically; for example, "World War, 1939–45 — Aerial Operations," "World War, 1939–45 — African Campaign," "World War, 1939–45 — Causes." The cards for the books on the history of a country are arranged chronologically rather than alphabetically: "United States — History — Colonial Period," "United States — History — French and Indian War," "United States — History — Revolution." With this arrangement, the reader is able to turn at once to the cards on the particular phase of the subject in which he is interested.

Sometimes a book contains material on more than one subject or represents a collection of the works of different authors. In that case, a card is made for each part of the book. This is called an analytical card.

Subject analytic:

```
333      GRAZING
            in
         Cheyney, E.G. and Schantz-Hansen,
         Thorvald
            This is our land. N.Y. Webb, 1946.
            p. 173-99.
```

This card means that there is material on grazing in the book *This Is Our Land* by Cheyney and Schantz-Hansen. It is found on pages 173–199. What is the call number of this book?

Author analytic:

```
822.8 Anderson, Maxwell, 1888-
        Winterset
          in
      Quinn, A.H. comp.
        Representative American plays from
      1767 to the present day. 6th ed.
      rev. and enl.  N.Y. Appleton, 1938.
        p. 1101-38.
```

Who wrote the play *Winterset?* What is the title of a
book in which you can find it? Who compiled the book?
On what page does this play start? What is the call number
of the book?

When looking up material in the card catalogue, you may
find that the catalogue uses a different name for a subject
or person from the one with which you are familiar. In
such case, the catalogue refers you to the name it uses. For
instance, if you want to find a book by Elswyth Thane,
and look under her name, you will find a card like this:

```
  Thane, Elswyth, pseud.
        see
Beebe, Elswyth Thane (Ricker)
```

This means: in order to find the books by Elswyth
Thane, in this library, you must look under her real name,
Elswyth Thane Beebe. You then turn from the T's to the
drawer that contains the B's, and there you will find her
books listed. This is called a *cross reference.*

Cross references are used also to tell you that you can
find additional material on a subject by looking up other
related subjects. For example:

```
  ANIMALS,
      see also
DOMESTIC ANIMALS; PETS; also names of
special animals (e.g. DOGS, SQUIRRELS)
```

This card tells you that if you want more books about animals than those listed under the subject "Animals," you should look up the other topics listed on the cross-reference card.

EXERCISE. Write the answers to the following questions:

1. What are the call numbers of the books by Edward Ellsberg?
2. Who wrote *Les Misérables?*
3. What is the latest book on economics in your library?
4. Find a play that appears in a collection of plays. Who is the author of the play and what is its title? What is the call number of the book in which you found it?
5. Can you locate three books on submarine action in World War II? List them alphabetically by author.
6. Does your library have an up-to-date book on personal grooming? What is the name of it?
7. Can you find two books on the government of your state? Name them.
8. Are there any cookbooks in the library? List three of them with the author, title, and call number of each.

There are a number of printed indexes that supplement the card catalogue. If your library catalogue does not have analytical cards, you must use these indexes to locate works in collections, such as plays, short stories, and biographies. You will find these aids by looking up the call numbers in the catalogue. Some of the most useful ones are:

ESSAY AND GENERAL LITERATURE INDEXES

Firkins, *Index to Plays*
Index to Short Stories
Lenrow, *Readers' Guide to Prose Fiction*
Logasa, *Biography in Collections*
Index to One-act Plays
Sutton, *Speech Index*

Lib 3   General Reference Books

As mentioned above, reference books may not be removed from the library because they are in constant use. They are written to provide information rather than to be enjoyed. Their arrangement enables the reader to find information with the least possible expenditure of time and effort. A good reference book is arranged either alphabetically or with a detailed index.

Each reference work has its own particular arrangement. You will save considerable time by observing certain rules in using them:

1. Notice whether the book is arranged alphabetically. If it is, turn to the correct place in the alphabet. If the book uses a different word for your subject from the one that you are using, there will be a cross reference from the word that you are looking for to the one used by the book, just as in the card catalogue. After you have read the material on your subject, look at the end of the article to see whether there is a list of related subjects for additional information. After you have traced all the references provided, see whether the book has an index. If it has, you may be able to locate additional information through its use.

2. If the book is not arranged alphabetically, look at the table of contents to find the page where the index starts. If you cannot locate the index through the table of contents, you will be obliged to hunt for it. Usually it appears at the back of the book. When you find it, read the note at the top of the first page. This note is important since it tells you how to use that particular index. If you are using a set of books of more than one volume, look first to see whether the index is in a separate volume. There are cross references in the indexes just as there are in the card catalogue and the encyclopedias.

With the exception of the unabridged dictionaries (see page 139), the encyclopedias are the most important reference books in the library. They contain information on all subjects, in concise form. The best ones for your use are *The Encyclopedia Americana* and the *Encyclopædia Britannica*. In these works, each article is written and signed by an authority on the subject. *The World Book Encyclopedia* is also good but is written in a less scholarly manner. The *Lincoln Library of Essential Information* is an authoritative work also but with only brief information on each subject, as it consists of only one volume. When seeking information on a subject in which it is important to keep up-to-date, such as science, always check the date of publication of the reference work.

Since it is impossible to revise these books every year and insert new facts, encyclopedias are kept up-to-date by yearbooks. One of these is issued each year. In it the subjects which are treated in the main set are rounded out by the addition of new facts which have come to light or events which have taken place during the year. The yearbooks are usually kept on the shelf beside the encyclopedia which they supplement.

EXERCISE. Follow these directions:

1. Make a list of the general encyclopedias in your library. Since there is no author for encyclopedias, list them alphabetically by title. After the title of each, note the date of publication and the number of volumes.
2. Locate the latest yearbook for each encyclopedia and find the answers to these questions: Who won the Pulitzer prize for the novel last year? What was the greatest advance made in aviation during the year preceding this one?
3. Use the gazetteer of an unabridged dictionary to find the size of Texas and that of Rhode Island. Find the capitals of Tasmania and Luxemburg.

Lib 4   Specialized Reference Books

Since encyclopedias and other general reference books cover the entire realm of knowledge, they cannot treat each subject fully enough to satisfy all your requirements. When you need fuller or more detailed information in any field, consult the reference books in that particular field.

Below is a list of the most important ones in each field. When using the books, remember the methods for locating material in general reference books.

STATISTICS

> *Statistical Abstract of the United States*
> *The World Almanac*

EXERCISE 1. Follow these directions:

1. Examine *The World Almanac* for the current year and answer the following questions: What is the official flower of your state? Who was Secretary of State during the administration of President Cleveland? Who won the National League pennant last year?

2. Using the *Statistical Abstract of the United States,* find the answers to the following: How many tons of coal were mined in the United States during the year 1942? How many colleges are there in this country?

BIOGRAPHY

> *American Authors, 1600–1900*
> *British Authors of the Nineteenth Century*
> *Current Biography*
> *Dictionary of American Biography*
> *Dictionary of National Biography* (British)
> *Lippincott's Pronouncing Biographical Dictionary*
> *Twentieth Century Authors*
> *Webster's Biographical Dictionary*
> *Who's Who*
> *Who's Who in America*

EXERCISE 2. By using the reference books on biography, see whether you can find the answers to these questions:

1. What is the pseudonym of William Sydney Porter?
2. What is the address of your favorite actress?
3. What are the chief characteristics of the poetry of Walt Whitman?
4. Where was John Alden's home before he emigrated to America?
5. What governmental position was held by each of the following writers: Hawthorne? Howells? Robinson?

HISTORY

Cambridge Modern History
Dictionary of American History
New Larned History for Ready Reference, Reading, and Research

EXERCISE 3. Find the answers to these questions:

1. What were the provisions of the Missouri Compromise?
2. When and where was the first free public school established?
3. What relation was Mary Queen of Scots to Queen Elizabeth?
4. What war was terminated by the Peace of Westphalia?
5. What was the purpose of the Monroe Doctrine?

LITERATURE

Bartlett's *Familiar Quotations*
Cambridge History of American Literature
Cambridge History of English Literature
Granger's *Index to Poetry and Recitations*
Oxford Companion to American Literature
Oxford Companion to Classical Literature
Oxford Companion to English Literature

EXERCISE 4. Find the answers to these questions:

1. Who is an American poet of the colonial period?
2. What was revolutionary about the poetry of Wordsworth?

3. Who said, "A rolling stone gathers no moss"?
4. Why do some people think that Sir Francis Bacon wrote the plays of Shakespeare? What do you think?
5. Who wrote the poem "The Highwayman"?

SCIENCE

    Chemical Rubber Company, *Handbook of Chemistry and Physics*

    Hackh, *Chemical Dictionary*

    Hiscox, *Henley's Twentieth Century Book of Formulas, Processes, and Trade Secrets*

    Van Nostrand's Scientific Encyclopedia

EXERCISE 5. Answer these questions:

1. What is the chemical composition of a ruby?
2. What fuel gives the greatest exhaust velocity when burned in a combustion chamber?
3. What is a good moth repellent?
4. What is the specific gravity of grain alcohol?

GOVERNMENT

    Official Congressional Directory

    United States Government Manual

    State Manuals. These are issued by the state governments. The title varies with the state.

EXERCISE 6. Can you answer these questions?

1. Does your state government publish a manual? If so, what is the title? How often is it published?
2. How often does your state legislature meet?
3. What is the length of the term of the governor? Is he permitted to succeed himself?
4. Who are the members of the Supreme Court of the United States?
5. In what Congressional district do you live?
6. Who are the United States senators from your state?

MUSIC

    Grove's Dictionary of Music and Musicians

EXERCISE 7. What is the difference in form between German and Italian opera?

PLACES

    Every unabridged dictionary contains place names, with location and pronunciation.

    Adams's *Atlas of American History*

    Encyclopædia Britannica World Atlas

    Goode's School Atlas

    Lippincott's *Complete Pronouncing Gazetteer and Geographical Dictionary of the World*

    Shepherd's *Historical Atlas*

EXERCISE 8. Answer these questions:

1. Where and what is Andorra?
2. What is the population of Trinidad?
3. Can you trace the route followed by Lewis and Clark from the Mississippi River to the Columbia?
4. What are the seven wonders of the ancient world?

THE ENGLISH LANGUAGE

    Fowler, *A Dictionary of Modern English Usage*

    Mawson, *Roget's International Thesaurus of English Words and Phrases*

    Vaille, *How Shall I Pronounce It?*

    Webster's Dictionary of Synonyms

    Weseen, *Crowell's Dictionary of English Grammar and Handbook of American Usage*

EXERCISE 9. Which book or books would you consult to find the answers to these questions:

1. What is another word for *damage?*
2. What is said about the usage of "It is I" or "It is me"?
3. What other words can be used to mean *hope? fear? doubt?*
4. What is meant by such terms as *nominative absolute? gerund?*

Lib 5   Magazines

The back numbers of magazines provide a great store of useful and interesting information.

Magazines appear at regular intervals — every week, every month, quarterly. Several consecutive issues make a volume. The number of issues in a volume depends upon the magazine. Each volume has a number, beginning with "one" when the magazine starts publication. The volume number appears on each issue. Usually the paging is continuous for the entire volume. Libraries often bind the back numbers of their magazines into book form, usually adding a title page and an index to each volume. The volume numbers are then marked on the backs, and the volumes are shelved as books.

How will you find the magazine articles that will be of use to you? Fortunately, it is not necessary for you to go through the index of each magazine, for a number of combination indexes are published.

The one which indexes the magazines most commonly used is the *Readers' Guide to Periodical Literature*. This is an alphabetical list which includes authors, subjects, and titles of magazine articles. In the front of each number of the *Readers' Guide*, there is a list of the magazines indexed and a table of abbreviations used. Here is a specimen entry:

TOYS
Guide to the best in toys. V. W. Marx. il
Parents Mag 35:34-5+ D '48

This means that there is an article titled "Guide to the Best in Toys" by V. W. Marx. It appeared in *Parents' Magazine*, Volume 35, pages 34 and 35, with a continuation on a later page. This issue was dated December, 1948. The article is illustrated. It was located by looking under the subject "Toys" in the *Readers' Guide*.

Large subjects are subdivided in the *Readers' Guide;* and cross references are used, just as they are in the card catalogue.

The *Readers' Guide* is published every two weeks. The one published at the end of a month contains the entries that were in the former one plus the new material for the last two weeks. When the latest *Guide* is received in the library, the former, smaller one, is discarded. Every few months, a larger one is published which contains entries for the preceding months. The smaller ones are then discarded. At the end of a year, all this material is gathered into a bound volume. The dates covered by the magazines indexed are plainly marked on the back of each number of the *Readers' Guide.* If you want to find an article on an event which occurred last November, you will use the *Readers' Guide* that covers magazines published during that month. If you wish to locate all the magazine articles on a certain subject, such as "Inflation," start with the latest and smallest number of the *Readers' Guide* and work back to the earliest volume.

You can discover which magazines your library keeps on file by using the card catalogue.

If your library keeps its magazines on the open shelves or in cupboards which are accessible to the reader, you may go there to get the ones you need. If, on the other hand, they are kept in locked cupboards or in the stacks, you must make a list, accurately furnishing the volume, the number, and the exact date of each one. Then ask a librarian to get them for you.

There are other indexes for more specialized magazines; but, as a rule, these are found only in larger libraries. If you go to a library which has these indexes, the librarian will be glad to direct you to them. You will use them just as you do the *Readers' Guide.*

EXERCISE. Follow these directions:

1. Look up "United States" in the *Readers' Guide*. Make a list of the subtopics under this subject.
2. Find a magazine article about the latest Presidential election.
3. Find a picture of a contemporary stage setting for *Hamlet*.
4. Locate in a recent magazine a poem by R. P. Tristram Coffin.
5. Find the most recent article available on UNESCO.

Lib 6   Pamphlets

Pamphlets are small, paper-backed books. Sometimes they contain valuable material not to be found in bound volumes. Some libraries keep them in boxes, which are classified and placed on the shelves with the books on the same subject. Others keep them in filing cabinets, arranged alphabetically by subject. Where does your school library keep them?

EXERCISE. Make a list of five pamphlets, giving the name of the author, if possible, the title, the publisher, and the date of publication.

Review Exercises

DEWEY DECIMAL SYSTEM

1. Draw a floor plan of your library, putting in the Dewey Decimal numbers to show where the books of each class are shelved.
2. Find one book in each of the following classes. Write the name of the author, the title, and the date of publication: 940.1, 942, 970.1, 973.2, 540, 570, 590, 750, 780, 796.33, 821, 353, 170, 220, 620, 640, 822.

CARD CATALOGUE

Choose a topic. Make a list of all the books that your library has on that topic. Arrange your list alphabetically by author.

REFERENCE BOOKS

Decide which of the reference books will be most likely to answer each of the questions below. Check the book to see whether your guess was correct. Give the answer to each question.

1. How many feet are there in a rod?
2. How should you pronounce *Pepys?*
3. Where will you find the lines, "Oh wind, if winter comes, can spring be far behind?"
4. What is the address of the Government Printing Office?
5. What is the place of Amy Lowell in American literature?
6. What was accomplished by the Council of Trent?
7. What is face powder made of?
8. What horse won the Kentucky Derby last year?
9. What is the highest mountain peak in the United States?
10. What is the purpose of the Fort Peck dam?

READERS' GUIDE TO PERIODICAL LITERATURE

1. Make a list of the magazines that are kept on file in your library. Which ones are bound?
2. Choose a topic of current interest. Make a list of all the magazine articles that were published on that topic during the past year. Give author, title, magazine, date, and pages. How many of these magazines are to be found in your library?

THE RESEARCH PAPER

VALUE

The research paper is known by several different names — term report, term paper, long theme; but each name carries the same meaning. Because no one ever knows all that he should know or wants to know, the research paper can bring the personal satisfaction that additional information always provides. Moreover, because it necessitates research, the comparison and contrast of ideas, the organization of points to be discussed, the formulation of opinions as a result of evidence, the research paper can develop good habits of thinking.

R P 1   Choosing a Subject

In choosing a subject for a research paper, there are four important points to be considered.

1. The subject should require research.

The research paper differs from the ordinary composition in that it is based on research. A paper that is based

349

only upon the opinion of the writer should not be called a research paper; more properly it should be called an essay, a theme, or a composition.

EXERCISE 1. Which of these topics would require research and, therefore, could be the basis of a paper?

1. Folk Poetry	11. Origin of Baseball
2. Dilemma at a Cafeteria	12. Hats Reflect Personality
3. Cartooning	13. Johnny Appleseed
4. Jazz	14. Contour Farming
5. Dull Conversationalists	15. Grandmothers
6. The Grasshopper	16. Mardi Gras
7. On Being in Love	17. Cold Shower Baths
8. Story of Stamps	18. Pennsylvania Dutch Customs
9. Christmas Shopping	19. Ambitions of Childhood
10. Charleston Architecture	20. Discovery of Oil

2. The subject should not be too broad for proper treatment.

A subject for a research paper should be narrow enough to be treated adequately in two or three thousand words.

EXERCISE 2. Reduce each of the following general topics to suitable subjects for research papers:

1. Poetry	6. Communication	11. Greece
2. Music	7. Transportation	12. Science
3. Astronomy	8. The Movies	13. Mark Twain
4. Dams	9. Shakespeare	14. Revolutionary War
5. Architecture	10. Painting	15. Railroads

3. The subject should be interesting to the writer and should be within his range of understanding.

EXERCISE 3. Which of the following would you like to know more about, and which do you believe deal with material you would understand?

1. Aegean Civilization	3. Comets
2. Gauguin	4. Binocular Instruments

5. Costume Design
6. Symbolism
7. Criminal Law
8. Gyroscope
9. Tapestry
10. Women's Suffrage

11. Glacial Period
12. Relativity
13. Helmets
14. Spectroscopy
15. Flight
16. Cubism

4. The research material to be used in developing the subject must be available.

No matter how interesting or worth while your chosen subject may be, it is useless if your library does not have source material dealing with it. Before you definitely decide upon a subject for a research paper, it is usually wise to make a rapid survey of materials available. The card catalogue (pages 334 to 338) and the *Readers' Guide to Periodical Literature* (pages 345 and 346) can tell you at once whether you should proceed with your subject.

R P 2   Making Tentative Plans

There is no such thing as jumping into a research paper without some preliminary thought. After you have chosen a suitable subject and ascertained how much material is available on it, stop to think about it. Think about it *before you start reading*. Ask yourself what you would like to know about the topic and what you think others would be interested in learning.

If you are going to write a paper on "Jazz" or "Folk Poetry," there are certain obvious questions which you will want to have answered. Those questions, then, will direct your reading into specific channels.

JAZZ

1. What is the history of jazz?
2. How is jazz different from conventional music?
3. What has been its influence on modern music?

351

FOLK POETRY

1. What is the origin of folk poetry?
2. What are its characteristics?
3. What folk poetry do we have in the United States?

EXERCISE 1. Write three or four questions concerning each of the following topics which would act as a guide in your reading:

1. Stamp Collecting	8. Balloons
2. Diamonds	9. Masks
3. The Olympics	10. The Cotton Gin
4. Early American Art	11. The Blind
5. Cartooning	12. Transcendentalism
6. Rodeos	13. Mountain Climbing
7. Panama Canal	14. The Pony Express

EXERCISE 2. When you have chosen a topic for a research paper, write three or four questions about it which will indicate the direction of your reading.

R P 3   Taking Notes

On pages 329 to 347 you will find the ways to use a library painlessly and efficiently in your search for reference materials. Before you go to the library, it is wise to master the art of note taking. You will certainly not take notes on everything that you read, but you will take notes — and many of them — on the questions which you have decided are important.

The following system of note taking is easy:

1. Use 3″ × 5″ cards or slips of paper.
2. Make a separate card for each new fact.
3. In the upper left-hand corner, write the name of the author; underneath it write the name of the book, or of the magazine and article, and the page reference.

4. In the upper right-hand corner, write the topic.

5. Unless you want a direct quotation, put the idea in your own words. It is usually wise to take notes in words or phrases rather than in sentences.

6. If you want a direct quotation, be sure that you copy the statement *exactly*.

Here is an example of a card taking a direct quotation:

Spaeth, Sigmund   *Definition of*
                                     jazz

At Home with Music, p. 256

"In a broad sense, modernism and jazz amount to the same thing. Both may be most simply defined as the distortion of the conventional in music."

Here is a paragraph taken from Mr. Spaeth's book, followed by an example of notes that might be taken on it:

The same thing has happened in the other arts, and here also there seems to be a limit beyond which scientific experiment cannot go without a definite sacrifice of beauty. The futuristic and cubist schools of painting are now generally discredited, although many of the offshoots of impressionism continue to command attention and respect. The absurdities of modernistic furniture, sculpture, and architecture are no longer taken very seriously, and the silly, formless puerilities that have masqueraded as literature are gradually finding the oblivion that they deserved.[1]

[1] From *At Home with Music* by Sigmund Spaeth published by Doubleday & Company, Inc.

Spaeth, Sigmund   *Modernism in other arts*

At Home with Music, p. 257

    Experimentation in all the arts

    Futuristic and cubist schools of painting
       discredited

    Modernistic furniture, sculpture, architecture
       less popular

    Foolish experiments in literature now rejected

EXERCISE. Take suitable notes on these excerpts:

1. JAZZ is a name which, since the period of the World War of 1914 to 1918, has been generally and ambiguously applied to American popular dance music in common time. Borrowed from music, the word *jazz* was widely used with reference to American social mores during the decade following the war of 1914–1918 — the so-called "jazz age" — a period notable for, among other things, a financial boom, Prohibition, bootleggers' gang wars, mixed drinking in speakeasies, knee-length skirts, and parvenu display. The urban manners of the time are suggested in such novels as F. Scott Fitzgerald's *The Great Gatsby* and John Dos Passos' trilogy *U.S.A.* The word jazz has also passed into the language as a synonym for racy; thus, a writer may be said to have a jazz style, or a dress may be referred to as a jazzy costume.

Encyclopædia Britannica

2. A large part of our interest in ragtime, jazz, or swing is in the energetic rhythms. I don't mean that jazz is not at times very beautiful in every musical sense; there is no reason why it shouldn't be so always. But we need to remind ourselves more often than we do that though jazz rhythms are not the most subtle in the world, they are on the whole more subtle than those

354

we usually notice. Even the jazz which musically is very bad may legitimately attract through its rhythmic power.

JOHN ERSKINE

3. Jazz distorts the conventions of popular music just as modernism in general distorts those of the serious, classic type. A reminder of the general definition of music as the Organization of Sound toward Beauty will simplify the analysis of possible distortions.

SIGMUND SPAETH [1]

4. Nice last week was holding the first International Jazz Festival. Jazz fans from all over Western Europe (including G. I.s given special leave from Germany) flocked to it. In Nice's plum-plush opera house, they heard jazz from seven nations, including three brands of U.S. stuff.

Time [2]

5. Certain Negroid jazz improvisers have been widely admired for their inventiveness and virtuosity, both by dance musicians and others familiar with the idiom. A few of these may be mentioned (the names of Negroes are italicized): trumpets — *Louis Armstrong*, Leon "Bix" Beiderbecke; trombones — *Jay C. Higginbotham*, Jackson Teagarden; clarinets — "Pee Wee" Russell, Frank Teschmaker; saxophones — *Johnny Hodges*, Lawrence "Bud" Freeman, *Coleman Hawkins;* pianists — *Earl Hines*, Jess Stacy, *Teddy Wilson*.

Encyclopædia Britannica

Bibliography Cards

Since a bibliography is an essential part of a research paper, you can save a tremendous amount of time by taking the necessary information as you go along. All the books, magazines, and newspapers which you use in writing your paper should be listed in your bibliography. Consequently, *as you use them,* jot down the necessary information on

---

[1] From *At Home with Music* by Sigmund Spaeth published by Doubleday & Company, Inc.   [2] Courtesy of *Time*, Copyright Time Inc., 1948.

3″ × 5″ cards. Making a bibliography will then be simply a matter of copying your cards.

Notice that in this example even the call number of the book is included. Sometimes it is necessary to use a book a second time; it helps to have all the information.

```
Spaeth, Sigmund

At Home with Music

Doubleday, Doran and Company

Garden City, 1945
                                    780
pp. 256–261                         S732a
```

R P 4   Making an Outline

After you have done all the research and taken all the notes that you think are necessary, you are ready to make an outline. First arrange your cards in stacks according to the broad classifications in which they fall. Then arrange the cards in each stack in as logical a way as you know how. Obviously, there will be cards which do not seem to fit under any classification. Put them in a discard stack; you may find use for them later. The outline which you will make will show in skeleton form the organization of your findings and of your thinking.

The two kinds of outlines which you will use most frequently are the topic outline and the sentence outline.

1. The topic outline

FOLK POETRY

I. Theories of the origin of folk poetry, or ballads
    A. Communal beginnings
        1. No specific parenthood
        2. Outcropping of tribal song and dance

            B. Unknown author
                1. Not a literary person
                2. Songs elaborated by common folk
            C. Minstrels before time of recorded history
            D. Minstrels of later period
                1. Most authorities of this opinion
                2. Proof offered for this belief
                    a. Most ballads made in 16th century
                    b. Genius of individual poets seen, rather
                       than of groups
    II. Characteristics of folk poetry
            A. Subject matter
                1. History
                    a. Robin Hood ballads
                    b. "The Outlaw Murry"
                2. Romance
                    a. "Douglas Tragedy"
                    b. "The Gay Goss Hawk"
                3. Superstition and horror
                    a. "The Wife of Usher's Well"
                    b. "Lord Randal"
            B. Form
                1. Story simple and crude
                2. Plot highly condensed
                3. Use of verse and chorus
                4. Use of conventional descriptive terms
                    a. "wealthy wife"
                    b. "blude-reid wine"
                    c. "merry greenwood"
    III. Folk poetry in the United States
            A. Sectional poetry
                1. Southern Appalachian section
                2. New England
                3. Southwest

        B. Occupational and racial poetry
            1. Loggers
            2. Seamen
            3. Cowboys
            4. Miners
            5. Negroes
            6. Indians

2. The sentence outline

The sentence outline differs from the topic outline only in the use of complete sentences instead of topics. Here is the first section of the outline on "Folk Poetry" as it would appear in a sentence outline:

FOLK POETRY

I. There are four theories concerning the origin of folk poetry, or ballads.
    A. First, the poetry may have had communal beginnings.
        1. According to this theory, the poetry had no specific authorship.
        2. It was the outcropping of tribal song and dance.
    B. Second, the poetry had specific authorship, though now unknown.
        1. The authors were not of the literary class.
        2. Their work was elaborated upon by the common people.
    C. Third, the poetry was created by minstrels who lived before the time of recorded history.
    D. Fourth, the poetry was created by minstrels of a later period in history.
        1. Most authorities accept the fourth explanation of the origin of folk poetry.

2. The proof which they offer is convincing.
   a. They point out that most ballads were made in the 16th century.
   b. They point out, too, that the ballads show the genius of individual poets rather than the doubtful genius of groups.

EXERCISE 1. Complete the sentence outline in sections II and III.

EXERCISE 2. Arrange the following main topics and subtopics in good outline form:

Main topics

PECOS BILL

I. Is the legendary hero of the Southwest
II. Trained Widow-Maker, his famous horse
III. Fought a tornado once

Subtopics

Left a hole a hundred feet deep
Is mythical king of the cow business
Raised him from a colt on nitroglycerin and dynamite
Landed in a place now known as Death Valley
Cut his teeth on a bowie knife
Finally slid down from the tornado on a streak of lightning
Grew up with the coyotes
Could not be ridden by anyone else
Could speak coyote language
Climbed on the back of the tornado
Had trouble getting down from peak
Let a friend ride him once
Actually thought he was a coyote, too
Was thrown by Widow-Maker high into the air
Landed on Pikes Peak
Fought it across three states

Four Details in Outlining

1. Arrange main topics and subtopics in a logical or a chronological order.

All topics should dovetail so closely that the outline will show a gradual progression. If each topic is in exactly its right place, anyone can see at a glance the purpose and the plan of the paper.

2. Keep all main topics and subtopics in parallel form.

If a sentence outline is used, make sure that *all* the parts are in sentence form; there must be *no* exception. If a topic outline is used, make all the topics structurally alike; if one begins with a noun, the next should not begin with a past participle, and the next with a verb. Obviously, the use of adjectives and adverbs at the beginning of a topic does not change its structure.

POOR:
  A. Cut his teeth on a bowie knife
  B. Coyotes his first friends

BETTER:
  A. Cut his teeth on a bowie knife
  B. Grew up with the coyotes

3. Avoid the inclusion of any single subtopics.

You should never have a subtopic A without a B, or a 1 without a 2. Join a single subtopic with the topic under which it falls.

4. Indent each of the subtopics sufficiently to show all the major and minor parts at a glance.

EXERCISE 3. Put the following into correct outline form:

Main topics

CASEY JONES

I. Know few facts about his life

II. Has been immortalized in song

Subtopics

His name came from Cayce, Kentucky, near which he was born.

Has become a famous American ballad.

Others quickly picked up the song.

A famous engineer

Had an inimitable way of blowing a whistle.

Song sung in his grief after Casey's death.

Was a Negro engine wiper.

He loved Casey.

Was first sung by Wallace Saunders.

Casey was killed in a train wreck in April, 1900.

EXERCISE 4. Now is the time to make an outline for your term paper.

R P 5   Writing the Paper

1. Parts of the paper

Almost all forms of writing have three parts: an introduction, a body, and a conclusion.

The *introduction*, or beginning, sets the stage for what is to come. It may give an overall picture of the topic under discussion. It may give a pertinent quotation or an illustrative story. It may make a startling statement to intrigue the reader and encourage him to continue to the end. It is the "show window" for the paper and as such must indicate that the "wares" are both interesting and worth while.

The *body*, or middle, is the main part of the paper. The outline which you have made tells you step by step the contents of the body of the paper.

The *conclusion*, or ending, is the tying together of all the threads of thinking. It may summarize the points made, or it may restate the general premise of the paper. Neither the introduction nor the conclusion needs to be long, but both are vitally important since they are the first and last impressions of the reader.

2. Use of reference material

Many research papers fail because of too close adherence to the ideas of others. *The purpose of reference material is to start you thinking.* A paper that has an overabundance of quotations shows that the writer has not been doing enough of his own thinking. Decide first what *you* think; then use the opinions of others to bolster your ideas.

For example, suppose you wish to point out that ballads show an oral influence. You have these two quotations:

1. BALLAD, the name given to a type of verse of unknown authorship, dealing with episode or simple motif rather than sustained theme, written in a stanzaic form more or less fixed and suitable for oral transmission.

Encyclopædia Britannica

2. Many of them [ballads] sound as if they had been recited or sung by a leader with his hearers joining in the chorus.

BOAS AND SMITH

Using this material, you write the following paragraph. Disregard the numbers. They will be explained later.

Ballads must first have been sung and then must have been passed on orally from father to son and from son to his son. The form of many of the ballads is indicative of the oral influence. As Boas and Smith say, they "sound as if they had been recited or sung by a leader with his hearers joining in the chorus." [1] Even such an authority as the *Encyclopædia Britannica* speaks of the stanzaic form of the ballads as being "suitable for oral transmission." [2]

EXERCISE 1. Write a paragraph in which you make wise use of the following source materials:

1. Our Western music is still rhythmically crude — there is no other word for it.

JOHN ERSKINE

2. The serious modern music and jazz alike will supply a great quantity of all these distortions, sometimes with excellent effect and sometimes for no apparent reason beyond the love of distortion as such.

SIGMUND SPAETH

3. Here another frequent characteristic of Negroid jazz may be mentioned: two or more players often improvise melodies simultaneously on the basis of a known chord progression, each player being guided by his own feeling and the sound of his fellows. The result is what might be called an informal jazz "counterpoint," whose interweaving melodies, in different syncopated rhythms, are often as exciting to its devotees as they are confusing to unaccustomed ears.

Encyclopædia Britannica

EXERCISE 2. Choose several related notes which you have taken for your research paper, and use them in a paragraph as proof of a point you wish to make.

R P 6   Making Footnotes

In the paragraph on page 362 you probably noticed the slightly raised numbers 1 and 2 at the end of the quoted references. The numbers tell the reader to look at the bottom of the page for notes giving the exact source of the material. These references are known as *footnotes*.

The footnotes for the paragraph mentioned would read:

[1] Boas, R. P., and Smith, Edwin, *An Introduction to the Study of Literature*, Harcourt, Brace and Company, New York, 1925, pp. 23–24

[2] "Ballad," *Encyclopædia Britannica*, 1948, Vol. 2, p. 993

If a later reference to one of the books is made, the abbreviation *op. cit.* (*opere citato*, "in the work cited") may be used.

　³ Boas and Smith, *op. cit.*, p. 25

The abbreviation *ibid.* (*ibidem*, "in the same place") is also helpful. It may be used to refer again to the source given in the immediately preceding footnote. If you wished to refer again to the *Encyclopædia Britannica* reference, your footnote should read:

　³ *Ibid.*, pp. 984–986

Or if the page reference was the same in both quotations, the second footnote would simply read:

　³ *Ibid.*

Not all writers use such complete footnotes as suggested here. The *minimum* amount of information to be given is the following:

　1. *For a book:* author's name, title of the book, volume if there is more than one, and page reference

　2. *For a magazine:* name of the magazine, volume number if the magazine is bound or the date if it is not bound, and page reference

　3. *For an encyclopedia:* name of the encyclopedia, volume number, and page reference

EXERCISE. Practice writing footnotes by using references from several of your textbooks. Include among them one using *op. cit.* and another using *ibid.* After you have finished, check for these points:

　(1) Underlining of titles of books, magazines, newspapers, and the abbreviations of Latin terms

　(2) Correct use of capital letters, periods, and commas

Footnotes are generally set off from the rest of the page by a band of white space or by a rule.

R P 7   Making a Bibliography

A bibliography is a complete listing in alphabetical order of all the materials used in the preparation of a paper. There are several ways in which a bibliography can be compiled. Some persons like to organize the references under *Books* and *Magazines*. The following, however, shows the general plan:

Bibliography

"Dyango Music," *Time*, November 18, 1946, p. 53

Erskine, John, *What Is Music?* J. B. Lippincott Company, Philadelphia, 1944, p. 58

Goodman, Benny, and Kolodin, Irving, *The Kingdom of Swing*, Stackpole Sons, Harrisburg, 1939

Handy, William C. (ed.), *Blues*, Albert & Charles Boni, Inc., New York, 1926

Hobson, Wilder, *American Jazz Music*, W. W. Norton & Company, New York, 1939, pp. 18–64

"Jazz," *Encyclopædia Britannica*, 1948, Vol. 12, pp. 982–983

"Jazz Cult," *Harper's Magazine*, February–March, 1947, pp. 141–147, 261–273

"Nice Jumps," *Time*, March 8, 1948, p. 40

Panassié, Hugues, *Hot Jazz*, M. Witmark & Sons, New York, 1936

Ramsey, Frederic, and Smith, C. E. (eds.), *Jazzmen*, Harcourt, Brace and Company, New York, 1939, pp. 71–99

Sargeant, Winthrop, *Jazz, Hot & Hybrid*, Arrow Editions Cooperative Association, New York, 1938

Spaeth, Sigmund, *At Home with Music*, Doubleday & Company, Garden City, 1945, pp. 256–261

EXERCISE 1. Arrange the following for a bibliography:

encyclopædia britannica 1948 vol 2 ballad pp 993–996

reynolds horace the christian science monitor magazine hootenanny march 6 1948 p 8

r p boas and edwin smith an introduction to the study of literature harcourt brace and company new york 1925 p 23

the macmillan company new york 1947 john a lomax adventures
of a ballad hunter

archibald t davison katherine k davis and frederic w kempf
songs of freedom houghton mifflin company 1942 boston

a treasury of new england folklore pp 836–900 1947 crown publishers new york b a botkin

crown publishers new york 1944 b a botkin a treasury of american
folklore

boni margaret bradford fireside book of folk songs simon and
schuster new york 1947

life october 20 1947 pp 63–66 folk singers; mountain people
remember the old american music

EXERCISE 2. Make a bibliography of the following:

wright a h scholastic magazine may 12 1947 p 46 u s postage
stamps 100 years old

strange things happen by e a kehr in saturday evening post
may 17 1947 on p 57

poor mans stock market in newsweek june 9 1947 on p 70

kimble ralph a how to collect stamps grosset & dunlap 1933
new york pages 90 to 151

so youre collecting stamps by mannel hahn published by dodd,
mead & company 1946 pages 102–156 new york

the stamp and the story by sid elias and ab feins in scholastic
magazine dec 15 1947 on page 38

stiles k b america in stamps new york times magazine p 20 may 11
1947

EXERCISE 3. Find in the library several books that
contain bibliographies. Do they follow the form given in
this chapter? If they do not, make notes indicating the
ways in which they differ. What seem to be some of the
standards followed in all the bibliographies that you
study? Is there a reason for these similarities?

EXERCISE 4. Prepare the bibliography for your own
research paper.

R P 8   Choosing a Title

Some persons choose a title before they begin to write, and others decide upon one after they have finished. *When* the title is selected is unimportant, but the *title* itself is vitally important.

The ideal title is short, limited, and attention getting. Some writers actually choose titles like "An Investigation of the Status of Secular Literature in New England in the Seventeenth Century as Evidenced in the Diaries and Letters of the Puritan Theocracy." Don't handicap your composition with a title so long that no one will get beyond it. If your title has more than five words, shorten it.

Your title must not be so broad as to cover more material than your paper could. The reader is entitled to a warning, by the title, of how large a slice of life you are going to serve him.

Make your title striking. Word it so that it will attract attention. Try to make your readers sit up in wonder. Your title must be original, but it must not be so unusual that it will mislead. To be effective it must be significant.

EXERCISE 1. For each of the fourteen topics listed on page 352 write an interesting title.

EXERCISE 2. Collect ten titles of books or movies that you consider particularly effective. Be prepared to defend your choices.

EXERCISE 3. Reword each of these dull titles:

Conservation	Chain Stores
Labor Organizations	Compulsory Military Training
Federal Bureau of Investigation	Analytical Geometry

EXERCISE 4. Choose a suitable title for your own research paper.

R P 9   Revisions

There is nothing sacred about the first draft of any piece of writing. If your paper does not satisfy you in your most critical frame of mind, it should by all means be revised.

Ask yourself the following questions as you read your paper:

Title

1. Is the title interesting?
2. Does it give a fair indication of what will be discussed in the paper?

Introduction

1. Is the first sentence attention getting? Will it intrigue the reader?
2. Does the first sentence repeat the title or use a pronoun that refers to the title? If it does, rewrite the sentence.
3. Does the first paragraph take up too much space?
4. Can the reader tell that this is an *introduction* to the problem?

Body

1. Does the organization of the body of the paper follow the outline? Each section in the outline should be evident in the paper. However, the sections should not be set off by any special devices.
2. Has each of the sections been given the proper proportion of space?
3. Do transitional words, phrases, and sentences tie the parts together in a unified whole?
4. Does the topic sentence of each paragraph tell accurately what the paragraph will include?

Conclusion

1. Does the last paragraph tie together all the threads?
2. Is the paragraph too long?
3. Is the last sentence one of the strongest of the entire paper?

There are other questions, too, which you will be asking yourself. If you are not satisfied with the answers you give yourself, turn to the special sections in this handbook.

1. Does the paper show *unity* of tone? (See pages 222 to 230.)
2. Are the parts woven together so neatly that *coherence* results? (See pages 231 to 239.)
3. Does the paper possess the proper amount of *emphasis?* (See pages 252 to 261.)
4. Is the *spelling* correct? (See pages 189 to 212.)
5. Are the *capitalization* and *punctuation* correct? (See pages 99 to 136.)

Review Exercises

EXERCISE 1. Reduce each of these general topics to one which could be covered adequately in a research paper:

Birds	World War II
Benjamin Franklin	The Rubber Industry
Great Philanthropists	

EXERCISE 2. On a $3'' \times 5''$ card, take notes on the following paragraph from page 176 of *A Treasury of American Folklore:*

The American genius for invention has produced its hero in Paul Bunyan. Although he handles nature like a toy and accounts for the bigness of certain American geographical features, such as Puget Sound, he is primarily a work giant whose job is to invent logging. By reason of his having to start from scratch, there is something primordial about him; but unlike most Titans, he combines brain with brawn, and employs both for the good of mankind. He has gone a long way from the giant of nursery tales whose chief purpose was to scare little children and be slain by the hero.

B. A. BOTKIN

EXERCISE 3. Outline a chapter in one of your texts.

EXERCISE 4. If you had used a quotation from the paragraph given in EXERCISE 2, what kind of footnote would you have made for it?

EXERCISE 5. Look in the library for source material on one of the following topics. Use books, magazines, and the encyclopedia; and do not be satisfied until you have found at least ten different sources. Make a correct bibliography of the references.

1. A Planet	6. FM
2. Penicillin	7. Valley Forge
3. Blank Verse	8. Babe Ruth
4. Gold Rush Days	9. Madame Chiang Kai-shek
5. Army Training Courses	10. The Gallup Poll

EXERCISE 6. Study the opening and closing paragraphs of a number of articles from such magazines as *The Atlantic Monthly, Harper's Magazine, The New Yorker.*

MECHANICS

MANUSCRIPT MATERIALS

Your school probably has a standard requirement for theme papers. It is a distinct convenience for your instructors to handle papers the same size and quality: papers are less likely to become lost or to get ruffled edges. It will also add to the comfort and convenience of your instructors if you use black or blue-black ink. Don't expend imagination on materials; save your originality for the *content* of your writing.

You will find that typewritten work is always happily received. Therefore, if you can operate a typewriter, type your manuscripts. Be sure that your typewriter is working properly and that you have a black ribbon that will produce clear-cut, legible print. Use white paper of standard size, $8\frac{1}{2}$ by 11 inches. A good quality will make clean erasures possible.

If graphs or sketches are a necessary part of your paper, they should be included. Never, however, should they be used as a mere decoration. Gone are the days when students were expected to submit decorative papers.

371

Mech 1   Arranging the Parts

EXAMPLE SHOWING PLACEMENT OF PARTS:

John Smith
American Literature
January 15, 19—

Hilarious Adventure and Exaggeration

Mark Twain is frequently praised for his satires on the lace-curtain brand of culture and his depiction of the lazy life of the Mississippi River Valley. Most Americans, however, love him for another reason. The Mark Twain who told tales of high adventure and of unbelievable straight-faced exaggeration is the one who has endeared himself to all.

Mark Twain's fame began with a fantastic tale called "The Celebrated Jumping Frog of Calaveras County" (1865). According to Jones and Leisy, "Clemens claimed to have heard the story from one of the hangers-on at Angel's Camp." [1] It seems that the plot of the story appeared in "A Toad Story" published in the Sonora *Herald* twelve years before.[2] Whatever its source may have been, the tale very quickly gained national fame. Its amazing spirit of exaggeration

[1] Jones, Howard Mumford, and Leisy, E. E., *Major American Writers*, Harcourt, Brace and Company, New York, 1935, p. 1209
[2] *Ibid.*

1. Placement of the heading

Themes should be headed in the way prescribed by your instructor. Usually themes carry the name of the student at the top of the page, the title of the course immediately below it, and the date under that, all placed either at the extreme right or at the extreme left.

2. Placement of the title

Leave a space between the heading and the title. The title, which should be brief, should be centered on your paper. You will remember, of course, that the first word and all important words of a title should be capitalized and

372

that no end punctuation is necessary unless the title is a direct question or an exclamation.

3. Placement of the first line

It is customary to leave a space between the title and the first line of the body of the writing.

4. Use of margins

Neat margins improve the appearance of a manuscript. If you are using ruled paper, follow the margins indicated. With unruled paper, whether you are writing or typing, allow ample margins at the top, bottom, and sides. Never crowd a page.

5. Indentation of paragraphs

In handwritten material, the first word in each paragraph is usually indented about one-half inch from the left-hand margin. In typed material, the indention is usually five spaces.

In some schools, students are asked to number the paragraphs of their themes to correspond with the topics in their outlines. In that case the number should be indented as though it were the first word.

6. Numbering of pages

The first page is not numbered. Succeeding pages are numbered with Arabic numerals in the upper right-hand corner.

7. Placement of footnotes

Footnotes should appear at the bottom of the page to which they refer. Leave space between the text of your theme and the footnotes, so that the footnotes will point out references and not. appear to be part of the text. See also page 364.

8. Placement of bibliography

The bibliography goes at the end of the theme. It may be on a separate sheet of paper, or it may immediately follow the closing of the theme proper. In the latter case, leave a space between the closing of the theme and the title "Bibliography."

Mech 2   Legibility

If you write in longhand, try to write legibly and neatly. All doubtful letters should be written with particular care. Decorative strokes distract the reader's attention from the content. Avoid using circles over i's and j's and odd lines through t's and x's.

If you use the typewriter, type on one side of the paper only and double-space your material.

Type footnotes single-spaced, to distinguish them further from the text of the theme. If you wish, you may use a horizontal line to separate them from the text, rather than the space recommended above.

The bibliography is usually single-spaced, with double spacing between items.

Mech 3   Checking Spelling

Before making the final copy of your theme, it is always a wise plan to check spelling. In your concern about expressing your ideas, you may have made thoughtless mistakes in spelling. Such errors will show up when you read your paper with only spelling in mind. Check all doubtful words in one of two ways: recall the rule that governs the spelling of the word, or look up the word in the dictionary. For a detailed study of spelling rules, see pages 194 to 200.

EXERCISE. The following letter is bad in many ways. Make all necessary corrections.

4684 Hickory Street
Nashville 6, Tenessee
Febuary 10, 19—

Super Sales Corpration
Magnolia and Main Streets
Nashville 2, Tennesee

Genelmen:

I saw you're advertisement in the newspaper for a stenogapher-bookeeper. I think I am qualifyed for the position as I have studied typeing, short-hand, bookeeping besides the usal coarses in highschool. I am neet and acurate. I reely want to be a privite secetary, but I am willing to begin at the bottem if it dosent take to long.

Hopeing to here favoribly from you soon, I remane

Yours truely,
Marianne Floyd

Mech 4   Checking Capitalization and Punctuation

If you read your theme aloud before copying it, you will probably spot careless errors. Refer to the punctuation rules on pages 107 to 133 whenever you are in doubt. Watch your capitalization as you copy the final draft. Beware of indiscriminate capitalization; apply only the definite rules given on pages 100 to 105.

EXERCISE. Copy the following paragraph, inserting the proper capitalization and punctuation:

like another outstanding short story writer o henry wilbur daniel steele was born in greensboro north carolina steele is a master technician he is so economical of his materials that the reader must get much of the story by reading between the lines for this reason a second reading of his stories is often more enjoy-

able than the first reading if you are not familiar with steeles
short stories you will want to hunt for surprise or footfalls

Mech 5   Making Corrections

Make corrections and erasures neatly. If more than two
or three occur on a page, rewrite the page. Here are a few
correction symbols that you will find helpful: To insert a
word, place a caret (∧) below the line and insert the word
over it, above the line. To close a space, draw a linking line
(⌒) across the top of the space. To separate words, use a
slanting bar (/). To correct a transposition of letters, draw
a hooking line (∼) between the letters to be transposed. To
indicate a paragraph that you have failed to indent, use
the paragraph symbol (¶).

> short-
> O. Henry is a famous ∧ story writer.
> He is noted for his unusual surprise endings.
> The short-story form is/largely an American development.

Mech 6   Abbreviations

With a few exceptions (noted below), it is not good form
to use abbreviations in general writing.

**Use abbreviations for these titles when they precede proper
names: Mr., Mrs., Messrs., Dr., Rev., and St. (saint).**

Never use these abbreviations unless they are part of
proper names.

> WRONG: My dear Dr.   Dear Rev.
> RIGHT: My dear Dr. Swanson   My dear Doctor
>   Rev. John Smith

**Use abbreviations for *Junior* and *Senior* and for college de-
grees attached to proper names.**

> RIGHT: John Jones, Jr.   Walter Taylor, Ph.D.

Use these abbreviations with numerals only: B.C., A.D., A.M., P.M.

> WRONG: It happened B.C.
> RIGHT: 1000 A.D.   9:30 A.M.   10 P.M.

For the abbreviations of periods of time, such as A.M., P.M., B.C., A.D., printers generally use small capital letters. Avoid other abbreviations in ordinary writing.

WRONG	RIGHT
Chas.	Charles
across the St.	across the street
Tues.	Tuesday
U.S.A.	the United States of America
Penn.	Pennsylvania
this A.M.	this morning

Abbreviations that are proper in tabulated lists, footnotes, and bibliographies are not considered good form in sentences.

Correct for tabulation:

> Ala.   Ark.
> Ariz.   Colo.

Correct in footnotes:

> *Ibid.*   *Op. cit.*

Correct in bibliographies:

> F. B. Millett, *Contemporary American Authors*, Harcourt, Brace and Company, New York, 1940, p. 450
> Davis, Elmer, "Roosevelt and Hopkins," *The Saturday Review of Literature*, Vol. XXXI, No. 43, pp. 7–9; 35–38

EXERCISE. Correct the errors in the following sentences:

1. The Rev. read some verses from saint Luke.
2. Since the Dr. was out last Mon. morning, I called Mister Patton.

3. They called him Jack Johnson, Junior, to distinguish him from Jack Johnson, Senior.
4. He went to school in the A.M. and held down a job in the P.M.
5. Chas. wanted to be a Dr.

Mech 7   Numbers

As a general practice, write out numbers. Use figures for the following:

1. Dates and times of day with A.M. and P.M.

    April 9, 1912   8:30 A.M.

2. Street numbers and postal zones

    203 Center Street, Seattle 41, Washington

3. Telephone numbers

    GLendale 3–0776

4. Page references

    Pages 1, 7, 19–21.

5. Numbers and sums of money that cannot be expressed in two or three words

    7,453,103 $19.95

In a series of numbers, use all figures or all words. If any one of the numbers is complicated, use figures throughout.

> WRONG: Room 101 gave $1.35; 104, fifty cents; 105, $2.73; 110, three dollars.
> RIGHT: Room 101 gave $1.35; 104, $.50; 105, $2.73; 110, $3.00.

Never begin a sentence with a figure. Either spell out the number or revise the sentence.

> WRONG: 16 seniors made scores of 90 or above.
> RIGHT: Sixteen seniors made scores of 90 or above.

EXERCISE. Copy the following sentences, making corrections wherever they are necessary:

1. When my father enrolled 30 years ago, there were fewer than 300 students in school.
2. Refer to pages sixteen, twenty-one, and thirty.
3. 8:30 was convenient for all 10 of them.
4. By coincidence he lived at 4400 Pleasant Drive, and his telephone number was PLeasant four thousand four hundred and one.
5. What famous ride took place on April eighteen, seventeen hundred seventy-five?

Mech 8   Syllabication

To keep the right-hand margin from becoming too irregular, it is sometimes desirable to divide a word. When a word is divided, place the hyphen at the end of the line, never at the beginning of the next line.

Divide words between syllables only.

The following rules cover most cases. If you are still in doubt, consult the dictionary.

1. Do not divide words of one syllable.

thought   stopped   reign

2. Do not separate a single letter from the rest of a word.

WRONG: a-bout   e-lision   i-cy   room-y

3. Seldom set off two letters, except prefixes like _un_ or suffixes like _ly_.

WRONG: au-to   wa-fer   ru-in
RIGHT: like-ly   un-satisfactory

4. Divide words so that the parts will be pronounceable.

WRONG: mus-ic   powd-er   wind-ow   wo-men

5. When a single consonant comes between two syllables, join it to the second syllable.

RIGHT: antici-*p*ate   compe-*t*ent   liga-*m*ent

However, a consonant that ends a single, stressed syllable is usually attached to it.

RIGHT: e*l*-egant   sa*t*-irize   sta*t*-ure

6. Divide two consonants between syllables. (A pair of consonants like *ch, ph, sh, th,* which have a single sound, are treated as a single letter.)

RIGHT: co*m*-*m*is-*s*ion   ru*n*-*n*er   i*n*-*t*el-*l*ect   ju*n*-*k*et
RIGHT: ar-*ch*i-tect   tel-e-*ph*one   en-*ch*ant

7. Divide between a prefix or a suffix and the root word, regardless of the rules for consonants between syllables. When a final consonant is doubled before a suffix, the additional consonant goes with the suffix.

RIGHT: *dis*-satisfy   *in*-duct   beau-ti-*ful*
RIGHT: shop-*p*ing   al-lot-*t*ed   swim-*m*ing

8. Divide compound words between the parts.

RIGHT: runner-up   worth-while   right-handed

9. Do not further divide a hyphenated word. A second hyphen is confusing.

WRONG: self-ad-dressed   mid-Vic-torian

10. Do not divide proper nouns or separate the initials of a name from the name itself.

WRONG: John-son   John-ny   C. C.-Mat-thews

EXERCISE. Copy the following words, placing a hyphen between syllables in words where it is permissible. For additional practice, use the spelling lists on pages 207 to 210.

abiding	convenient	R. H. Berkshire
achievement	elegy	sale
apple	fussy	semicolon
armistice	innocent	skipped
benefited	nothing	thoughtless
bibliography	parable	uncounted
coarse	precipitous	undernourish

EXERCISE. Open this book to any page except one devoted to the hyphen; run your eyes down the right-hand margin and copy the first ten divided words you can find. Do the divisions conform to the rules you have just studied? After each word, list by number the rule that applies.

Mech 9 Italics

Use italics (indicated by underlining) for names of books, magazines, newspapers, long plays, musical productions, and works of art.

Quotation marks, rather than italics, are used for short stories, magazine articles, chapter titles, booklets, poems, and songs. For illustrations see page 127.

George Babbitt is the main character in *Babbitt*.

Before the production of *Bound East for Cardiff*, Eugene O'Neill did reporting for the New London, Connecticut, *Telegraph*.

Alfred Drake sang "Oh, What a Beautiful Morning!" from *Oklahoma*.

George W. Bellows first achieved fame with his painting *Stag at Sharkey's*.

EXERCISE. Copy the following sentences, underlining all words that should be italicized:

1. Anne in White, Bellows's portrait of his daughter, was reproduced in Life magazine.

2. Elmer Davis reviewed Roosevelt and Hopkins by Sherwood in The Saturday Review of Literature.
3. She had sung in half a dozen operas, including Carmen and Madame Butterfly.
4. Robert Sherwood wrote Abe Lincoln in Washington as a radio sequel to his play Abe Lincoln in Illinois.
5. Carl Sandburg worked on the Chicago Daily News while writing Abraham Lincoln, a three-volume biography.

Use italics for names of ships, aircraft, and trains.

Gripsholm   *The Spirit of St. Louis*   *Portland Rose*

Use italics for words, letters, or figures referred to by name.

He noticed that the *a*'s and *e*'s did not print clearly.
There were three *16*'s in the column.
Bookkeeping is the only English word with three consecutive double letters.

EXERCISE. Copy the following sentences, underlining all words that should be italicized:

1. The Queen Mary sailed from New York to Southhampton.
2. The Old Beauty and Others by Willa Cather was reviewed in The New York Times as well as in The Atlantic Monthly.
3. His mother warned him to mind his p's and q's.
4. His favorite train was the Super Chief.
5. E is the most frequently used letter in the English alphabet.

Use italics for foreign words and phrases.

Many words and phrases of foreign origin have been added to the English language and are no longer italicized. When you are in doubt about the status of a word, consult a recent dictionary. If the word appears in the main vocabulary section and is not set off in any way, it should not be italicized. If it appears in the special section dealing with foreign words and phrases or if it is set off in the main section, it should be italicized.

RIGHT: *à droite*   *tempus fugit*   *ma chère*   *adsum*
RIGHT: connoisseur   amateur   trousseau   matinee

EXERCISE. According to the dictionary, which of the following words should be italicized?

alamode	de luxe	pax vobiscum
bon voyage	debut	post-mortem
café	on dit	protégé
cherchez la femme	passé	répondez s'il vous plaît
dachshund	patio	tout de suite

It is inadvisable to use italics for emphasis. Emphasis can better be obtained through careful arrangement of the sentence structure.

POOR: *John* wrote the speech; *Bill* did not.
BETTER: John, not Bill, wrote the speech.

EXERCISE. Copy the following sentences, underlining all words that should be italicized:

1. Although Jack London belonged by birth to the bourgeoisie, he allied himself early with the proletariat. 2. Temperamentally he inclined to "red-blooded" stories and a Sturm und Drang romanticism. 3. Inspired by Melville's Moby Dick, London shipped on the Sophie Sutherland on a sealing voyage. 4. Later he was off to the Klondike, where he found no gold but did gain an intimate knowledge of the frontier locale in which his first successes in fiction were to be won. 5. In 1900 his first volume, The Son of the Wolf, a group of Alaskan adventure stories, was published. 6. In 1903 appeared his masterpiece, The Call of the Wild, in which he illustrated the biological trait of atavism — that is, the reappearance in an animal of the instincts and habits of its remote ancestors. 7. The civilized dog, Buck, after being torn from de luxe surroundings in California, is sent to the savage environment of the Far North, there to struggle for survival under the law of club and fang. 8. London's vision of beauty and of brutal adventure lifts The Call of the Wild from the level of mere

entertainment to that of true literature.   9. London later turned
to socialism, lecturing from the platform, exposing the degrada-
tion of the slums in The People of the Abyss (1903) and preaching
the dogma of class conflict in The War of the Classes (1905).
10. Of his problem novels, the best known, although not the best,
is The Sea Wolf, a curious hodgepodge of adventure, philosophy,
and hokum.

Uniformity

Uniformity in the mechanics of a paper is exceedingly
important. Before handing in any piece of written work,
go over it for each of the following points:

INDENTATION. Do not indent varying amounts of space.

CAPITALIZATION. Do not write "Spanish *club*" one place
    and "Science *Club*" another.

PUNCTUATION. Do not write "truth, honesty, and justice"
    and then "English, history and algebra."

SPELLING. Do not write *theater* and then again *theatre*.

Review Exercises

EXERCISE. Rewrite the following excerpt from a term
paper, making all the corrections which you believe are
necessary:
                                            Ellen

BRET HARTE: A ROMANTIC IDEALIST.

Bret Harte gave to american readers a picture of the gold
rush days in California. His depiction included characters of all
sorts. Gamblers, liars, drunkards, and the like. And he placed
them in situations unlike anything American Readers had ever
heard of before. As a consequence Bret Harte very quickly became a literary sensation.

Was Bret Harte really a realist? Ask any 20 of your freinds,
and they will say that he was If however you study his stories
carefully you find although his principal characters are gamblers,
liars and drunkards they are nevertheless persons with drems in

thier hearts. Kentuck in The luck of Roaring Camp could not be called a first citizen but he was willing to give his life to save that of a baby. John Oakhurst in The Outcasts of poker Flat gave his life in the vane hope that he might save the lifes of others.

One authority in the field of the American Novel has said, Although he was not didactic, all of his stories are shot through with a romantic idealism which led him to discover honest gamblers.[1] Certainly we must agree with Doctor Jones as we analyze a number of Hartes characters. According to Jay B Hubbell Californians long questioned the accuracy of his picture of the miners.[2] They were miners but they were miners *plus*. In the cold light of reality, they were to good to be true.

An excelent example of Harte's romanticism can be found in the story Tennessee's Partner. The funeral address which is delivered in that story is one that any minister would be proud to claim. It came from the lips of an untutored man, a man who did not know the refinments of the english language and yet who was one who could speak profound truths as well as pull the heartstrings of the most hardened. The diseased was delivered to the earth beautifuly tenderly and sympathetically. A novelist of the realistic school would dwell upon the ugliness of life as seen in the outcasts of Poker Flat the luck of Roaring camp and Tenesse's Pardner The characters would be depicted in all their filth of mind, and heart, and spirit. There gamboling lying cheating would be piled up as proof that crime does not pay. Life would be all black not even a slight gray would be allowed

Harte's romantic method has softer edges than that used by the realist. His characters in moments of crisis always behave magnificent and because they do some noble deed there passed imperfections are over-looked.

[1] Jones, Howard Mumford, and Leisy, E. E. Major American Writers, 1935, Harcourt, Brace and Company, p 1274

[2] Jay B. Hubbell, American Life in literature, Harper & Brothers Publishers 1936, page 130, New York,

INDEX

387

Index

Index

Index

Index

Index

Index

(Par or ¶) THE PARAGRAPH *Pages 271–302*

Paragraph, Definition	Topic Sentence	Details	Transitional Devices	Methods of Development
Par	Par 1	Par 2	Par 3	Par 4
	Length	Kinds		
	Par 5	Par 6		

(Let) LETTER WRITING *Pages 303–328*

Business Letter	Friendly Letter
Let 1	Let 2

(Lib) LIBRARY TECHNIQUES *Pages 329–348*

Arrangement	Card Catalogue	General Reference	Special Reference	Magazines	Pamphlets
Lib 1	Lib 2	Lib 3	Lib 4	Lib 5	Lib 6

(RP) THE RESEARCH PAPER *Pages 349–370*

Subject	Plans	Notes	Outline	Writing
RP 1	RP 2	RP 3	RP 4	RP 5
	Footnotes	Bibliography	Title	Revisions
	RP 6	RP 7	RP 8	RP 9

(Mech) MECHANICS *Pages 371–385*

Arrangement	Legibility	Spelling	Cap. & Punc.	Corrections
Mech 1	Mech 2	Mech 3	Mech 4	Mech 5
	Abbreviations	Numbers	Syllabication	Italics
	Mech 6	Mech 7	Mech 8	Mech 9